THE TRUTH (with jokes)

Also by Al Franken

I'm Good Enough, I'm Smart Enough,
and Doggone It, People Like Me!

Rush Limbaugh Is a Big Fat Idiot
and Other Observations

Why Not Me?
*The Inside Story of the Making and Unmaking
of the Franken Presidency*

Oh, the Things I Know!
A Guide to Success, or, Failing that, Happiness

Lies, and the Lying Liars Who Tell Them
A Fair and Balanced Look at the Right

Al Franken The

Truth
(with jokes)

DUTTON

DUTTON
Published by Penguin Group (USA) Inc., 375 Hudson Street, New York, New York 10014, U.S.A.
Penguin Group (Canada), 90 Eglinton Avenue East, Suite 700, Toronto, Ontario M4P 2Y3, Canada (a division of Pearson Penguin Canada Inc.); Penguin Books Ltd., 80 Strand, London WC2R 0RL, England; Penguin Ireland, 25 St. Stephen's Green, Dublin 2, Ireland (a division of Penguin Books Ltd); Penguin Group (Australia), 250 Camberwell Road, Camberwell, Victoria 3124, Australia (a division of Pearson Australia Group Pty. Ltd); Penguin Books India Pvt Ltd, 11 Community Centre, Panchsheel Park, New Delhi - 110 017, India; Penguin Group (NZ), cnr Airborne and Rosedale Roads, Albany, Auckland 1310, New Zealand (a division of Pearson New Zealand Ltd); Penguin Books (South Africa) (Pty) Ltd, 24 Sturdee Avenue, Rosebank, Johannesburg 2196, South Africa

Penguin Books Ltd, Registered Offices: 80 Strand, London WC2R 0RL, England

Published by Dutton, a member of Penguin Group (USA) Inc.

First printing, October 2005
10 9 8 7 6 5 4 3 2 1

Graph on p. 31 from Mark J. Landau, et al., "Deliver Us From Evil," *Personality & Social Psychology Bulletin* (Vol. 80, No. 9) p. 1145. Copyright 2004 by the Society for Personality and Social Psychology, Inc. Reprinted by permission of Sage Publications, Inc.

 REGISTERED TRADEMARK—MARCA REGISTRADA

LIBRARY OF CONGRESS CATALOGING-IN-PUBLICATION DATA
has been applied for.

ISBN 0-525-94906-2

Printed in the United States of America
Set in Adobe Minion
Designed by Amy Hill

For two courageous women:

My Mom,

Phoebe Kunst Franken,

And my Mother-in-Law,

Frances Doyle Bryson.

Thanks for my life and my wife.

CONTENTS

THE TRUTH (with jokes)

When Al Franken asked me to write a foreword to this astonishing and profoundly moving book, he had only one condition: that I remain anonymous.

"Why?" I asked. "Having a big name like mine on your cover would be an enormous feather in any author's cap."

"That's exactly the point," he responded.

Al, you see, is too modest to want to call attention to the fact that he and I are such close friends. Typical Al. He always hides his light.

I reluctantly agreed to his condition, but in return I extracted one of my own. In exchange for concealing my famous identity, I demanded total control over the text of this foreword. I knew Al too well to give him the chance to edit out all the well-warranted praise I intended to heap on him. But even though this enthusiastic foreword will no doubt embarrass Al, I believe that you, the reader, deserve to know the full truth about this great American and about this book. I believe it to be not only the finest volume *he* has written, but perhaps the Great American Nonfiction Hardcover itself.

The Truth is a very different kind of book than the ones this multifaceted genius has given us before. Oh, it's funny. (How could Al Franken *not* write a funny book?) But it's more than that. Gone is the familiar cast of villains: the psychotic Ann Coulter, the sex-addicted Bill O'Reilly, the drug-addicted Rush Limbaugh. Consigned to their own personal hells by their failings as human beings, Franken mercifully leaves them be. Ann Coulter has been banned as effectively from these pages as from the intellectual salons to which she so desperately craves admittance.

In *The Truth*, the fish are bigger, and the fry is deeper.

Franken's targets this time include both people—Bush, Cheney, Rice, Rove, DeLay—and something new: ideas. In particular, the idea that the 2004 election meant that Franken's beloved America had moved to the right. Al Franken ain't buyin' it.

Using access to confidential documents and firsthand accounts, Franken weaves the *true* story of the Making of the President 2004, starring the Three Horsemen of the Republican Apocalypse: Fear, Smears, and Queers.

Franken shows more than *how* Bush won. He shows *what* Bush won. (Or in the case of a mandate, what he *didn't* win.)

But this story chronicles more than a rise. It chronicles a fall. And what a fall! Was Bush like Icarus, simply a man who dared to dream—a man who flew too close to the sun? Or like Daedalus, a man who equipped his son with unsafe wings made of easily melted beeswax?

As Franken makes clear, the answer is both—and neither.

If you doubt that Icarus has fallen, then I say these words to you: Terri Schiavo, Social Security, Ahmed Chalabi, Tom DeLay, and Iraq.

But this book is more than just a disconnected list of names, places, and topics. Far more. It is something new for Franken. And, I would argue, for literature. Here, Franken has taken a single stem cell—the English language—and grown from it a fully functional kidney with which to purify the blood of the body politic.

In the rarified sphere of contemporary general-audience nonfiction, few books live up to the promise offered by their title. Fewer still, their subtitle. But in *The Truth (with jokes)*, the author lives up to not only his title and his subtitle but, most important, to the name that appears on the cover. Al Franken.

Anonymous
New York, NY
August 13, 2005

Book One
The Triumph of Evil

1 | Election Day

November 2, 2004, 3:43 P.M.

It was a cool, misty day in Boston, Massachusetts, and TeamRadioFranken was riding high. And for good reason. We had just put on an excellent show. And we were about to take over the country.

Exit polls leaked to us by our sources in the bowels of the liberal media indicated that John Forbes Kerry, who you might recall was running for President of the United States on the Democratic ticket, was surging ahead of George W. Bush, who was about to become a one-term president like his loser father.

Our hard work had paid off. In the preceding seven months we had built an explosively popular radio network that, in our view at that moment, had fundamentally redefined American political discourse. In the 2000 election, the right-wing propaganda apparatus had succeeded in painting Al Gore as a serial exaggerator and political opportunist. But in 2004 we were there to fight back. And fight back we did. For three hours a day, five days a week, *The Al Franken Show* had counterattacked the

Republican noise machine with truth and comedy doled out with unbridled ferocity and glee. We had delivered the facts, and we had delivered the funny. And now we were tasting the sweet fruit of our labors. In fact, the exit polls suggested we were so far ahead, some us were privately wondering if we hadn't worked *too* hard in the preceding weeks and months. Perhaps we should have devoted more time to our families or hobbies.

Some might describe our mood as smug. Others might call it giddy. Both would be correct. There was a smug giddiness in the room, so smug and giddy that, as we planned for our November 3 broadcast, we didn't bother wasting even a minute sketching out a Plan B—what to say if Bush won rather than Kerry.

My staff was gathered around an oblong conference table in a back room at our hotel in Boston for our post-show meeting. Ideas for the next day's victory show were flying. Producer Ben Wikler thought I should start the show with an inspiring speech about not only what I and John Kerry had accomplished, but what the whole progressive movement had accomplished by working together. Executive Producer Billy Kimball thought I should use the moment to deliver a few leftover, gratuitous slams to the defeated and disgraced lame duck. Mostly, the staff wanted to spend the program crowing about our triumph and exulting in Bush's collapse.

Punch drunk with anticipation of the coming Democratic ascendancy, we cobbled together an opening monologue:

> As you have probably heard, John Kerry was elected President yesterday. We'll get to that soon. But first, I want to pick up where I left off with the case against George W. Bush. Now, as I was saying yesterday, nothing illustrates Bush's incompetence more than the looting of hundreds of tons of high-grade explosives from the al Qaqaa ammo dump. But it's not just incompetence.

The plan was that I would milk the conceit for a minute or so, and then my cohost, Katherine Lanpher, would talk me out of it. Then I'd take the high road for a moment—"This wasn't just a victory for John Kerry, it was a victory for a movement; the young people of America have changed the course of history forever; now's the time for healing and reconciliation after four years of bitterness"—and then we'd get into the good stuff: gloating. We'd play "We Are the Champions," and then play Bush's concession speech, and then play "We Are the Champions" again, this time singing along, and then play the concession speech with our snarky comments over it. "You blew it! You had it in your hand, and you blew it!" and "Hey, Karl Rove! Mister *GENIUS*!!!" . . . stuff like that.

Over gales of laughter, we started riffing. What jobs would former Bush administration officials take? Cheney, of course, would be CEO of Halliburton again. Colin Powell would collect board directorships. Bush would become senior vice president of Halliburton, after being rejected as commissioner of baseball.

And what about Rumsfeld? He'd honor us with a fake phone call and, as usual, he'd disrupt the interview by asking himself rhetorical questions. It might be my last chance to do my Rummy impression, which I had recently perfected.

Am I happy Kerry won? No.

Could the election be interpreted as a repudiation of the wars I mismanaged? Maybe.

Should I take responsibility? No. Why should I?

Will I be secretary of defense in the new administration? Probably not.

Am I going to leave the Pentagon? No way.

Are they gonna try to remove me? Sure.

Is this some kind of coup? You could call it that.

Have I gone crazy? You tell me.

We left the hotel for the Kerry victory party in Copley Square, high-fiving each other and feeling as if we were on top of the world. Little did we know that we were about to begin a nightmarish death spiral into the fiery pits of electoral obliteration. (Though not, as I will painstakingly document later in this chapter, by a substantial margin.)

Bouncing cheerfully into the lobby of the Fairmont Copley Hotel to pick up our press credentials, I spied a friend, a grinning Ed Markey. With Senator Kerry in the White House, the way would finally be clear for the tireless, handsome Massachusetts congressman to run for Senate. And from there, who knows? We bumped chests in the manner of victorious cavemen.

Next I saw Gene Sperling, former—and, now, future—economic adviser to the President. His face was alight. "We've done it," his glowing face seemed to say.

"We've done it!" I said to Gene.

"That's what I just said," answered Gene.

"Oh," I responded, "I thought that was just your face."

Gene shot me a weird look. But the awkwardness could not survive the building excitement we were both feeling. We hugged. More awkwardness as we disentangled ourselves, followed again by shared joy.

But tonight would not just be a celebration of the plum executive branch appointments that my friends and I would soon choose from. No, it was a victory for all of America, and indeed the world. Every American child would soon have health insurance. Every American ally would soon have reason to trust us again. Even Karl Rove, I mused expansively, would be better off in the long run under a Kerry administration. Though, I supposed, it might take him a while to realize it.

I crossed the street with my entourage of young producers and researchers, heading for our broadcast position in the southwest corner of

Copley Square. This was an exciting night for me, I reflected, but what really brought me satisfaction was seeing the jubilance surging through their young bodies. How many nights had I lain awake worrying that their expectations would be shattered? I had challenged them to give their all to this endeavor. And even if their all wasn't nearly as much as *my* all, they had come through. And now their sacrifice would be vindicated. Grizzled political veterans such as myself knew that the rigor of the campaign would now give way to the rigors of governance, but I wanted to let them have this moment. To savor it. They would learn about budget reconciliation and recess appointments in good time; tonight was a night for celebration. For revelry and drunkenness. For dewy young bodies entwined in an at-first-tentative, then urgent, embrace of love. Moistly thrusting . . .

A clap of thunder rumbled in the distance. Ah, I thought. A good omen. Mother Earth was about to be replenished, just like our drought-stricken political culture.

My phone rang. Felt. Mark Felt.[1] My secret inside source, who would be providing me with the exit poll numbers the minute they arrived on his desk. That afternoon, Felt's phone calls had delivered nothing but good news: Kerry was winning Pennsylvania! Kerry was winning Ohio! Kerry was winning Florida! I eagerly answered.

"What's the good news, Felt? Utah?"

But instead of good news, Felt delivered something very different. *Mixed* news. It looked like Florida was going to be a lot closer than early exit polls had indicated. Ditto for Ohio. And Utah was trending solidly red, though polls wouldn't close there for several hours.

Uh oh. Maybe I had misinterpreted the thunderclap and the blackening sky. As a chill rain began to fall, one word appeared in my mind: foreshadowing.

Still, most of the news had been good. Kerry didn't need *both* Ohio and Florida to win. He just needed one of them. And Ohio had lost over two

---

[1] "Mark Felt" is the alias I'm using in order to protect the identity of my real source, Judith Miller.

hundred thousand jobs during Bush's first four disastrous years in office. There's no way Ohio could go for Bush. Right? Right?

Hey! There's Barney Frank. It seemed like every Democratic congressman in Massachusetts was in Boston tonight. I went over to Barney for a chest bump to lift my slightly flagging spirits. But Barney was in no mood for such antics, and his chest bump lacked its usual brio.

"How's it looking, Barney?" I asked expectantly.

He looked glum. "Cautiously optimistic."

Cautiously optimistic? That's not good. That's an optimist's way of saying, "We're screwed." I've instructed my wife that if a doctor ever tells her that he's "cautiously optimistic" about my test results, she is to pull the plug immediately. I saw what happened to Terri Schiavo. I don't want to become a political football on the basis of cautious optimism.

Onstage, the Black-Eyed Peas had launched into "Let's Get It Started" (the politically correct version of their hit "Let's Get Retarded"), which had featured prominently in every meeting of five hundred or more Democrats during the campaign season. My staff was gamely bobbing and grooving in the freezing rain. No reason to give up hope yet. That's what Jesse Jackson would have told them if he had been there. Oh, he was. And he didn't look hopeful. Crud.

Another thunderclap rang out. Only this time it wasn't from the inky sky. It was a figurative thunderclap, emanating from the massive video screens flanking the stage. Tom Brokaw was telling us that Bush was doing much better in Florida's all-important I-4 corridor than he had in 2000. Political junkies like myself recalled that Florida had been extremely close in that election. So close that Bush had been forced to prevent the counting of ballots there in order to steal a victory, assume the presidency, and carry out his plan to invade Iraq.

The phone rang again. Felt. Mark Felt. He told me that Bush had done better than expected in the I-4 corridor. "Oh, is that important?" I asked caustically. "Next time, call me with something I *don't* know." So he did. Ohio was looking grim. I wish I could say I crushed the phone with my hand in disgust. But I didn't. I sensed that Felt still had a role to play. A sense that proved incorrect.

Pull it together, Al. You've got a job to do. Your Sundance Channel TV show starts in less than ten seconds. That's what Billy said to me. Ben, in turn, told me to take off the fluffy magenta scarf that a diehard fan had graciously knitted for me, and that I had felt an obligation to wear even during several television interviews earlier that evening. I'm not gay, but I sure looked gay with that scarf on. Off it went. Thanks, Ben. Camera time.

Putting on a brave, straight face, I looked in the camera and told America that I still believed we could pull it out. Was I lying? Only to myself. I *did* still believe we had a fighting chance in Ohio. Remember, the Red Sox had won the World Series. There was no reason Kerry couldn't rally in the Buckeye State as returns came in from the most populous, most Democratic counties. Despite the handicap of having gut-wrenchingly bad news to report, my broadcast was a smashing success, bringing laughter and courage to a blue America in dire need of succor.

Then things went downhill. I had tried to shield my staff and television audience from the bad news in Ohio, but now it was there on the big screen for all to see. About 12:45 A.M., a certain news channel whose name I am legally prohibited from mentioning—Fox—called Ohio for its preferred candidate, George W. Bush.

It's only Fox, I thought. Then NBC followed suit. It's only NBC, I thought. Only NBC. Hoo boy. The Kerry people, desperately looking for a network that would call Ohio for Kerry, had to settle for CNN calling Ohio a purple state. Wolf Blitzer and the CNN brass were taking the easy, intellectually honest, way out. Because Kerry could theoretically make up the gap once all the provisional votes had been counted, CNN refused to give Ohio to either side. The beleaguered crowd at Copley Square cheered. Could this be another 2000? At this point, that was our best hope. And as if on cue, John Edwards walked onstage and told us that the campaign would keep fighting until every ballot had been counted.

As the wet, cold, emotionally traumatized throng thronged out of the

Square, my team began discussing the logistics of a potential Ohio stake-out. Four years previously, the lack of an *Al Franken Show* broadcasting live from the Florida recount had cost the world's only remaining super-power its rightful leader.

"This is why we're on the air," I told my exhausted staff. "Get as much rest as you can over the next two hours. Then we'll swing down to New York, knock off a show, and then look at the county-by-county returns in Ohio to get a sense of the state of play. I don't know where this is taking us. Could be Columbus, could be Dayton. Who knows, it could be Kalama-zoo.[2] All I know is that our country needs us."

I had paced myself that fall in order to produce the maximum possi-ble political impact all the way through the election. In addition to my radio and TV shows, I had been traveling to swing states every weekend and speaking at fund-raisers on weeknights. I plotted it out so that I would stagger across the finish line and collapse dramatically in exhaus-tion on the night of November 2.

The exhaustion part of the plan worked fine. But I had forgotten one small detail: I had to do another show on November 3. The morning after what many had called the most important election in our lifetime, we piled into our inappropriately festive rock-and-roll tour bus and hit the road back to our studios in New York. Billy found a vial of cocaine wedged behind his seat cushion, an artifact, no doubt, from an eighties prom. It was empty. Billy threw it into the Charles River, where it sank without a trace. Another broken dream.

As I traveled through the dawn, a million thoughts went through my head. I never remember my dreams when I wake up, so I can't tell you

---

[2] I was not aware at the time that Kalamazoo is in Michigan. But that's what I said. I could easily have changed Kalamazoo to "Cincinnati" or "Cleveland," but I respect you, my readers, too much to give you anything but the truth. Also, I didn't want to leave myself open to Swift boat–style attacks on my integrity from my staff, who frankly I don't trust.

what they were, although I'm pretty sure my teeth crumbled at some point.

We arrived at our New York studios at ten. Though we stank, there would be no time to shower before our broadcast. There is nothing unusual about this, but I wanted to mention it anyway in the interest of full disclosure. That's the difference between us and them. As I scanned the newspapers and the Internet, wheels in my head turned. Was there a way to pull the baby out of this burning building? Was there a way to land this plane in the fog? Kerry was only 136,000-odd votes short in Ohio, and his camp contended that up to 250,000 provisional ballots had yet to be counted. "I've been in worse jams," I told Katherine with false bravado. If 20 percent of the provisional ballots were invalidated, we would need to win only 86 percent of what remained. This was doable. Things were looking up.

At 11:10 A.M., the Kerry campaign, looking at the same numbers we were looking at but through slightly less rose-colored goggles, announced that Senator Kerry had called President Bush to concede. The baby was staying in the fire. The plane had flown into some high-tension power lines and burst into flames itself.

All my work had been for nothing.

I took a slug of Jim Beam and headed to the studio. It would be the most difficult show anyone had ever attempted. Still, my indefatigable sense of humor rescued the day. Katherine looked on with admiration as I opened the broadcast:

> It's Wednesday, November 3, and *The Al Franken Show* is on the air. First, the good news: Ralph Nader did not swing a single state. As for the bad news, that's why we invented the Oy Yoy Yoy show. Joining us for wailing and gnashing of teeth, we've got *New York Times* columnist Paul Krugman, *New York Observer* writer Joe Conason, and American Enterprise Institute resident scholar Norm Ornstein. We're putting the

gallows back in gallows humor—as *The Al Franken Show* starts now.

Home run. Thank God I was on the air. The healing had begun.

Kerry's concession speech was beautiful. Bush's, however, was hardly a concession speech at all. It made me sick. But even worse was Cheney's speech introducing Bush. The dust had not yet settled on the most narrow election victory by an incumbent president in the history of the republic. Bush's edge was 2.5 percent, smaller even than Woodrow Wilson's pathetic 1916 victory margin of 3.2 percent. Now, I'm no partisan. But it really chapped my ass when Cheney claimed a "broad nationwide victory" and a "mandate" for Bush's "clear agenda."

Mandate? We couldn't even tell who'd won until the afternoon after the election. In 1936 FDR had a mandate. In 1956 Eisenhower had a mandate. In 1964 Johnson had a mandate. In 1972 Nixon had a mandate. In 1984 Reagan had a mandate. In 1996 Clinton had beaten Dole by 8.5 percentage points. More than three times Bush's margin. I knew mandates. Mandates were a friend of mine. And you, 2004, were no mandate.

Surely, this pretension to a mandate was just a rhetorical flourish on the vice president's part. It came in a moment of such palpable joy and excitement that many watching feared that his heart would explode. The vice president knew as well as anyone how close the election had been; we could forgive him a moment's hyperbole. But surely no one would echo it.

But I had forgotten the right-wing hacks. That same day, Bill Bennett wrote on *The National Review Online*: "Bush now has a mandate." Tucker Carlson agreed: "It is a mandate." Peggy Noonan on Fox's *The Sean Hannity Show*[3] that night had a similar view: "He has, I would argue, a man-

---

[3] The show might not really be called that, but I'm too lazy to look it up. I think that's it.

date now." Hack rag *Weekly Standard* editor Bill Kristol staked out perhaps the most counterintuitive position: "In one sense, we think it an even larger and clearer mandate than those won in the landslide reelection campaigns of Nixon in 1972, Reagan in 1984, and Clinton in 1996."[4]

The next morning's *Wall Street Journal* ran an editorial titled "The Bush Mandate" proclaiming that "Mr. Bush has been given the kind of mandate that few politicians are ever fortunate enough to receive." Of course, *The Wall Street Journal* editorial page had also implied that Bill Clinton had murdered Arkansas teenagers by running them over with a train,[5] a claim even more outlandish than the Bush mandate fabrication.

As depressing as it was to see the hacky right-wing hackocracy fall into hackstep—and very depressing it was—I expected this kind of thing from them. I could take it. I could steel my stomach because I knew that my fellow travelers in the Mainstream Media wouldn't buy it either.

With that in mind, I turned from the *Journal* to the website of that liberal standard bearer, *TIME* magazine. Uh oh:

> This time, of course, his claim of a popular mandate is incontrovertible.

Upsetting—but maybe this was just a fluke. *TIME* magazine, while *very* liberal, would sometimes feint rightward to fool the suits upstairs. It had been feinting rightward for almost seventy-five years. But I knew I could find a levelheaded, liberal assessment in the pages of the reliably lefty *Jew York Times*.

---

[4] In grudging fairness to Kristol, I should explain his argument before completely dismissing it. He wrote that "while the Nixon, Reagan, and Clinton victory margins were much, much bigger," Bush's victory was more impressive because he was "a war president" who couldn't run a "smiley-face campaign," but rather had to be "serious and substantive." Thus, his victory was an "ideological confirmation" not unlike FDR's in 1936. I'll just point out one glaring problem: In 1972, WE WERE AT WAR. Remember, Bill? Vietnam. You were in favor of it. Maybe you don't remember because you weren't there. You were in college with me, and with your roommate Alan Keyes. You were probably getting high all the time, that's why you don't remember it. There. I was grudgingly fair to you.
[5] See *Lies, and the Lying Liars Who Tell Them,* chapter 19.

Wrong again. David Sanger was toeing the party line all right. The wrong party. "Mr. Bush no longer has to pretend that he possesses a clear electoral mandate. Because for the first time in his presidency he can argue that he has the real thing." I appreciated Mr. Sanger acknowledging Bush's four-year record of pretending he had won in 2000. But it seemed to me that Mr. Sanger had drunk the pretend Kool-Aid.

My head spinning, I turned to Doyle McManus and Janet Hook of the *Los Angeles Times*. No liberal dice. They used a similar "now Bush doesn't have to pretend anymore" formulation:

> Four years ago, George W. Bush won his first term with fewer votes than his opponent, but governed as if the nation had granted him a clear mandate to pursue conservative policies. This time, Bush can claim a solid mandate of 51% of the vote, which made him the first presidential candidate to win a clear majority since 1988—a point Bush aides made repeatedly Wednesday.

The Bush strategy that McManus and Hook pointed out (claiming that 51 percent was a solid mandate) had obviously worked with McManus and Hook. It was true that in '96, Clinton had received only 49.24 percent of the popular vote—short of the 50.01 percent necessary for a clear majority, much less the 50.73 percent racked up by George W. But Clinton had been in a three-way race with the late (?) Ross Perot. No well-funded third-party candidate had run in 2004, despite the best efforts of Republicans to pump up Ralph Nader. And Clinton received 379 electoral votes. Bush had won 286.

I was getting sick. Where was the liberal media in my hour of greatest need? Maybe I had been right in my last book, *Lies, and the Lying Liars Who Tell Them*, even without meaning to be. Maybe there really isn't such a thing as the liberal media. Is this why my last book was so successful? Because I had hit upon, entirely by chance, a hidden, but profound, truth about the American political scene?

There was only one way to find out. I turned to CNN, which Republican House Majority Leader Tom DeLay had so aptly described as the Communist News Network. Ah, there was Wolf Blitzer, a loyal foot soldier in the left-wing media army. What's he saying? He was talking about Bush. "He's going to say he's got a mandate from the American people, and by all accounts he does."

By *all* accounts? So CNN was on their side, too. The darkness overwhelmed me. If CNN, the *LA Times*, *The Jew York Times*, and *TIME* magazine were all claiming that George "2½ percent" W. "Smallest Margin in History" Bush had a mandate, then it was just Air America alone on the left. Air America, and, it goes without saying, National Politburo Radio.

Slumping back in my chair, I switched on NPR's *Morning Edition* and recognized the voice as Renee Montagne's. "The President's people are calling this a mandate. By any definition I think you could call this a mandate."

Suddenly my despair turned to rage. My head was in greater danger of exploding than even Cheney's heart. What the hell was going on?!

Bush had won in a squeaker. Predictably, he was trying to spin it as a landslide. But the press, instead of laughing and throwing beer bottles, or grabbing their crotches and saying, "Mandate?! I got your mandate right here!", was going along with him. Bush said on November 4, "Let me put it to you this way: I earned capital in the campaign, political capital, and now I intend to spend it." Not true, right? Obviously not true. But it was reported with a straight face. That's where he got his political capital— from a spineless press corps that gave it to him.

How could Bush have actually won political capital? How could he have earned a mandate? Well, he could have won more states. He could have won more votes. But here's the thing. He didn't. He won by the skin of his teeth. (In 2000, he won by stealing the skin off Gore's teeth.) It was like Karl Rove had picked up a fumble in the end zone and here George W. Bush was doing the Ickey Shuffle. The referees of the media—the Wolf Blitzers, the Renee Montagnes, the David Sangers—should have penalized him for excessive celebrating. But George W. Bush, the luckiest member of the luckiest family in the history of the world, had somehow managed to enlist the referees in his touchdown party. George W. Bush was claiming a sweeping mandate and, against all reason, he was getting away with it.

And what did he say his mandate was for? At the top of his list was Social Security and tax "reform." Which in Bush-speak means Social Security privatization and more tax cuts for the rich. That wasn't the agenda he had campaigned on. Sure, he'd mentioned those issues on the stump, in passing. But the headlines and the roars of the handpicked crowds came from his core message: Terrorists want to kill you, my opponent is a flip-flopper, and only I can protect you and your spouse from the menace of gay marriage. Or, in my preferred vernacular, rhyme: fear, smears, and queers.

So not only was Bush inventing a mandate, and not only were the right-wing media dutifully parroting it, and the mainstream media slavishly echoing it, but now George W. Bush, for the first time the duly elected President of the United States, was announcing to the nation that he intended to use his imaginary political capital to lay waste to the very pillars of middle-class prosperity that allowed his constituents to buy televisions on which to watch his darkly triumphant press conference. It was the ultimate irony. FDR giveth. And GWB taketh away.

I swore then and there, if memory serves, to fight this bastard every step of the way. Setting my jaw, I turned to Katherine.

"It's time to do this," I said.

"You're right." There was an unexpected softness to her voice. A weariness, laced with exhaustion, tinged with resignation, with an undercurrent of relief. "Time to give up. We've had a good run. We tried, and we . . . we failed."

I could hardly believe my ears. Was this the Katherine Lanpher who had sat, and fought, by my side for these seven long months? Was this the Katherine Lanpher who had laughed at some of my jokes, even when Air America Radio was a hairsbreadth away from collapse?

No. No, it was not. This was a Katherine Lanpher badly in need of a bucking up.

"No, Katherine. If we quit now, they'll have won."

"But they have won."

"Have they, Katherine? Have they really?"

"Yes."

"Hmm."

There was a pause. Then I remembered the talking points that Democratic strategist Paul Begala had once slipped me after an especially dispiriting guest appearance on *Crossfire*: "Never stop fighting. Never stop believing. And don't stop thinking about tomorrow."

"Katherine, we're going to keep fighting. We're going to keep believing. And no matter what happens, Katherine, we're never, ever, going to stop thinking about tomorrow. We've got two million listeners out there who are hurting just as bad as we are. And we've got a nation to fight for and a world to save. Let the Tom Brokaws and the Ted Koppels do the giving up. The world needs us now, perhaps more than ever."

The tears streaming down her face told me that I wouldn't be going solo after all. At least not yet.

I decided to re-up with Air America for another two years. Not only that, but I would honor my book contract with Dutton, and not merely by slapping together a collection of show transcripts as Bill O'Reilly had done in his number one bestseller *The O'Reilly Factor*. No. I would work tirelessly on two tracks. By day I would present the first draft of history, in the form of broadcast journalism. By night I would labor over the second draft of history: this book. (I would leave the third draft to the historians. And the fourth draft to the revisionists.)

I knew we needed a fresh direction. But to understand where we might be going, we had to understand where we had been.

In the early nineties, American politics had been defined by competing views on the American economy. In the late nineties, politics had coalesced around one man's penis. But after 9/11, George Bush had made a decision. The country was as united as it had ever been. The world was at our side. Bush could have challenged us all to live up to our highest ideals, in a spirit of mutual purpose and mutual sacrifice. That might have won him reelection, the way it did for FDR. But Bush and Cheney and Rove decided that the clearest path to victory ran not to the City on a Hill but rather through a cemetery and past a haunted house. Instead of telling us that we had nothing to fear but fear itself, they would tell us that it was just a matter of time before the terrorists would strike again. There was a new ghost haunting the American political landscape. A terrifying ghost.

A ghost called Fear.

2 | How Bush Won: Fear

Most of you probably know me first as an author of immensely popular political satire. Others of you are no doubt devoted fans of my Air America Radio show, which has succeeded against all odds. There are still others who, when they hear "Al Franken," think "best speaker I've ever heard at a high-end corporate event." And, of course, there are millions who know me from my work in the salad days of *Saturday Night Live*. But the place I feel I've had the most impact is on the silver screen.

A great actor can communicate more humanity in a few moments on-screen than a corporate speaker can at a thousand industry conventions. In my roles as Baggage Handler #2 in *Trading Places* and Reporter #2 in the remake of *The Manchurian Candidate*, I drew upon every tool at an actor's disposal to maximize the impact of my performance.

You're probably familiar with such tools as "line memorization" and "not looking into the camera." But true actors, from Sir Laurence Olivier to Dame Judi Dench, know that these tools are mere child's play as compared to "sense memory," in which an actor digs deep to summon up an experience from his past, reliving the powerful emotions of that moment in order to communicate a truth so personal it's universal.

This is a book, not a film. But in order to write this chapter on fear, I feel it necessary to retrieve the most terrifying moment in my own life.

This is a true story.

The year was 1974. Tony Orlando & Dawn were hot. Nixon was on his way out. And "being gay" meant "being happy," not "being homosexual." They were innocent times. As a struggling comedian, I lived in what was considered a "shitty" neighborhood in Los Angeles. And late one night, after hanging out with some "gay" friends of mine, who by chance were also homosexual, I bid my pals good-bye and walked out into the warm and inky darkness of East Hollywood, heading home.

I was alone. I could hear my footfalls and my heartbeat. Turning a corner, a mere block from the relative safety of my shitty apartment, I came face to muzzle with a pack of wild dogs.

Shit.

How'm I going to get to my shitty apartment?

These dogs looked mean. And mangy. And *hungry.*

Street dogs. Los Angeles street dogs. I had thought they were a myth.

If I turned and ran, there was no way I could outrun them. I would be torn to shreds. But if I attacked them head-on, sure, I might win their respect, but still, I'd be torn to shreds. I didn't think I was going to make it. But I did make a mental note that if I did make it, this would be a great sense memory of fear.

The fear saturated every cell of my body. My heart pounded. My lungs heaved. Even now, as I write, my eyebrows are twitching and my sweat glands are unleashing rivulets of liquid terror.

At that moment, I was a Bush voter.

As I remember back, I would have given anything for this fear to lift. If only the fear could be vanquished, I would have gladly voted against my own economic interests. To relieve the crushing fear, I would have voted to do away with my own reproductive rights. To escape the fear, I would have ignored not only my own health care needs, but those of my parents and my children. And *their* children. If only I could get past these dogs!

And that is almost literally the choice that Bush offered America's voters on November 2, 2004: Vote Republican, or be ripped apart by dogs. Or to be precise, wolves. In the campaign's final stretch, Bush unleashed an advertisement he had saved for the crucial moment—an ad that, according to his henchmen, was the ad that tested best of all, that convinced the most swing voters to vote their way. The ad, which played like a trailer for a horror movie, showed flashes of wolf fur and fangs amid the leafy shadows of a deep, dark forest. An ominously somber announcer voiced the script:

> In an increasingly dangerous world . . .
> Even after the first terrorist attack on America . . .
> John Kerry and the liberals in Congress voted to slash America's
> intelligence operations by 6 billion dollars . . .
> Cuts so deep they would have weakened America's defenses.
> And weakness attracts those who are waiting to do America
> harm.

At this point, a group of wolves lounging in a grassy clearing arose and began advancing toward the viewer.

And then the tagline:

> I'm George W. Bush and I approve this message.

Scary.

The ad was dishonest. First of all, the "first terrorist attack on America" was left deliberately vague. Most viewers would think it was a reference to

9/11. Historians might have thought it was talking about the sinking of the *Lusitania* or the scalping of Goodie Pinkerton. In fact, the only thing the ad could possibly be referring to was the 1993 World Trade Center bombing. In 1994, Kerry *had* introduced a deficit reduction package that included a onetime $1 billion cut in intelligence, to be followed by a four-year inflation-adjusted freeze.[1] But in those days, everyone who was anyone on Capitol Hill was cutting intelligence spending. For example, the next year, Florida Republican Congressman Porter Goss cosponsored a bill cutting intelligence personnel by 20 percent over five years. But did Bush run negative ads against Porter Goss? No. He put him in charge of the CIA.

The advertisement's power didn't come from its (fake) facts. It came from its scary wolves. Some say the "Wolves" ad was modeled after Ronald Reagan's "There's a Bear in the Woods" spot. Perhaps. That was scary, too. But to me, it resonated with that night in Hollywood, thirty years before—and for millions of Americans, it resonated with the scary wolves of fairy tales like "Little Red Riding Hood" and "The Three Little Pigs." As Karl Rove knew very well, many of the "security moms" to whom the ad was targeted had read these same stories to their children mere minutes before turning on the television. The implication was clear. Kerry was the pig who had built his house out of straw (intelligence cuts). While Bush was the smart pig who had built *his* house out of bricks (invading Iraq).

Fear was Bush's ace in the hole. The Bush campaign wanted Americans to believe that if John Kerry was elected president, their families would be killed by terrorists. They tied everything back to this essential point, from policy differences to character issues. By the end of the campaign, Bush's speechwriters had distilled this terrifying message into a stump speech as elegant, efficient, and deadly as a ticking Swiss watch wired to a time

---

[1] Because the total intelligence budget is classified, it's impossible to know how deep Kerry's cuts really would have gone. But the best estimate is that his cuts would have amounted to about 3.7 percent.

bomb. Here's an excerpt from Bush's address at Tinker Field in Orlando, Florida, on October 30, 2004:

> A president must not shift in the wind; a president has to make tough decisions and stand by them. Especially in a time of war, mixed signals only confuse our friends and embolden our enemies. All progress on every other issue depends on the safety of our citizens. Americans will go to the polls Tuesday in a time of war and ongoing threats. The terrorists who killed thousands of innocent people are still dangerous, and they're determined to strike. The most solemn duty of the American president is to protect the American people. If America shows uncertainty or weakness in these troubling times, the world will drift toward tragedy. This is not going to happen on my watch.

Or, as Dick Cheney had put it more succinctly seven and a half weeks earlier:

> It's absolutely essential that eight weeks from today, on November 2, we make the right choice, because if we make the wrong choice then the danger is that we'll get hit again, that we'll be hit in a way that will be devastating from the standpoint of the United States, and that we'll fall back into the pre-9/11 mindset, if you will, that in fact these terrorist attacks are just criminal acts and that we are not really at war.

As obnoxious as that was, I thought his next comments, which were not so widely reported, were even worse:

> Further, we have very credible intelligence that tells us that if Kerry wins, the following states will be hit: Ohio, Florida,

Pennsylvania, Wisconsin, Minnesota, and New Mexico. What's more, terrorists are also threatening to attack any state in which the Democrats pick up a Senate seat.

The implication was clear. A Kerry victory would cost millions, if not hundreds of millions, or even billions, of lives.[2]

Enhancing the terrifying effect of these terror remarks was a steady drumbeat of terrifying terror alerts. From the first terror alert on February 12, 2002, until the November 2, 2004, election, the Bush administration raised the nationwide threat level to orange, meaning a "high risk of terrorist attack," six times.

For the record, during that period there were no terrorist attacks. Also for the record, there have been no nationwide orange alerts since the election. Also for the record, former Homeland Security Secretary Tom Ridge has now gone on the record to say that he didn't know why they kept issuing alerts. A few months after leaving office, Ridge complained that there was often only flimsy evidence to justify raising the threat level, but that he was overruled by other administration officials, like Attorney General John Ashcroft, master of the frightening press conference. As Ridge put it, "There were times when some people were really aggressive about raising it, and we said, 'For that?' "

Could it be that the "that" in question might have been Bush's reelection rather than credible threat information? Could it be that terror alerts like the August 1, 2004, warning, which was based almost entirely (if not entirely entirely) on intelligence obtained prior to 9/11, were more geared toward freaking people out than protecting them? Could it be, as cynics charged, that the much-vaunted Homeland Security apparatus was less about homeland security and more about politics?

---

[2]After my last book, some of younger and/or less bright readers complained that they couldn't tell when I was joking and when I was merely reporting true things in a comedic manner. The quote from Cheney about "making the right choice," while cartoonishly inflammatory, is real. The quote about terrorists attacking swing states, is, to my knowledge, just something I made up.

Sorry, cynics! Asked about a possible political motive the day after the suspiciously unwarranted August 1 alert, Tom Ridge was firm: "We don't do politics in the Department of Homeland Security."

On the other, cynical, hand, it did come out after the election that Ridge had met with hotshot Republican pollsters Frank Luntz and Bill McInturff just four days before embarking on the first of his sixteen trips to ten swing states at the height of the campaign season.[3]

We know about the meetings with the GOP pollsters because the Associated Press filed a Freedom of Information Act request for Ridge's daily appointment calendars, a request that Ridge's staff conveniently failed to comply with until three days after he left office. What we don't know is whether Luntz specifically focus-group-tested the phrase "We don't do politics in the Department of Homeland Security."

The terror alerts served no purpose other than to remind people that they could be incinerated at any moment. But that reminder was exactly the point. It's an old saw in politics that you don't change pants in mid-shit. So the Bush administration was determined to keep every American shitting his or her pants as frequently as possible in the months leading up to the election.

The "mid-shit" maxim is actually backed up by decades of peer-reviewed social science research, specifically in a little-known but actually real subfield of social psychology known as "Terror Management Theory," or TMT. Google it. It's fascinating. But in case you don't have a computer, let me save you some trouble.

TMT argues that much of human behavior and human culture can be understood as a response to the fear of death. Duh. Among other things, TMT predicts that death-related thoughts drive people to affirm their preexisting cultural worldview (boo gay marriage!) and to support "charismatic/visionary" leaders (Bush) over "task-oriented" leaders (Kerry) or "relationship-oriented" leaders who emphasize the need for people to

[3] In fairness, Ridge also made twenty appearances in nine non-swing states during the campaign season.

work together and accept mutual responsibility (Kerry). The predictions of TMT have been borne out by more than 175 published experiments. As compared to, say, the number of peer-reviewed studies concluding that human beings have nothing to do with global warming, which is zero.

Of all the TMT studies I've read (two), my favorite is "The Effects of Mortality Salience and Reminders of 9/11 on Support for President George W. Bush," which appeared in the September 2004 issue of the *Personality and Social Psychology Bulletin*. In a series of experiments conducted on student volunteers from across the political spectrum, the authors found that reminders of death generally or 9/11 specifically caused subjects to view Bush more favorably.

The first experiment divided the students into two groups to test whether thinking about death affected their politics. The control group was asked to describe the experience of watching television. Members of the second group were asked to "describe the emotion that the thought of your own death arouses in you" and to "jot down, as specifically as you can, what you think will happen to you as you physically die and once you are physically dead."

Both groups were then asked to read and evaluate a short essay praising Bush and endorsing the war in Iraq. Most of the people in the television group disagreed with the essay. Most of those in the death group agreed with it. Math nerds will be interested to know that the effect size was both large ($\eta^2 = .55$) and statistically significant ($p < .001$).

In the second experiment, the subjects were divided into three groups. In order to prime their subconscious thought patterns, one group was assigned to write about death, another about 9/11, and the third, the control group, about pain. (The scientists substituted "pain" for "watching television" to make sure that Bush's bump in the first experiment came from thinking about death specifically and not just from thinking about something unpleasant. If I were conducting the experiment, instead of pain, I would have made the unpleasant thing something very specific—like having to give Kentucky Senator Mitch McConnell a foot rub.)

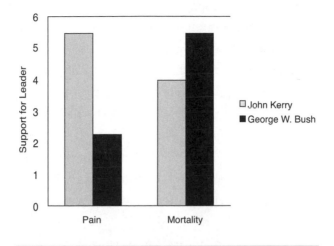

Support for President George W. Bush and presidential candidate John Kerry as a function of priming condition.

In this experiment, the subjects prompted to think about pain preferred Kerry by a more than a two-to-one margin. Those thinking about death or 9/11 preferred Bush by a landslide. The effect of thinking of death or 9/11 worked on liberals, moderates, and conservatives alike.

The Terror Management theorists who authored this study concluded:

> The present findings support the views of many theorists who have noted that political allegiances are not always based on the balanced, rational forces of self-interest suggested by the Jeffersonian notion of democracy but also on the operation of nonrational forces of which we are not always aware.

Hence, the wolves.

And it worked. The wolves blew Kerry's house down. Bush's margin in the 2004 election came from the ranks of the terrified.

I know. You think Bush won on "moral values." That myth came from one terribly designed exit poll, in which 22 percent of respondents looked at a list of "issues" and chose "moral values" as the most important one.

And 80 percent of those people voted for Bush. For the next month, we were subjected to Republican talking heads crowing about how Democrats were "out of touch" on the "moral values issue."

There were any number of problems with the "moral values issue" issue. For starters: To me and apparently to some other people, the economy is a moral issue. During the first three years of Bush's presidency, 4.3 million Americans—including a million-plus children—fell into poverty. I, for one, don't blame the kids. Yet of the 20 percent of the voters in this exit poll who said "economy/jobs" was the most important issue, 0 percent were considered "moral values" voters. And 80 percent of them voted for Kerry.

Ditto for Iraq, health care, and education, which Kerry won with 73 percent, 77 percent, and 73 percent, respectively. Does anyone think there's a moral dimension to people dying in Iraq, to eighteen thousand unnecessary deaths each year because of the lack of health insurance, or to kids getting crummy educations in crumbling schools? Anybody? Anybody?

Even if we pretend to accept the 22 percent moral values number as valid, that still doesn't mean that Bush won on that "issue." I will permit my colleagues at the prestigious Tory magazine *The Economist* to administer the coup de grâce:

> That 22% share is much lower than it was in the previous two presidential elections, in 2000 and 1996. Then, 35% and 40%, respectively, put moral or ethical issues on top, and a further 14% and 9% put abortion first, an option that was not given in 2004. Thus, in those two elections, about half the electorate said they voted on moral matters; this time, only a fifth did.

Okay? All right? So it wasn't moral values, asshole. (Although coarse language may have played a role.) It was terror. *Terror.*
TERROR!!!
Guess how many people in 2000 said that terrorism was their number one reason for voting? I'll give you hint. It was zero. That's right. Why the

change? Does the date 9/11/01 ring any bells? You may know it as "9/11." I think that's why the terrorism issue became prominent. You know I'm right.

Every one of the roughly 23 million voters who thought terrorism was the number one issue (if you believe this stupid exit poll) is a person who used to think something *else* was the number one issue. That is, before 9/11, and Bush's constant reminders of 9/11, scared the shit out of them. Some of these people were probably "moral values" voters in 2000. Some of them were probably "economy/jobs" voters. And a lot of them were probably "non" voters. That is, they didn't vote. But now they did. And even though, as I'll prove in the next chapter, 9/11 happened while Bush was president, that's not what mattered. What mattered was that through the skillful use of scary wolves and other subconscious and not-so-subconscious "priming" techniques, Bush, Rove, Limbaugh, and company had ensured that on November 2, 2004, as they entered the voting booth, Americans had one thing on their minds. Voting. Voting for that guy, the one who's gonna protect them from terrorism.

On that day, on that terrible day—11/02—86 percent of terrorism voters went for Bush.

3 | Bush's Little Black Dress

On September 10, 2001, President George W. Bush's approval rating was hovering at around 50 percent. On September 12, 2001, to my knowledge, no poll was conducted. I don't blame the pollsters. All of us were still devastated by the previous day's attack, and many offices were closed.

But by September 14, Frank Newport, editor in chief of the Gallup Poll, had pulled himself together enough to put another survey in the field. His findings stunned an already stunned nation. Bush's approval rating had shot up to 86 percent. A week later it reached 90 percent, the highest ever recorded since the Gallup Poll first asked, "Do you approve or disapprove of the way Franklin Delano Roosevelt is handling his job as President?" And *that* was way back during the Roosevelt administration!

What had Bush done in those critical days to become so spectacularly popular? Well, he had stood on a pile of rubble and delivered a rallying cry via bullhorn that I thought was genuinely stirring. Also, he had made me and two hundred million-plus other Americans cry with his speech at the

National Cathedral. And then he had declared a war on terror. (Although it turned out he meant "Iraq.") Then, he called the war on terror a "crusade," which to many listeners, sounded like "Crusade"—which is probably why he didn't get all the way up to 100 percent.

But something else had happened in the period between September 10 and September 14 that was more important than all those other things combined. George W. Bush had failed to prevent the most deadly terrorist attack in American history.

In my last book, *Lies and the Lying Liars Who Tell Them*, in the chapter "Operation Ignore," I laid out in great detail how the Bush administration had ignored the terrorist threat until it was too late. The 9/11 Commission did an even better job than I did. Of course, they had more time, a bigger staff, and subpoena power. As an official, bipartisan body, the 9/11 Commission couldn't come right out and say, as I did, that Bush had dropped the ball on terrorism over and over again from the minute he came into office. But anyone who reads the report can't come to any other conclusion.

To me, the most infuriating passage deals with Bush's nonreaction to the August 6 Presidential Daily Brief, memorably titled "Bin Laden Determined to Strike Inside U.S." The brief warned, among other things, that "al Qaeda members—including some who are U.S. citizens—have resided in or traveled to the U.S. for years, and the group apparently maintains a support structure that could aid attacks." Even worse, "FBI information . . . indicates patterns of suspicious activity in this country consistent with preparations for hijackings or other types of attacks, including recent surveillance of federal buildings in New York."

The 9/11 Commission reported:

> [The President] did not recall discussing the August 6 report with the Attorney General or whether [then National Security Adviser Condoleezza] Rice had done so. He said that if his advisers had told him there was a cell in the United States, they would have moved to take care of it. That never happened.

If advisers had told him there was a cell? Can someone please tell me what else "al Qaeda members have resided in or traveled to the U.S. for years," maintaining "a support structure that could aid attacks," could possibly mean?

Furthermore, the 9/11 Commission found that following the August 6 PDB,

> We have found no indication of any further discussion before September 11th between the President and his advisers about the possibility of a threat of al Qaeda attack in the United States.

It is my firm belief that President Bush never read the August 6 PDB. Or if he did, he did not have the reading-retention skills to pass the sixth-grade No Child Left Behind high-stakes exam. And it's hard to imagine any higher stakes.

Not convinced? Answer this question: If he had read the PDB, why did Bush go into the classroom at the Emma E. Booker Elementary School just after Condoleezza Rice had told him that a commercial plane had struck the World Trade Center?

I know what you're thinking. "*Nobody* thought it was terrorism at that point! *I* certainly didn't." Yeah, but, like the President, *you* hadn't read the PDB! You see?

CIA Director George Tenet was eating breakfast at the Hay-Adams Hotel in Washington that morning. When *he* heard about the first plane, he immediately asked, "Was it an attack? It sounds like an attack," and then told his breakfast-mate, "This is bin Laden. His fingerprints are all over it." Of course, Tenet had been trying to alert Bush to the terrorist threat for months. But I contend that anyone who had really absorbed the PDB ("hijacking," "buildings in New York," "Bin Laden Determined to Strike Inside U.S.") would have put two and two together and come up with "yikes!"

Now, you might be thinking to yourself, "Sure, Al. Very clever. But the PDB wasn't such a big deal. After all, the 9/11 Commission—a source that you yourself have cited—says that 'the President told us that the August 6 report was historical in nature.' Condi Rice made the same point *eight times* in her own testimony to the 9/11 Commission. Why would Bush have remembered something that was merely historical in nature? It's not like it was talking about a current and serious threat. *That's* the kind of thing Presidents remember, not boring old historical briefs."

Very clever, reader. You're clearly smarter than the readers of Sean Hannity's books. I welcome this battle of wits. But I'm afraid I'm still one step ahead of you. The 9/11 Commission directly debunked the Bush/Rice "historical" claim on page 260 of its report:

> Two CIA analysts involved in preparing this briefing article believed it represented an opportunity to communicate their view that the threat of a bin Laden attack in the United States remained both current and serious.

If, in fact, the PDB was meant to reflect a "historical" threat, the title would have been "Bin Laden *Used to Be* Determined to Strike Inside U.S., *But Not Anymore!*" That would have been historical. That's the kind of memo you know you don't have to waste a lot of time following up on.

And why exactly would people bother to prepare historical memos for Bush anyway? It's not like the previous day's PDB had been titled "Battle of Trafalgar Ends Threat of Napoleonic Invasion of British Isles."

Ah, you're finally seeing things my way. About time. But let me drive this point home a little further, with a quote from former vice president Al Gore, from a speech delivered on Monday, October 18, 2004, at 12:30 P.M.:

> In his famous phrase, George Tenet wrote, "The system was blinking red." It was in this context that the President himself was presented with a CIA report with the headline, more alarming and more pointed than any I saw in eight years of daily CIA briefings: "Bin Laden Determined to Strike in the U.S."

So it's pretty clear that either Bush didn't read the PDB, or its extraordinary importance didn't register. (Possibly, this was because he hadn't read any *other* PDBs.)

Why does this matter? For one thing, if Bush *had* processed the PDB, at the very least we all would have been spared the collective embarrassment of watching our leader freeze at his greatest moment of crisis. If Bush had realized that the first WTC strike was a terrorist attack, he would never have entered the classroom. Why he remained in the classroom for five to seven minutes even after hearing about the *second* attack remains a mystery. Bush did tell the 9/11 Commission that he "felt he should project strength and calm until he could better understand what was happening." But there's no way he could better understand what was happening by reading *The Pet Goat*, unless, of course, *The Pet Goat* had been written by Nostradamus, or by whoever had written the August 6 PDB.

But that's not the main thing. The main thing is that he might have reacted back on August 6, and initiated the kind of government-wide alert that had thwarted the planned Millennium attacks. Back to Al Gore's speech:

> The only warnings of this nature that remotely resembled the one given to George Bush were about the so-called Millennium threats predicted for the end of the year 1999 and less specific warnings about the Olympics in Atlanta in 1996. In both cases these warnings in the President's Daily Brief were followed, immediately, the same day—by the beginning of urgent daily meetings in the White House of all of the agencies and offices involved in preparing our nation to prevent the threatened attack.
>
> By contrast, when President Bush received his fateful and historic warning of 9/11, he did not convene the National Security Council, did not bring together the FBI and CIA and other agencies with responsibility to protect the nation, and apparently did not even ask follow-up questions about the warning.

Of course, Al Gore had a dog in this fight. Maybe his view was jaundiced by the experience of having the presidency stolen from him. Better to hear it from a Republican-chaired, bipartisan, unanimous report based on thousands of hours of rigorous investigation. Don't you think? So if you're sick of partisan spin, here's the *real* story—straight from the 9/11 Commission. As you'll note, it's the same as Gore's, although more detailed and less angry.

> In the period between December 1999 and early January 2000, information about terrorism flowed widely and abundantly. The flow from the FBI was particularly remarkable because the FBI at other times shared almost no information. That from the intelligence community was also remarkable, because some of it reached officials—local airport managers and local police departments—who had not seen such information before and would not see it again before 9/11, if then. And the terrorist threat, in the United States even more than abroad, engaged the frequent attention of high officials in the executive branch and leaders in both houses of Congress.

Like Gore, the 9/11 Commission contrasts this period with the months preceding the September 11 attacks:

> In the summer of 2001, DCI Tenet, the Counterterrorist Center, and the Counterterrorism Security Group did their utmost to sound an alarm, its basis being intelligence indicating that al Qaeda planned something big. But the Millennium phenomenon was not repeated. FBI field offices apparently saw no abnormal terrorist activity, and headquarters was not shaking them up.

In other words, Clinton put the government on high alert and stopped a deadly attack. Bush did nothing.

Could 9/11 have been prevented? We'll never really know. But if Bush had shaken the trees like Clinton had, Washington might have found out about the Phoenix memo, which warned of suspected terrorists enrolling in flight schools, or about the FBI agent in Minneapolis who tried to warn HQ that Zacarias Moussaoui might "take control of a plane and fly it into the World Trade Center." The CIA and the FBI might have shared information about Nawaf al-Hazmi and Khalid al-Mihdhar, who helped hijack American Airlines flight 77. The CIA had their photographs, but they were never put on the terror watch list and they were allowed to board the plane. In his book *Intelligence Matters*, former Senate Intelligence Committee Chairman Bob Graham identified twelve instances when the 9/11 plot could have been discovered and potentially foiled.

Why did they achieve no better than a disappointing 0-for-12 hit rate in preventing 9/11? It's because the Bush administration was focused on other national security matters.

Most of all, they *loved* Star Wars.

During the transition, Clinton personally told Bush that "by far your biggest threat is bin Laden and al Qaeda," and Sandy Berger (Clinton's national security adviser) told Condi Rice that she would spend more time on bin Laden and al Qaeda than on anything else. But despite these warnings, or maybe because of them, the Clinton-hating Bush team decided to shift its focus to missile defense.

In fact, Condi Rice was scheduled to give a speech on this very topic on September 11, 2001, at Johns Hopkins University. As the *Washington Post* reported on April 1, 2004, Rice's speech was intended to address "the threats and problems of today and the day after, not the world of yesterday." But the text of the speech, which was never delivered, contained not one word about the actual threat of "today," which, as became clear that day, was al Qaeda. Here's the *Post*:

> The address was designed to promote missile defense as the cornerstone of a new national security strategy, and contained no

mention of al Qaeda, Osama bin Laden or Islamic extremist groups, according to former U.S. officials who have seen the text.

The Bush administration has never allowed the full text of that speech to become public, even though it would have been public if she had been able to deliver it. My guess is that it's being withheld on national security grounds. After all, America's enemies might be emboldened if they knew just how far the Bush team's heads were up their asses during that critical period.

Many of us would look back at the events leading up to that horrible day and draw many lessons. The first of those lessons is to pay attention to your Presidential Daily Briefs. Another good one: If the Director of Central Intelligence tells you "the system is blinking red," ask him what he'd like you to do about it. Also, if you insist on appointing Dick Cheney head of your Counterterrorism Task Force, make sure Cheney actually calls a meeting. Many, including me, have argued that Bush's failure to do these things during his first eight months in office might have made the difference between preventing and not preventing the attacks.

But while you and I were sifting through old intelligence reports to understand what had gone wrong, he was looking at his poll numbers.

Bush took away a very different lesson: *Take advantage of 9/11. 9/11 is good to you. If you want to invade Iraq, if you want an excuse for a rotten economy, if you want to get reelected—don't forget: 9/11 is the gift that keeps on giving.*

As I documented in the previous chapter, Bush used 9/11 to scare people. But that's not all. He used it for pretty much everything. As the wife of blogger Dwight Meredith observed, 9/11 became Bush's "little black dress." Meaning he could slip it on for almost any occasion. Bush put on his little black dress to accuse Senate Democrats of not being sufficiently patriotic, to unravel Americans' civil liberties, to make the case for drilling in ANWR, and even as an excuse not to allow prescription drugs to be reimported from Canada. In the lead-up to the Iraq War, he went a step further and accessorized his little black dress with a strand of Richard Perles.

He also wore his little black dress with pumps—when he was pumping his economic record. And, boy, did it need pumping. As late as January 2005, Bush was still the first president since Herbert Hoover not to have created one single new net job. I think this might have had something to do with his policy of borrowing hundreds of billions of dollars in order to provide tax cuts to the rich, who then invested the money in a particularly non-economically-stimulating fashion, by buying the bonds issued to pay for their tax cuts. But Bush had a more fashionable explanation for the job loss. As he said on October 6, 2004: "Because of the attacks of September 11 nearly a million jobs were lost in three months."

Now, according to something called the Bureau of Labor Statistics, which provides statistics related to labor, the number of jobs reported lost either directly or indirectly because of 9/11 was 125,637. Sixty-two percent of those jobs were in either the air transportation or hospitality industries.

The 9/11 excuse for the prescription drug reimportation ban, for which the little black dress was borrowed by one of Bush's henchmen, was just as nakedly false. In fact, it was debunked as soon as it was reported. Witness this AP report from August 12, 2004:

FDA WARNS OF TERRORIST PRESCRIPTION DRUG TAMPERING

WASHINGTON (AP)—"Cues from chatter" gathered around the world are raising concerns that **terrorists might try to attack the domestic food and drug supply, particularly illegally imported prescription drugs,** acting Food and Drug Administration Commissioner Lester M. Crawford says.

In an interview with The Associated Press, **Crawford said Wednesday that he had been briefed about al-Qaida plans** uncovered during recent arrests and raids, but declined further comment about any possible threats.

Here's the next paragraph of that article:

> "While we must assume that such a threat exists generally, **we have no specific information now about any al-Qaida threats to our food or drug supply**," said Brian Roehrkasse, spokesman for the Homeland Security Department.

Who do you suppose had "briefed" Lester M. Crawford about al Qaeda plans to "attack" imported drugs? Apparently not the same the person who had briefed Brian Roehrkasse. At any rate, Mr. Crawford explained to the AP that the possibility of such an attack was the most serious of his concerns about drug reimportation.

My briefings indicate that the administration opposed drug reimportation because of an even more serious concern than the nonexistent threat of al Qaeda tampering with Canadian Lipitor: It would cut into the profits of their contributors in the pharmaceutical industry. Worse yet, it would make these drugs available at a lower price to Medicare recipients who desperately needed them, and as was no secret, Bush—like all Republican politicians—hated the old. Almost as much as he hated the young.

But the little black dress was at its most powerful when it was used to seduce America into invading the defanged, hapless Middle Eastern dictatorship known as Iraq.

Why would we go to the trouble of invading that country? Didn't we remember that George H. W. Bush had warned us in 1999 that taking Baghdad after the first Gulf War "would have been disastrous"? Or that Dick Cheney had said in 1991 that such an invasion would get us "bogged down in the quagmire inside Iraq?"[1]

---

[1] The entire quote is even more damning: "I think that the proposition of going to Baghdad is also fallacious. I think if we were going to remove Saddam Hussein we would have

Perhaps Iraq had somehow gotten far more dangerous during the intervening years. But that couldn't be it. After all, Colin Powell and Condoleezza Rice had both recently explained that Iraq posed no threat at all. As I'm sure you'll remember, Colin Powell had addressed this very issue in a Q&A session with reporters at the Ittihadiya Palace in Cairo, after meeting with Egyptian Foreign Minister Amre Moussa on February 24, 2001. His response to a question about the sanctions on Iraq rings as true today as it did then:

> The sanctions exist—not for the purpose of hurting the Iraqi people, but for the purpose of keeping in check Saddam Hussein's ambitions toward developing weapons of mass destruction. . . . And frankly they have worked. He has not developed any significant capability with respect to weapons of mass destruction. He is unable to project conventional power against his neighbors.

Five months later, Bush's national security adviser chimed in with a similarly clear-eyed analysis. Here's what Condi Rice told CNN's Wolf Blitzer on the twenty-ninth of July:

> In terms of Saddam Hussein being there, let's remember that his country is divided, in effect. He does not control the northern

---

had to go all the way to Baghdad, we would have to commit a lot of force because I do not believe he would wait in the Presidential Palace for us to arrive. I think we'd have had to hunt him down. And once we'd done that and we'd gotten rid of Saddam Hussein and his government, then we'd have had to put another government in its place. What kind of government? Should it be a Sunni government or Shi'i government or a Kurdish government or Ba'athist regime? Or maybe we want to bring in some of the Islamic fundamentalists? How long would we have had to stay in Baghdad to keep that government in place? What would happen to the government once U.S. forces withdrew? How many casualties should the United States accept in that effort to try to create clarity and stability in a situation that is inherently unstable? I think it is vitally important for a president to know when to use military force. I think it is also very important for him to know when not to commit U.S. military force. And it's my view that the President got it right both times, that it would have been a mistake for us to get bogged down in the quagmire inside Iraq."—Dick Cheney, the Washington Institute's Soref Symposium, April 29, 1991.

part of his country. We are able to keep arms from him. His military forces have not been rebuilt.

But on September 11, 2001, the world changed. Overnight, Iraq developed a massive stockpile of, as Bush would describe them, "the most lethal weapons ever devised." It was an accomplishment that put the Manhattan Project to shame.

It got worse. Saddam's fascistic, rigidly secular government had suddenly developed a relationship with the fanatically religious terrorist group al Qaeda. As President Bush explained to the nation in a speech at the Cincinnati Museum Center on October 7, 2002, Iraq and al Qaeda now "had high-level contacts that go back a decade." In fact, he said in a separate speech, "you can't distinguish between al Qaeda and Saddam when you talk about the war on terror." The world faced a new and terrifying threat. The threat that, as the President warned that October evening, "Iraq could decide on any given day to provide biological or chemical weapons to a terrorist group or to individual terrorists."

Such a threat would have seemed implausible on 9/10. But if 9/11 had taught us anything, we learned from Bush and Cheney, it was that Iraq could strike at any moment through its partners in the al Qaeda terrorist network. Foolish "experts" could jabber all day long that the real threat was from small groups of fanatical "non-state actors" unaffiliated with any government and therefore immune to the threat of conventional military retaliation. But Bush and Cheney knew better. 9/11 was a wake-up call about Iraq, which coincidentally many of their neoconservative friends had been hoping to attack for several years.

The outlook could hardly have been bleaker. In Cincinnati, Bush laid out the cold, hard facts. "We learned that Iraq has trained al Qaeda members in bomb-making and poisons and deadly gases."

But poisons and deadly gases were child's play compared to the threat the President would unveil next:

The evidence indicates that Iraq is reconstituting its nuclear weapons program. Saddam Hussein has held numerous meetings with Iraqi nuclear scientists, a group he calls his "nuclear mujahideen"—his nuclear holy warriors. . . . If the Iraqi regime is able to produce, buy, or steal an amount of highly enriched uranium a little larger than a single softball, it could have a nuclear weapon in less than a year. . . . Saddam Hussein would be in a position to pass nuclear technology to terrorists. . . .

We've experienced the horror of September the eleventh. We have seen that those who hate America are willing to crash airplanes into buildings full of innocent people. Our enemies would be no less willing, in fact, they would be eager, to use biological or chemical, or a nuclear weapon. . . . Knowing these realities, America must not ignore the threat gathering against us. Facing clear evidence of peril, we cannot wait for the final proof—the smoking gun—that could come in the form of a mushroom cloud.

Dear God.

Nuclear holy warriors! And a smoking gun in the form of a mushroom cloud!

Thank goodness they didn't have a softball of uranium yet! It made you think about what it would be like to die in a nuclear conflagration. It primed you to think about the emotion that the thought of your own death aroused in you, and specifically, what you thought would happen to you as you physically died and once you were physically dead. How could Americans manage such terror?

Fortunately, the 2002 midterm elections were only a month away. Frightened Americans had an opportunity to manage their mortal fear by voting Republican and electing senators like Saxby Chambliss of Georgia, Jim Talent of Missouri, Elizabeth Dole of North Carolina, John Sununu of New Hampshire, and my personal favorite, Norm Coleman of Minnesota.

Then the third shoe dropped. In Bush's State of the Union Address on

January 28, 2003, he told the nation that "the British government has learned that Saddam Hussein recently sought significant quantities of uranium from Africa."

"Significant quantities?" Sounded bigger than a softball. Maybe Saddam had sought as much as a football, or worse yet, a basketball of uranium. A nuclear "slam dunk" could be coming in a year, or sooner. And sooner it was. A scant two months later, Cheney dropped the bomb about the bomb they might drop. On the March 16 *Meet the Press*, he told NBC's gullible Tim Russert, "We believe he has, in fact, reconstituted nuclear weapons."[2]

It was time to attack Iraq or die at the hands of Saddam's nuclear mujahideen. The United States and a brave coalition of equally determined allies chose the only rational option.

(Attack.)

Polls throughout 2003 found that huge swaths of Americans believed Iraq was involved in 9/11. In a March 7–9 poll conducted by *The New York Times* and CBS News, 45 percent of interviewees agreed with the statement that "Saddam Hussein was personally involved in the Sept. 11, 2001 terrorist attacks." This idea came from somewhere. As *The Christian Science Monitor* reported, "Right after Sept. 11, 2001, when Americans were asked open-ended questions about who was behind the attacks, only 3 percent mentioned Iraq or Hussein."

Long after the war started, the right-wing media started bleating that the Bush administration had never actually claimed that Iraq and 9/11 were linked. This isn't true. Cheney had told a credulous Tim Russert on *Meet the Press* that it was "pretty well confirmed" that Mohammad Atta, 9/11's lead hijacker, "did go to Prague and he did meet with a senior official of the Iraqi intelligence service in Czechoslovakia last April, several months before the attack." Cheney's claim was quite the bombshell, and was widely reported at the time. In yet another *Meet the Press* appearance,

---

[2]He later said that he misspoke, and that he'd meant to say "reconstituted his nuclear program."

Cheney told a wide-eyed Russert what success in Iraq would mean: "We will have struck a major blow right at the heart of the base, if you will, the geographic base of the terrorists who have had us under assault now for many years, but most especially on 9/11."

Bush made it official. In his letter to Congress on the eve of the war, he concluded that attacking Iraq was "consistent with the United States and other countries continuing to take the necessary actions against international terrorists and terrorist organizations, including those nations, organizations, or persons who planned, authorized, committed, or aided the terrorist attacks that occurred on September 11, 2001."

So Bush and Cheney did explicitly link Iraq to 9/11 on several occasions, especially when speaking to the naive Russert. But most of the time, they took great pains to imply it without coming out and saying it. They knew the public would make the link for themselves. And if the public was too slow, their jackals in the right-wing press would connect the dots for them. So the implication was all they needed. Every time the Bushies talked about Iraq, they talked about the lessons of September 11. *The Christian Science Monitor* wrote on March 14:

> In his prime-time press conference last week, which focused almost solely on Iraq, President Bush mentioned Sept. 11 eight times. He referred to Saddam Hussein many more times than that, often in the same breath with Sept. 11.

How many times did he mention Osama bin Laden in the same press conference? Zero times. In fact, during the whole of 2003, George W. Bush publicly mentioned Osama bin Laden four times. Every time in direct response to a question about Osama bin Laden.

The truth is that Iraq wasn't just not involved in 9/11. Saddam's regime and al Qaeda weren't working together *at all.*

Although these two villainous gangs of goons had, in fact, met a few times to compare notes, they had abandoned any hopes of collaborative evildoing when they realized that their aims were in "ideological conflict." That quote is from a top secret British intelligence memo that was leaked to the BBC in early February 2003, just in the nick of time to stop the march to a disastrous war.

News of the memo, which concluded that there were no current links between Saddam's regime and the al Qaeda network, made headlines around the world—headlines like "No Link Between Iraq Regime and al Qaeda," which appeared in the *Press Trust* of India on February 5, 2003. And "No Iraq-Osama Link" in Australia's *Gold Coast Bulletin,* and "Experts Scorn Saddam Link to al Qaeda" in *The Scotsman,* a paper published by a man in Scotland, and "British Intelligence Report Rejects Current Iraq–al Qaeda Link" in the Chinese Xinhua Newswire.

It also made the news here in the United States. The memo was mentioned in the *Village Voice* and in the *LA Weekly,* which many have called the *Village Voice* of Los Angeles. The mainstream press covered it, too. On February 5, you'll remember, Colin Powell told the United Nations, "Iraqi officials deny accusations of ties with al Qaeda. These denials are simply not credible."[3] The next day, Congressman Bernie Sanders of Vermont brought up the leaked memo on CNN's *Crossfire,* although Tucker Carlson blew past it, no doubt to move on to something more important. The *Washington Post* mentioned it in the last two paragraphs of a page 15 story on February 8 in its widely unread Saturday edition. Not only that, but the BBC's Gordon Corera mentioned it in passing in a brief appearance on the February 6 *Today Show* to explain why Brits "just aren't convinced" about the link, and Sheila MacVicar, reporting from London on February 5, mentioned it while chatting with Wolf Blitzer after Powell's presentation. Also, there was a Cleveland *Plain Dealer* op-ed, and a wire story that appeared in Salt Lake City's *Deseret News.*

That's it. Believe it or not, Fox didn't mention it all. Neither did the

---

[3] Powell would later say of the speech, which was written by the vice president's office, "It turned out that the sourcing was inaccurate and wrong, and in some cases *deliberately misleading.*" Emphasis mine.

liberals at ABC, CBS, *The New York Times*, NPR, or PBS. So don't get me wrong. I'm not accusing Fox of any bias here. I took care of that in my last book. And look what happened.

Once we'd invaded Iraq on false pretenses, you'd think the Bushies would have been satisfied with what they'd pulled off. It was impressive. Clinton hadn't been able to mislead his country into war, and he was a political master.

So on the day when Bush landed on that aircraft carrier dressed in a flight suit with a stuffed codpiece, most of us expected him simply to crow about how he fooled everyone and then to explain what we were really doing there. Instead, he declared the war over, and mentioned September 11 not once, not twice, but three times. And he mentioned al Qaeda, not twice, not thrice, but four times. I could hardly believe it. He was sticking to his story. When would he give up the ruse?

> The liberation of Iraq is a crucial advance in the campaign against terror. We've removed an ally of al Qaeda, and cut off a source of terrorist funding. And this much is certain: No terrorist network will gain weapons of mass destruction from the Iraqi regime, because the regime is no more.[4]
>
> In these 19 months that changed the world, our actions have been focused and deliberate and proportionate to the offense. We have not forgotten the victims of September the eleventh— the last phone calls, the cold murder of children, the searches in the rubble. With those attacks, the terrorists and their supporters declared war on the United States. And war is what they got.

Bin Laden must have been furious. Here he had gone to all this trouble to murder thousands of Americans, and Saddam—Saddam, the infidel!—

---

[4]There was also another reason why no terrorist network would gain weapons of mass destruction from the Iraqi regime. Can you guess what it was? Here's a hint. It was the same reason that no terrorist network could get a signed Mickey Mantle rookie card from the Iraqi regime.

was getting all the credit! Who was the head of al Qaeda?! Who was *funding* al Qaeda?! Somewhere along the Afghanistan-Pakistan border there was a very angry terrorist mastermind that day.

Amazingly, as the months passed and Iraq–al Qaeda connections repeatedly failed to materialize, Bush and his friends in the right-wing media continued to flog them. *The Weekly Standard,* edited by the nefarious neocon William Kristol, ran an article ironically titled "Case Closed." The article summarized a memo leaked by Undersecretary of Defense for Policy Douglas Feith. "Osama bin Laden and Saddam Hussein had an operational relationship from the early 1990's to 2003," Feith wrote. "There can no longer be any serious argument about whether Saddam Hussein's Iraq worked with Osama bin Laden to plot against America." His memo contained fifty bullet points of supposed links between Iraq and al Qaeda.

As *Newsweek* reported, "many of these reports were old, uncorroborated and came from sources of unknown if not dubious credibility, U.S. intelligence officials say." While the *Standard* reported this as new information, *Newsweek* concluded that Feith's memo was just a collection of "recycled shards of old, raw data that were first assembled last year by a tiny team of floating Pentagon analysts . . . whom Feith asked to find evidence of an Iraq–al Qaeda connection."

This didn't stop the right-wing media from waving the story hysterically whenever anyone pointed out that Bush's case for war was a mirage. To this day, Sean Hannity, for example, mentions that article an average of 12 million times a show.

The National Commission on Terrorist Attacks Upon the United States, better known to shorthand enthusiasts as the 9/11 Commission, closed the case on "Case Closed" and filed it in a drawer marked, "Dustbin of History." As it concluded on page 66 of its Final Report:

> The reports describe friendly contacts and indicate some common themes in both sides' hatred of the United States. But to date we have seen no evidence that these or the earlier contacts

ever developed into a collaborative operational relationship. Nor have we seen evidence indicating that Iraq cooperated with al Qaeda in developing or carrying out any attacks against the United States.

This revelation was first made public in a 9/11 Commission Staff Statement in June 2004. The administration immediately started backpedaling, but not in the way you might imagine. Instead of admitting that its earlier claims were unfounded, it denied that it had actually made its earlier claims.

You'll remember, for example, the bombshell Cheney had dropped on the unsuspecting Tim Russert on the December 9, 2001, *Meet the Press*:

> RUSSERT: A couple articles have appeared which I want to get you to react to. The first: "The Czech interior minister said today that an Iraqi intelligence officer met with Mohammed Atta, one of the ringleaders of the September 11 terrorist attacks on the United States, just five months before the synchronized hijackings and mass killings were carried out." . . .

> CHENEY: Well, what we now have that's developed since you and I last talked, Tim, of course, was that report that—it's been pretty well confirmed that he did go to Prague and he did meet with a senior official of the Iraqi intelligence service in Czechoslovakia last April, several months before the attack. Now, what the purpose of that was, what transpired between them, we simply don't know at this point, but that's clearly an avenue that we want to pursue.

Now, here's the backpedaling. Three days after the 9/11 Commission staff statement, Cheney emerged from the shadows to be interviewed by Gloria Borger on CNBC's *Capital Report*:

BORGER: Well, let's get to Mohammad Atta for a minute because you mentioned him as well. You have said in the past that it was, quote, "pretty well confirmed."

CHENEY: *No, I never said that.*

BORGER: Okay.

CHENEY: *I never said that.*

BORGER: I think that is . . .

CHENEY: *Absolutely not.* What I said was the Czech intelligence service reported after 9/11 that Atta had been in Prague on April 9 of 2001, where he allegedly met with an Iraqi intelligence official. We have never been able to confirm that nor have we been able to knock it down, we just don't know.

Bush was pirouetting with equal dexterity.

The reason I keep insisting that there was a relation between Iraq and Saddam and al Qaeda: because there was a relationship between Iraq and al Qaeda.

Uh huh. And . . . ?

The administration never said that the 9/11 attacks were orchestrated between Saddam and al Qaeda. We did say there were numerous contacts between Saddam Hussein and al Qaeda.

Can you imagine if Bush had tried to get us to go to war by citing a handful of fruitless meetings? Donald Rumsfeld had more meetings with Saddam Hussein than Osama bin Laden had. Or to put it a slightly different way, Saddam Hussein had more meetings with Donald Rumsfeld than with Osama bin Laden. See? Slightly different.

But the Bushies bounce back quickly. Like Luke Skywalker heeding the disembodied voice of Obi-Wan Kenobi to use the Force, George W. Bush heard his own disembodied voice, whispering to him from two and a half years earlier:

> *Use 9/11, George. Don't forget to mention 9/11. 9/11 is your best friend. Use it. Use your friend. That's what you do with your friends, George. You use them. Use them for your own political gain. Do you understand what I'm saying, George? Use 9/11. Use it! For example, use it at the Republican National Convention. Have the convention in New York, where 9/11 happened. Except the Pentagon part of 9/11. And the Pennsylvania thing. But no one remembers those, really. Do they? Hard to say. Also, don't mention bin Laden. It's just 9/11, 9/11, 9/11. Oh! And give your convention speech from Ground Zero, through a bullhorn.*

Karl Rove could always tell when the President's inner voice had gone too far. He let Bush do everything but the part with the bullhorn at Ground Zero.

And so, as the Democrats organized their national convention around the positive, uniting, uplifting theme of "Reliving the Vietnam War," the fiendishly clever Republicans went with "9/11/24/7."

The 9/11 theme didn't mean that Madison Square Garden's men's room attendants would be breaking out the Osama bin Laden urinal cakes. No, this new-and-improved 9/11 theme would not pin the blame on one specific man or group. Instead, the Republican Convention would revolve around the epic, historic clash between the enemies of freedom on the one hand and George W. Bush on the other.

For three days, a parade of inspiring speakers invoked the painful memories of the attacks that had occurred only blocks away. They celebrated the

President's decisive leadership in attacking people who had nothing to do with the attacks, and warned of impending terrorist strikes on our homeland that could only be prevented by electing the President to a second term.

Critics would later claim that the name "Osama bin Laden" was not uttered by a single speaker at the RNC. This is a lie as despicable as any falsehood foisted upon the American people by a war-hungry, unelected child of privilege. As an equal opportunity debunker, I see it as my job to expose the lies of lying liars on *either* side of America's blue-red political divide. In fact, Osama bin Laden *was* mentioned. Twice. Once by Republican up-and-comer Speaker of the House Dennis Hastert on August 30 at approximately 11:23 A.M., and once by Republican down-and-outer New York Governor George Pataki on September 2 at 9:44 P.M.

Because neither was broadcast on network television, it's possible that some Americans may have missed their denunciations of America's most deadly nemesis. But fortunately, they would get to listen to the next best thing. Denunciations of the man whom Bush had successfully apprehended.

In books like this one, too often cases are made on the basis of anecdotes and generalities. For example, in Bernard Goldberg's biased *Bias*, the author relies on a story about a colleague calling Gary Bauer "a little nut from the Christian group" as proof of a media-wide anti-Christian, anti–short people, anti-nut conspiracy. See? I started this paragraph with a generality and tried to prove it with an anecdote. That kind of sloppiness doesn't cut it here.

I don't want you to take my word for it that the major Republican National Convention speakers systematically conflated 9/11 with Iraq. No, I want to prove it to you. Using not soft, disputable words, but cold, hard numbers. Numbers that, admittedly, represent the use of words, but numbers all the same. Because numbers, unlike words, can never be "spun." Especially when those numbers are collected and presented in strict accordance with the Scientific Method.

Hypothesis. Major speakers at the 2004 Republican National Convention mentioned Saddam Hussein, Iraq, terrorism, terrorists, terror, and/or

9/11 (hereafter referred to as "conflation words") more frequently than they mentioned Osama bin Laden.

Null hypothesis. The speakers used conflation words the same number of times as they mentioned Osama bin Laden.

Methodology. Major speeches from the Republican National Convention were analyzed by a team of one researcher (Ben), who tracked iterations of key words.

Results. See Fig. 1. All numbers have been rounded to the nearest integer.

Figure 1: Word Frequency in Major Republican National Convention Speeches

SPEAKER	SADDAM/IRAQ	TERROR(ISM/ISTS)	9/11	OSAMA
McCain	8	3	4	0
Giuliani	10	41	11	0
Laura Bush	8	3	2	0
Schwarzenegger	3	3	0	0
Cheney	7	8	5	0
Zell Miller	3	3	1	0
George Pataki	5	2	10	1
Bush	18	16	4	0
Total	62	79	37	*Uno*

Analysis. Major speakers at the 2004 Republican National Convention used conflation words 17,800 percent more frequently than they mentioned Osama bin Laden. The statistical likelihood of this occurring by chance is less than 0.0000000008331 percent. A lot less.

Case study. Here's a passage from the beginning of Rudolph Giuliani's address on the first night of the convention. As you'll see, the former New York City mayor is a master conflater. Watch how skillfully he gives the false impression that Iraq had been involved in 9/11:

> It was here in 2001 in lower Manhattan that President George
> W. Bush stood amid the fallen towers of the World Trade Center

and said **to the barbaric terrorists who attacked us,** "They will hear from us."

They have heard from us! They heard from us in Afghanistan and we removed the Taliban.

They heard from us in Iraq and we ended Saddam Hussein's reign of terror.

Conflation accomplished. Brain scientists tell us that "what fires together, wires together." Giuliani had gotten those 9/11-Iraq neurons firing and wiring beautifully. Then, Giuliani continued his list of places where "the barbarians who attacked us" have now heard from us, but in a way that gave him plausible deniability should anyone ever accuse him of claiming that Iraq was involved in 9/11:

They heard from us in Libya and without firing a shot Gadhafi abandoned weapons of mass destruction.[5]

They are hearing from us in nations that are now more reluctant to sponsor terrorists.

Who are "they" at this point? Who exactly is hearing from us? And what exactly are they hearing? Is he saying al Qaeda is in Libya? I don't think so. Suddenly, everything is very vague. "The barbaric terrorists who

---

[5] This, by the way, is a complete misrepresentation. (I'd say deliberate misrepresentation, but Giuliani probably had no idea what he was talking about.) As Flynt Leverett, who served on Bush's National Security Council, explained in a January 23, 2004, *New York Times* op-ed, Libya gave up its WMD not because of the war in Iraq, but because of negotiations that began in secret during the Clinton administration. In fact, Leverett pointed out that Libya's story was an argument *against* Bush's foreign policy approach, because Libya was offered a carrot (lifting of sanctions and normal diplomatic relations) and not just a stick. As Leverett wrote, "Until the administration learns the real lessons of the Libyan precedent, policy toward other rogue regimes is likely to remain stuck in the mud of ideology." Qadhafi was playing his cards brilliantly by agreeing to disarm just days after Saddam was captured—all of a sudden, he went from evil rogue dictator to poster boy for the war in Iraq. If, after reading this footnote, you're still skeptical, Google "Flynt Leverett" and "Why Libya Gave Up on the Bomb." Then write me a nice note of apology. I'll make sure your note is included in my *Collected Papers*, which will be released seventy-five years to the day after my death.

attacked us" are now, apparently, people in any nation that is now or has ever been involved in sponsoring any terror activity of any kind. Such as Northern Ireland or Saudi Arabia.

Conclusion. Republicans are shameless dicks. No, that's not fair. Republican *politicians* are shameless dicks. My hypothesis is correct. Or, if you want to be scientific, we fail to reject the hypothesis and we reject the null hypothesis.

Not only was my hypothesis correct, but the larger point that preceded the hypothesis is correct as well. They conflated Iraq and 9/11. It wasn't that they were confused. They were the confus*ers.* And many in the American public became, unwittingly, the confus*ees.*

Bush and his surrogates would continue to tie 9/11 to Iraq throughout the fall, pausing only to eat and sleep or, in Bill Bennett's case, gamble. Bush conflated them so much that his own neurons, to the extent that they fire at all, began to fire and wire together in the same pattern that he was trying to create in the electorate. Since all of his events were in front of prescreened crowds and his most nakedly dishonest lines were getting the biggest applause, perhaps it was only natural that he would show his hand at the worst possible moment: at the first presidential debate.

It was September 30. Bush was ahead. The race was his to lose. All he had to do was not look like a fool, and it would be clear sailing through November. *Just don't look like a fool.* It was that voice again. But this time, it wasn't coming from inside himself. Nor was it God. No, it was coming from the bulky transmitter under his suit coat.[6]

Don't look like a fool. Also, stop saying, "It's hard work."

As always, Karl was right. The President grimaced. Ah: The moderator was asking a question.

LEHRER: Mr. President, new question. Two minutes. Does the Iraq experience make it more likely or less likely that you

---

[6]Here's the truth about the transmitter. There wasn't a transmitter. If they wanted to use a transmitter, they could have used a much smaller transmitter. You can get really tiny ones. Also, the Secret Service told *The Hill* that the bulge was caused by a bulletproof vest.

would take the United States into another preemptive military action?

BUSH: I would hope I never have to. I understand how hard it is to commit troops. Never wanted to commit troops. When I was running—when we had the debate in 2000, never dreamt I'd be doing that.

But the enemy attacked us, Jim, and I have a solemn duty to protect the American people, to do everything I can to protect us.

Kerry saw an opening.

KERRY: Jim, the President just said something extraordinarily revealing and frankly very important in this debate. In answer to your question about Iraq and sending people into Iraq, he just said, "The enemy attacked us."

Saddam Hussein didn't attack us. Osama bin Laden attacked us.

As Kerry proceeded to methodically dissect Bush's arguments, the President looked stunned. Even more stunned than he had looked throughout the rest of the debate. Finally, it was his turn to respond.

LEHRER: Thirty seconds.

A wounded, peevish president snapped:

BUSH: First of all, of course I know Osama bin Laden attacked us. I know that!

After the debate, the polls would swing back toward Kerry. It would take a month of rock-solid 9/11-Iraq conflating to restore Bush's lead. That, plus the smearing and queering detailed in chapters to come.

It's a cliché to say that the Bush administration's use of language is Orwellian. After all, the "Healthy Forest Initiative" won't make forests healthy. Much to the contrary. It will make them *gone*. And the pro–air pollution Clear Skies Initiative is designed to clear the skies of birds. And then there's the slogan of Bush's newly created Ministry of Truth: "War is Peace. Freedom is Slavery. Ignorance is Strength." All of those things can be justly described as Orwellian. I mean, who's he kidding?

But Newspeak isn't the only thing Orwellian about this presidency. In Orwell's dystopian classic *1984*, the totalitarian state of Oceania is kept in a state of permanent war by Big Brother, who is the oldest of four sons of a former president. Big Brother's younger brother Younger Brother is really named Jeb, and is much smarter than Big Brother. Eerie, right? Anyway. Back to the permanent war. It doesn't matter who the enemy is or whether the enemy is actually threatening Oceania; the important thing is to keep the population thinking that it is under attack from an external threat. And just like in *1984*, where the enemy is switched from Eurasia to Eastasia, Bush switched our enemy from al Qaeda to Iraq. Bush's War on Terror is a war against whomever Bush wants to be at war with.

It wasn't enough just to scare people. Terror Management Theory suggests that, when frightened, the public yearns for a resolute, infallible leader. Had I been a Republican, my suggestion would have been former New Jersey Governor Thomas Kean, who had chaired the 9/11 Commission so masterfully. Knowing that Tom Kean was in charge would certainly have given *me* psychic relief from the specter of my own mortality. But the Bush administration insisted that the role of fearless leader be played by President Bush himself. I know. I can't explain it either. But that's the choice they made. And I guess it worked.

From the beginning of the Bush campaign, George Bush was portrayed as a steadfast leader who would never flip or flop. Flip-flops like his rejection and then embrace of a Department of Homeland Security; his rejection, then embrace, then rejection of steel tariffs; his embrace, then rejection of mandatory caps on carbon dioxide emissions—these were conveniently erased from the historical record by Ken Mehlman and his stooges at the Ministry of Truth.

No, George W. Bush had to be re-created as a man who had never changed his mind, never made a mistake, and never once swerved from the path of sure-footed certainty.

This approach faced its greatest test during Bush's April 13, 2004, press conference, when a handsome young *TIME* magazine correspondent, one John Dickerson, asked a question that seemed at the time to catch Bush totally off guard:

> **DICKERSON:** After 9/11, what would your biggest mistake be, would you say, and what lessons have you learned from it?
>
> **BUSH:** Hmmm—(pause)—wish you would have given me this written question ahead of time, so I could plan for it. (Laughter.) Uh—(really long pause)—John—(short pause)— I'm sure historians will look back and say, gosh, he could have done it better this way, or that way—(short pause)— Uh—(extraordinarily long pause)—You know, I just, uh— (pause that would normally be considered long, but in this context seemed reasonably brief)—I'm sure something will pop into my head here in the midst of this press conference with all the pressure of trying to come up with an answer, but—(mercifully short pause)—it hadn't yet. I, uh—(long pause, followed by a rambling defense of how he handled Afghanistan and Iraq).

To observers like myself, the President's fumfering answer seemed colossally dumb. It seemed to reinforce all the flaws that I believed would lead to his sure electoral defeat: his inability to accept responsibility, the yammering inarticulateness that frankly was an embarrassment to our once-proud nation, and the smug laziness betrayed by the fact that he hadn't prepared for a question that any seasoned politician should have expected.

As it would turn out, to my tremendous amusement and subsequent depression, I was wrong on the last point. Amazingly enough, Bush had seen the question coming and had prepared for it.

The New York Times reported two days later:

> Mr. Bush's advisers said that the President had anticipated the line of inquiry at the news conference.
>
> One adviser said the White House had examined polling and focus group studies in determining that it would be a mistake for Mr. Bush to appear to yield.

Not only did the *Times* article shed new light on Bush's "no mistakes" fumfer-thon, it also illuminated two other exchanges in the same press conference. Asked how he felt about dwindling support in the polls for his misbegotten war in Iraq, Bush responded:

> BUSH: And as to whether or not I make decisions based upon polls, I don't. I just don't make decisions that way.

And, a few minutes later:

> BUSH: If I tried to fine-tune my messages based upon polls, I think I'd be pretty ineffective. I know I would be disappointed in myself.

By the Republican National Convention, the doctrine of presidential infallibility had grown to mythic proportions. And no one's nose was browner than the well-proportioned snout of former New York Mayor Rudolph Giuliani. On that first night, when Giuliani won the Mortality Salience Award by mentioning terror forty-one times, he also related an anecdote that combined both the unabashed Bush-worship and the histrionic dishonesty that undergirded so much of the campaign's rhetoric. Speaking of, of course, 9/11, he said:

At the time, we believed we would be attacked many more times that day and in the days that followed. Spontaneously, I grabbed the arm of then Police Commissioner Bernard Kerik and said to Bernie, "Thank God George Bush is our president."

And I say it again tonight. Thank God George Bush is our president.

When Giuliani said that, I was watching from the floor of the convention there in Madison Square Garden with my radio producer, Ben Wikler. Spontaneously, I grabbed his arm and said to Ben, "He made that up." And as would later become clear, I was right.

Giuliani's bestseller, *Leadership*, had opened with, as *Publishers Weekly* described it, "a gripping account of Giuliani's immediate reaction to the September 11th attacks." Given Giuliani's well-known political ambitions, you just know that his book would contain any story that would please prospective Republican primary voters. For example, on page 52, he wrote: "I thought it so important that George W. Bush defeat Al Gore that I campaigned for Bush even during the course of my radiation treatment for cancer." But the "Thank God George Bush is our president" line, which would make headlines when Giuliani used it at the Republican Convention, was nowhere to be found in *Leadership*. In fact, the name "Bush" makes a total of zero appearances in the twenty-eight-page "gripping account" of that fateful morning.

I know from experience that a smart author never leaves out a dramatic and/or self-serving anecdote. For example, you'll notice that, above, I related the anecdote about grabbing Ben's arm and telling him that Giuliani made up the anecdote about grabbing Kerik's arm.

Kerik, whom Giuliani would recommend to be Bush's director of Homeland Security, had set up a love nest in an apartment across the street from the World Trade Center site that had been donated for the use of weary rescue workers. He had been grabbed many times near Ground Zero, it seems. But never by Giuliani.

Wrestling with the fear triggered by the Republican Convention's 116 prime-time references to terror or 9/11, the viewing public was in desperate need of a charismatic leader who could restore them to "psychological equanimity in the face of death," as Terror Management Theorists Cohen, Solomon, Maxfield, Pyszczynski, and Greenberg put it in "Fatal Attraction: The Effects of Mortality Salience on Evaluations of Charismatic, Task-Oriented, and Relationship-Oriented Leaders." Summarizing the ideas of cultural anthropologist Ernest Becker, they wrote:

> For terror management purposes, people need a supremely confident leader who has a grand vision and can provide self-worth through identification with the leader and the leader's vision.

George W. Bush was ready to deliver.

At Madison Square Garden, President Bush strode purposefully to the podium, a podium on which the presidential seal partially obscured a semi-subliminal cross. His brow was furrowed. Not in confusion, as in the debates. No, it was furrowed with steely resolve. True to form, the President made no apologies for his inaction before 9/11. Rather, he called the nation's attention to the attitude he adopted immediately after:

> Since that day, I wake up every morning thinking about how to better protect our country. I will never relent in defending America, whatever it takes.

He displayed his light touch:

> Some folks look at me and see a certain swagger, which in Texas is called "walking."

In Minnesota, we call it "a swagger." In New York, they call it "being an asshole." That's the difference between Minnesota and New York. And Texas.

He walked—or swaggered—his audience through the horror of 9/11 one more time, and darkly hinted at the possibility of future attacks if America were to make the wrong choice:

> If America shows uncertainty or weakness in this decade, the world will drift toward tragedy. This will not happen on my watch.

And then he hit the gusher—the supreme confidence in himself and his country, a confidence so blindingly bright that it could lift the spirits of a cowering nation. A nation cowering because of the previous speakers. He ended on a note so uplifting that if I didn't know anything about him, it would have made me think he was fantastic:

> Like generations before us, we have a calling from beyond the stars to stand for freedom. This is the everlasting dream of America and tonight, in this place, that dream is renewed.
>
> Now we go forward, grateful for our freedom, faithful to our cause, and confident in the future of the greatest nation on earth.

The crowd went nuts. And with good reason. Before them stood, not just a politician with a great speechwriter, but a *leader*, a man's man who had displayed the fortitude, the iron will, the unyielding resolve necessary to deliver the speech exactly as written.

The speech was the final shrink-wrapping on the packaging that had been chosen over eggies at Karl Rove's Breakfast Group nearly eighteen months before: The man who had shrunk from duty in Vietnam, who had been asleep at the wheel from January 20 through 9:12 A.M. on September 11, 2001, who had lied us into a disastrous, unnecessary war and simultaneously failed to create jobs despite a series of unprecedented wartime tax cuts for the rich that were driving us deeper and deeper into debt—this man had become Resolute Man, a superhero whose one defining characteristic was his unyielding commitment to appearing resolute.

But on its own, it wasn't enough. Seeming resolute would only take Bush halfway there. For Bush to be elected once and for all, the GOP and the right-wing media would have to package his opponent as well. Through smears, lies, and unceasing attacks, they would have to define him as a weakling, as a coward—as a spineless wimp who would get us all killed.

They would have to turn a war hero into a flip-flopper.

4 How Bush Won: Smear

Although I am writing this chapter with John and Teresa Heinz Kerry literally looking over my shoulder, and although John and Teresa are financing the research, publication, and bulk-buying of this book with the $15 million left over from the campaign, this chapter is in no way a definitive defense of John Kerry's run for the White House.

Yes, I will be debunking a few of the most outrageous and often slanderous charges that were leveled against the senator during the 2004 election. But I won't make excuses for what was at best an excellent campaign, but one that not infrequently wandered into a fog of vagueness and abstraction.

Hold on. John wants to write something about the leftover $15 million.

This is John Kerry. First of all, if you voted for me, thank you for voting for me. As you may have read earlier in this book, I received more votes for President of the United States of America than any Democrat who has ever had the honor of winning from this country's

Democratic primary voters that great honor bestowed only once every four years—the mantle of standard-bearer for our party, the party of the people.

Okay, this is Al again.

Hang on, Al. But I harbor no bitterness toward those who did not vote for me. Any American who exercises his franchise, or her franchise, is a living testament to the greatness of our framers' vision: a federal republic united by the spirit and vision of "we the people." And to those nonvoters, to you I say this: Come, join our celebration of democracy. Experience the challenge and the promise of self-government. For though ours is a nation of laws, not of men, those laws are only as wise and as just as are the elected legislators who write and revise them each year in the halls of Congress.

Okay, this is Al again. John had to catch a plane for a ribbon-cutting in Manchester. But I think John was about to address the criticism from some quarters that his campaign should have spent every dime that it raised, and maybe even gone into debt, rather than leaving $15 million in the bank on Election Day. I'll bet his response would have been that the leftover money was being kept as a strategic reserve, which would have been a godsend if they had had to fight a recount battle. Think about it. If Gore had saved a little dough for Florida, he might be serving a second term today, 9/11 might have been averted, and our troops would already be returning home triumphantly from Darfur.

But I'm getting off track. What I'm saying here is that I'm not going to get bogged down responding to every little criticism of Kerry. He did some things very well, and other things—let's just say I wish he'd done those differently. Like the things he screwed up. I wish he had done those things differently.

No, the point of this chapter is this: For the last five elections, at least, the

Republicans have gone after the Democratic nominee with constant, vicious, dishonest character attacks. 2004 was worse than usual, but it's always ugly. We've got to expect it, be ready for it, and know how to beat it. This chapter tells the story of how the Republican smear machine took a war hero with a record of unflagging support for our troops and convinced a slim majority of voters that he was a sniveling traitor running for president in order to dismantle our armed forces, ban the Bible, and raise taxes enough to award himself tens of millions of additional unearned medals. I present this story not just to shock you, not just to make you laugh and cry alternatingly or maybe even at the same time, not just to set the record straight—but to rouse you, to prepare you for battles ahead. The only vaccine powerful enough to inoculate you from Republican lies is the truth. If you run for president as a Democrat, they're going to come after you. They're going to come after you no matter who you are. Even if it's you, Hillary. You may not believe it now. But if you read the rest of this chapter, I hope you'll come away convinced. This chapter is both sword and shield. Enjoy.

Tom Oliphant was mad. And when Tom Oliphant gets mad, close observers of Tom Oliphant can often detect a slight tilt to the usually perfect horizontal set of the mild-mannered *Boston Globe* columnist's signature bow tie. Sitting across from Tom that hot August day in Air America's roasting craphole of a studio, I could see he was mad indeed.

Nearly forty years of journalistic experience informed Oliphant's elegant rage. He had covered Kerry since his return from Vietnam and his emergence as an antiwar leader. He knew Kerry's story chapter and verse and he had heard these attacks before. This time, something had changed.

The Swift Boat Veterans for Truth (or as I like to call them, Swift Boat Veterans for "Truth," or Swift Boat Veterans "for" Truth, or better still, the "Swift" "Boat" "Veterans" "for" "Truth," because every word they said was a lie) had been slinging their feces at Kerry like gorillas for months. But that's not why Tom was mad. Gorillas everywhere always throw their feces. Tom was mad because of the way the media had responded. Here's what he told me:

> Let me see if I can explain myself with a little conciseness here, but make the point about what's happened to my business.
>
> Take the first Purple Heart. There's a guy in the first TV commercial who says, "I know he's lying about that because I treated him." Say a guy like that walks into your office in a newspaper, and he says, "I got this story for you. I treated John Kerry for that wound, and he's lying about what happened."
>
> And you say, "Well, Jesus, that's interesting, guy. What do you got? Anybody else back you up? You got some corroboration?"
>
> "Well, no."

Tom's even voice had grown soft. Soft, with an edge.

> "How about a document? You treated him. You know, maybe there's a piece of paper that says, gee, you treated him."
>
> "Well, no. I don't have a document. There is this document, but it says somebody else treated him."

I laughed. That was funny. But Tom's eyes were burning.

> Now, at that point, the way I was raised: "Thank you very much for coming in."

Tom pointed toward the door of the studio, as if to invite the imaginary Swift Boat Liar to get the hell out.

> You know, we've put a million stories in our wastebaskets over the years, because they don't . . . check . . . out.
>
> Today, we publish, or we broadcast, the mere *fact* of the accusation, regardless of whether it's filled with helium.

Tom invested the word "fact" with all the scorn he could muster.

> *That's* what's changed in our business. We served as transmis-
> sion belts for this stuff without ever inquiring into its accuracy.
>   "How did this happen?"

That was me. As a professional radio host, I've learned to ask open-ended, rather than "yes-or-no" questions. It's a trick of the trade.

Tom responded concisely. More in anger than in sadness.

> Because that's the way the news business runs now.

Tom's face was red and his bow tie practically vertical. No, it was spinning. And his face was purple like a beet. I hope I've illustrated the extent of his anger through these metaphors.

Anyway, the point is Tom was pissed off.

It was August 26. The book *Unfit for Command: Swift Boat Veterans Speak Out Against John Kerry* had topped the best-seller list for three weeks. The Republican National Convention was about to start. We had that to look forward to. For weeks, political news coverage had been dominated by "the mere fact of the accusation." The mainstream media had finally begun doing what they should never have had to do—debunk the scurrilous charges that Kerry had not earned his military decorations in Vietnam. They never should have *had* to debunk these charges because the charges should never have been given any play in the first place. The charge that Bush had been involved in a series of chainsaw massacres while serving as governor of Texas didn't get any coverage in the 2000 election. That charge was equally untrue and equally unworthy of coverage. But the treatment it received was very different.[1]

---

[1] One key difference was that, unlike the scurrilous Texas chainsaw story, the Swift Boat Veterans for Truth were the beneficiaries of a nationwide publicity campaign initially financed by Karl Rove's inner circle of political donors. The Texas chainsaw story never got a thin dime from the Gore money men. This is a mistake we shan't repeat.

The responsible newspapers did eventually jump on the debunk wagon. On August 20, the *LA Times* put it pretty simply: "Military documents and accounts of crewmates who did serve with Kerry support the view put forth by the candidate and his campaign—that he acted courageously and came by his five medals honestly." Two days later, the *Washington Post* carried a 4,100-word opus under the headline "Swift Boat Accounts Incomplete; Critics Fail to Disprove Kerry's Version of Vietnam War Episode." And the same week, *The New York Times* moved the story further by exposing the incestuous relationship between the supposedly non-Bush-run Swift Boat Vets and their slutty older sisters in the Rove-run Bush campaign:

> A series of interviews and a review of documents show a web of connections to the Bush family, high-profile Texas political figures, and President Bush's chief political aide, Karl Rove.

And for good measure, the *Times* tossed in some debunking of its own:

> The strategy the veterans devised would ultimately paint John Kerry the war hero as John Kerry the "baby killer" and the fabricator of the events that resulted in his war medals. But on close examination, the accounts of "Swift Boat Veterans for Truth" prove to be riddled with inconsistencies. In many cases, material offered as proof by these veterans is undercut by official Navy records and the men's own statements. Several of those now declaring Mr. Kerry "unfit" had lavished praise on him, some as recently as last year.

It was nice. But it was late. And that's not just my opinion. That's what a hissing Tom Oliphant said that day in our studio:

> I don't really care what *The New York Times* did last Friday, or the *Post* did the day before or Sunday. It was late.

Long before the mainstream press had debunked each and every charge made by John O'Neill and his swarm of psychotic lying vermin (the Swift Boat Veterans), those charges had been played over and over again on Fox, on talk radio, and in right-wing rags, and had burrowed their way into America's collective brain stem to lay their eggs of pure evil. Vermin. Vermin, indeed.

Let's just take one of those egg-laying charges and crack it open.

The Swift Boat Vets claimed in *Unfit for Command* and on countless right-wing talk radio shows and countable right-wing cable TV shows that, as with all his other decorations, Kerry received his Silver Star not on the basis of valor, but on the basis of scheming, treachery, and lies. And by shooting a nearly naked, wounded, and possibly unarmed child in the back.

The official naval citation for Kerry's Silver Star says that "an enemy soldier sprang up from his position not ten feet from Patrol Craft Fast 94 and fled. Without hesitation, Lieutenant (junior grade) KERRY leaped ashore, pursued the man behind a hooch, and killed him, capturing a B-40 rocket launcher with a round in the chamber" and commends Kerry for "extraordinary daring and personal courage . . . in attacking a numerically superior force in the face of intense fire."

The Swiftees saw it differently. Even though they didn't actually see it. Because they weren't actually there.

Here's how they tell the story in their awful book:

> Kerry's boat moved slightly downstream and was struck by a rocket-propelled grenade in its aft cabin. A young Viet Cong in a loincloth popped out of a hole, clutching a grenade launcher which may or may not have been loaded, depending on whose account one credits. Tom Belodeau, a forward gunner, shot the Viet Cong with an M-60 machine gun in the leg as he fled. At about this time, with the boat beached, the Viet Cong who had been wounded by Belodeau fled. Kerry and Medeiros (who had many troops in their boat) took off, perhaps with others, following the

young Viet Cong as he fled, and shot him in the back, behind a lean-to.

Then they editorialize about it:

> Whether Kerry's dispatching of a fleeing, wounded, armed, or unarmed teenage enemy was in accordance with the customs of war, it is very clear that many Vietnam veterans and most Swiftees do not consider this action to be the stuff of which medals of any kind are awarded; nor would it even be a good story if told in the cold details of reality. . . .
>
> The citation statement that Kerry attacked "a numerically superior force in the face of intense fire" is simply false. There was little or no fire. . . . The lone, wounded, fleeing young Viet Cong in a loincloth was hardly a force superior to the heavily armed Swift boat and its crew and the soldiers carried aboard. . . .
>
> Commander George Elliott, who wrote up the initial draft of Kerry's Silver Star citation, confirms that neither he nor anyone else in the Silver Star process that he knows realized before 1996 that Kerry was facing a single, wounded young Viet Cong fleeing in a loincloth. While Commander Elliott and many other Swiftees believe that Kerry committed no crime in killing the fleeing, wounded enemy (with a loaded or empty launcher), others feel differently. Commander Elliott indicates that a Silver Star recommendation would not have been made by him had he been aware of the actual facts.

How had Commander George Elliott come to learn these "actual facts"? By talking to the Swift Boat Vets. Who weren't there. Nevertheless, in July 2004, Elliott signed an affidavit affirming that their account of the facts was correct.

When a skeptical *Boston Globe* reporter named Michael Kranish asked the Swift Boat Vets to back up their claims, they produced—guess what?—Elliott's affidavit. Which was based solely on what they'd told him.

But Kranish didn't take the Swiftees' word for it. Maybe because Elliott had told the *Globe*, as recently as June 2003, that Kerry's Silver Star was "well deserved" and that he had "no regrets or second thoughts at all about that."

When Kranish actually reached him, Elliott said, "It was a terrible mistake probably for me to sign the affidavit with those words. I'm the one in trouble here." He also said, "I knew it was wrong."

Mysteriously, that very night, the obviously very stable ex-commander reversed himself again. Kind of. He signed *another* affidavit, this one presumably not "wrong" and "a terrible mistake." As the *Boston Globe* reported the next day, Elliott's new affidavit reiterated that "had I known the facts, I would not have recommended Kerry for the Silver Star simply for pursuing and dispatching a single wounded Viet Cong," although he graciously added, "I do not claim to have any personal knowledge" of what happened.

Elliott's re-re-reversal, almost unprecedented in affidavit history, was quickly and unquestioningly picked up by the Drudge Report, from whence it exploded into the right-wing blogosphere, radiosphere, and asshole-on-TV-o-sphere (Fox News Channel's *The Sean Hannity Show*).

So if Elliott wasn't there, and the Swift Boat Vets weren't there, who *was* there? I mean, obviously, Kerry was a medal-chasing glory hound whose account only a fool could take seriously. Then there was Mike Medeiros, who corroborated Kerry's account. He didn't think Kerry had merely capped a "fleeing, wounded enemy (with a loaded or empty launcher)." He told historian Douglas Brinkley that "the VC guy was a lethal threat. He still had the B-40 rocket launcher in his hands."

But he also told the *Washington Post* that Kerry "was a great commander. I would have no trouble following him anywhere." So how can you trust *him*?

And Belodeau, the machine gunner who wounded the "fleeing teenager in the loincloth," was dead. Very convenient, don't you think?

Then there was Fred Short. He was on the boat, too. "Kerry saved our lives," he told Brinkley. "The guy was dangerous, and there were others waiting." But how can you trust him? He obviously felt beholden to Kerry, because he believed Kerry had saved his life. You save a guy's life, he'll say anything for you!

Ditto for all the other guys on Kerry's boat, all of whom sided with Kerry. Not trustworthy at all.

Of course, Kerry's PCF-94 wasn't the only Swift boat on the Dong Cung tributary of the Bay Hap River on February 28, 1969. PCF-43 was commanded by Lieutenant j.g. Donald Droz. But Droz died in battle on April 12 of that year. And PCF-23 was commanded by one William B. Rood—but he wasn't talking.

Lacking a credible referee who could determine which side was right—the Bush-donor-funded Swift Boat Character Assassins, or the Kerry crewmates who were actually there—the media kept treating the smear campaign as a "he-said, she-said" story. Fox's popular Bill O'Reilly exemplified the relativistic spirit of the age when he told Jim Rassman, the former Green Beret whom Kerry had saved from certain death in another much-lied-about incident that led to Kerry's Bronze Star, "You see it one way, and you're sincere, and you're correct. They see it another way, but they may also be sincere and correct."

For every story on the Fox News Channel, there were a hundred stories on right-wing talk radio.

The hackery reached an apex in one four-day period from August 17 to August 20, when every episode of Fox News Channel's *The Big Story with John Gibson* (5 P.M.), *Special Report with Brit Hume* (6 P.M.), *The O'Reilly Factor* (8 P.M.), and *The Sean Hannity Show* (9 P.M.) "reported" on the Swiftees.

With one single shining exception. On August 20, Bill O'Reilly took a break from the character assassination of Kerry and turned his focus to Kerry's character assassination of Bush. "Kerry's got to know what's going on," O'Reilly opined. "He's got to know MoveOn.org and all those people are assassinating characters all over the place. . . . I don't think the Republicans have done that. . . . Do you know of any conservative right-wing websites that do what MoveOn.org does?"

Other than that, it was wall-to-wall "Why Is John Kerry Lying?", "Will John Kerry's Lies Hurt Him?", and "John Kerry: the Man and His Lies."

Finally, the previously silent William B. Rood, commander of PCF-23, couldn't stands it no more.

Now, Bill Rood probably wouldn't use a phrase like "I couldn't stands it no more," especially in such a serious context. He is, after all, an editor on the metropolitan desk of the *Chicago Tribune*, which is an utterly humorless paper. No, when Rood decided to break his thirty-five-year public silence by publishing a 1,760-word account of the encounter that led to Kerry's Silver Star, he used phrases like "it's gotten harder and harder for those of us who were there to listen to accounts we know to be untrue, especially when they come from people who were not there."

Here's how Rood described the "fleeing, wounded, armed, or unarmed teenage enemy" incident, which, for brevity's sake, I will hereafter refer to as the "loincloth affair":

> As we headed for the riverbank, I remember seeing a loaded B-40 launcher pointed at the boats. It wasn't fired as two men jumped up from their spider holes.
>
> We called Droz's boat up to assist us, and Kerry, followed by one member of his crew, jumped ashore and chased a VC behind a hooch—a thatched hut—maybe 15 yards inland from the ambush site. Some who were there that day recall the man being wounded as he ran. Neither I nor Jerry Leeds, our boat's leading petty officer with whom I've checked my recollection of all these events, recalls that, which is no surprise. Recollections of those who go through experiences like that frequently differ.
>
> With our troops involved in the sweep of the first ambush site, Richard Lamberson, a member of my crew, and I also went ashore to search the area. I was checking out the inside of the hooch when I heard gunfire nearby.

Not long after that, Kerry returned, reporting that he had killed the man he chased behind the hooch. He also had picked up a loaded B-40 rocket launcher, which we took back to our base in An Thoi after the operation.

Okay. So the rocket launcher was loaded. And the guy who had the launcher may not have been wounded. And he wasn't alone. In fact, Rood wrote:

The man Kerry chased was not the "lone" attacker at that site, as O'Neill [coauthor of *Unfit for Command*] suggests. There were others who fled. There was also firing from the tree line well behind the spider holes and at one point, from the opposite riverbank as well. It was not the work of just one attacker.

In other words, it was kind of a dangerous place to be on a Friday afternoon. Not like a "casual Friday" at the Alabama Air National Guard base, where George W. Bush wouldn't later go. Also, Rood addressed the whole "loincloth" issue—the very loincloth that gives the "loincloth affair" its name:

John O'Neill, author of a highly critical account of Kerry's Vietnam service, describes the man Kerry chased as a "teenager" in a "loincloth." I have no idea how old the gunner Kerry chased that day was, but both Leeds and I recall that he was a grown man, dressed in the kind of garb the VC usually wore.

Grown man? No loincloth? Loaded rocket launcher? Other attackers firing from behind the tree line and on the opposite riverbank? It seemed like Rood's version agreed with what "he" (Kerry) said, not with what "she" (O'Neill) said.

If only there were some *other* people there, besides Kerry, his crew, and the nonpartisan journalist William Rood, who had steadfastly refused to get involved until, as he put it, the Swiftees' claims started "splashing doubt" on his own record and, worse, "hurting crewmen who are not public figures and who deserved to be honored for what they did." If only there was someone without an axe to grind. Someone almost entirely indifferent to American politics. But who else could have been there, in Vietnam?

Hmm.

Vietnam . . . Vietnam . . . Was there anybody in Vietnam during the Vietnam War, besides the American troops?

Think. Think, Franken.

I was stumped. But Ted Koppel wasn't. He took a *Nightline* crew to Vietnam, and talked to . . . *the Vietnamese.* Yes. That's why Ted Koppel is Ted Koppel.

The story ran on October 14. Koppel's team interviewed the villagers of Tran Thoi, along the Bay Hap river. Koppel, a gay anchorman who fusses constantly with his hair whenever the camera isn't rolling, was naturally interested in the loincloth-clad teenager.[2] Here's how ABCnews.com summarized Koppel's report on the villagers:

> They have no problem remembering Ba Thanh, the man who has been dismissed by Kerry's detractors as "a lone, wounded, fleeing, young Vietcong in a loincloth."
>
> "No, this is not correct," Nguyen Thi Tuoi, 77, told ABC News. "He wore a black pajama. He was strong. He was big and strong. He was about 26 or 27."

So the "loincloth affair" really should be called the "pajama affair." Or, my publisher suggests, "the pajama party."

Was the twenty-six- or twenty-seven-year-old Ba Thanh working alone, as the Swiftees claimed? Was there "little or no fire"?

---

[2] Actually, besides being a great journalist, Ted is one of the straightest guys I know (which could mean he's gay). Also, I have no evidence that he fusses with his hair.

"When the firing started, Ba Thanh was killed," [Viet Cong Commander] Tam said. "And I led Ba Thanh's comrades, the whole unit, to fight back. And we ran around the back and fought the Americans from behind. We worked with the city soldiers to fire on the American boats."

So it's not a teenager, no loincloth, *loaded* rocket launcher, *maybe* wounded, and certainly not alone. Kerry was definitely fighting "a numerically superior force in the face of intense fire," exactly as his Silver Star citation had said.

Debunking O'Neill's lies any further at this point is gratuitous. But please indulge me. *Unfit for Command*, you'll recall, makes a big deal out of the claim that Kerry supposedly shot Ba Thanh, the 26.5-year-old teenager, in the back. O'Neill writes:

> While Commander Elliott and many other Swiftees believe that Kerry committed no crime in killing the fleeing, wounded enemy (with a loaded or empty launcher), others feel differently.

Kerry's version of the story, which I am beginning to believe, holds that "he was running away with a live B-40 [rocket launcher] and, I thought, poised to turn around and fire it."

I don't know about you, but if I put myself in Kerry's position, that's when I shoot the guy. I don't wait for him to turn around.

Is that sporting? Hell, yes. Remember? It's a war. Under what rule of war does an armed enemy in a firefight become off-limits just because he's running away? I am fifty-four years old. I have seen hundreds, if not thousands, of war movies. In fact, I spent a great deal of the Vietnam War watching war movies. And I've never seen a single war movie in which it's not okay to shoot a fleeing enemy in the back.

Does John O'Neill know some secret Geneva Convention governing the shooting of people who aren't facing you? Is John O'Neill telling us that America could have saved thousands upon thousands of lives on D-Day if our troops had just *backed* up Omaha Beach?

"*Nein!* Don't shoot! Not until zey turn around! Ach, those Americans are so shmart!"

The debunking was complete. But the damage had already been done. (Even so, the right-wing media kept flogging the story.) Because the Swift Boat Vets had dominated sixty successive news cycles, what should have been Kerry's greatest strength became a defining liability.

Bush and his supporters spent a billion dollars creating a simple story line:

1. Bush was strong, patriotic, and steadfast.
2. Kerry was weak, French-like, and flippity-floppity.
3. Terrorists attack countries with weak presidents, so voting for Kerry meant almost certain death for your children.

At the outset of the campaign, Kerry's record as a decorated combat veteran made *him* seem strong, patriotic, and steadfast—especially when contrasted with Bush's own record of cowardice. It had to go. And go it went.

This wasn't the first time that the opponent of a Karl Rove candidate had been on the receiving end of a mysterious, quasi-independent smear campaign that had turned his strength into an albatross.

Back in 2000, during the South Carolina primary campaign, John McCain had the pleasure of hearing a Vietnam veteran, Thomas Burch, standing next to Governor George W. Bush, tell a crowd that McCain "came home and forgot us." He had the even greater pleasure of learning from the Bush grapevine that Bridget, the dark-skinned Bangladeshi girl that he and his wife Cindy had adopted from an orphanage run by Mother Teresa, was not an orphan at all, but rather his own illegitimate black daughter. South Carolina's Republican primary voters would be reminded of McCain's interracial indiscretions every time Bridget appeared on stage with her father and, I guess, stepmother.

Ugly? You bet. The worst thing Rove had ever denied any involvement in? Oh gosh, no.

In the November 2004 *Atlantic Monthly*, which came out just before the election, journalist Joshua Green went snorkeling in the cesspool of Karl Rove's political career. Being, as he was, entirely submerged in the Rove shit lagoon, Green managed to find stinky nuggets of political chicanery that had eluded me when I merely waded through the cesspool in my last book, *Lies, and the Lying Liars Who Tell Them.*

Although I didn't know it at the time, the stories I recounted in *Lies* about Rove bugging his own office in order to cast suspicion on his client's opponent, and swiping an opponent's letterhead in order to send out fake event invitations promising "free beer, free food, girls, and a good time for nothing" to homeless shelters—these were merely what we in the political sanitation industry call "floaters." The heavy, dark stuff always sinks to the bottom. And down in the dankest deepest depths, Joshua Green found something that, to me, best captures the full putrescence of Karl Rove's soul.

In the early 1990s, Rove arrived in Alabama eager to ruin the Alabama judicial system by injecting extreme, vicious partisanship into what had previously been an only *somewhat* vicious political culture. His plan succeeded. In his first year of operation there, he put three GOP candidates on what had been an entirely Democratic court for more than a century. Today, the court is entirely Republican. And not just Republican, but Roy Moore, 2.6-ton-Ten-Commandments-in-the-courthouse-rotunda Republican. It seemed like just another sparkling Rove success story. But in that first campaign season in 1994, there was a hitch.

Rove ran *four* candidates. One of them . . . *lost.*

The man who beat Rove's guy, Harold See, was Mark Kennedy, son-in-law of former Governor George Wallace. Don't like him so far, right? Neither did I, until I read Joshua Green's description of him. Check this out:

Kennedy had spent years on the bench as a juvenile and family-court judge, during which time he had developed a strong interest in aiding abused children. In the early 1980s he had helped to start the Children's Trust Fund of Alabama, and he later established the Corporate Foundation for Children, a private, non-profit organization. At the time of the race he had just served a term as president of the National Committee to Prevent Child Abuse and Neglect.

Pretty good, huh? Plus, he was a Kennedy! You're probably guessing that he beat Rove's candidate by trumpeting his heroic work advocating on behalf of the powerless. Well, you're kind of right. In fact:

Some of Kennedy's campaign commercials touted his volunteer work, including one that showed him holding hands with children.

Uh oh. Are you thinking what I'm thinking?

One of Rove's signature tactics is to attack an opponent on the very front that seems unassailable. Kennedy was no exception.

"We were trying to counter the positives from that ad," a former Rove staffer told me, explaining that some within the See camp initiated a whisper campaign that Kennedy was a pedophile.

Yep, you were right. But how do you smear a guy with that without having your fingerprints all over it?

"It was our standard practice to use the University of Alabama Law School to disseminate whisper-campaign information," the staffer went on. "That was a major device we used for the transmission of this stuff. The students at the law school are from all over the state, and that's one of the ways that Karl got the information out—he knew the law students would take it back to their home towns and it would get out." This would create the impression that the lie was in fact common knowledge across the state.

Ah. Smart.

Excuse me while I run away from my computer and vomit.

ONE MINUTE LATER

There. I vomited in the wastebasket. I had been planning to use my office bathroom, but I didn't make it.

Let's go back to Joshua Green. He talked to Kennedy's campaign manager, Joe Perkins.

> "What Rove does," says Joe Perkins, "is try to make something so bad for a family that the candidate will not subject the family to the hardship. Mark is not your typical Alabama macho, beer-drinkin', tobacco-chewin', pickup-drivin' kind of guy. He is a small, well-groomed, well-educated family man, and what they tried to do was make him look like a homosexual pedophile. That was really, really hard to take."

So even though Kennedy won in the end (by one percentage point), when his term was up, he decided not to run for reelection. He just didn't have the stomach for it.

When Green sat down with Kennedy, he met a man whose victory a spelling bee champion might call "Pyrrhic."

> Kennedy appeared to derive little satisfaction from having beaten Rove. In fact, he seemed shaken, even ten years later.

See? Rove took Kennedy's strength (touching the lives of kids) and used it against him (saying he was touching kids). Genius. What a pro.

Actually, I have to take another break. Hold on.

THREE HOURS LATER

This is Franni, Al's wife. I'm with him at the hospital. I told him this would happen if he looked too closely into the Karl Rove situation. This book is really taking a toll on Al, and I'm thinking of calling off the whole thing. Or maybe he could just focus on debunking lies from Rush or Sean Hannity. That always makes him happy. I hate to see him like this.

5 A Brief Recuperative Debunk

Lenox Hill Hospital—June 17, 2005

As you may have read in the press, I've been hospitalized with Rove-induced septic shock, and I am under orders from my wife and doctors not to discuss the Bush-Cheney '04 campaign until my organs are functioning properly.

At first, Drs. Vajpayee and Fischbein insisted that I take a break from all forms of political commentary. Franni just laughed, albeit a bit hysterically. She knew that was impossible. Besides, she pointed out, debunking right-wing jerks has historically had a therapeutic effect on me. After all, that's how *Rush Limbaugh Is a Big Fat Idiot* was born. Recovering from surgery for a knee injury incurred while tussling with some hecklers at a Harris Wofford rally.[1]

So we reached a compromise. I could debunk to my heart's con-

---

[1] Pennsylvania Senator Harris Wofford, a cofounder of the Peace Corps and former aide to both JFK and Martin Luther King, was defeated in 1994 by Rick Santorum. The knee injury story is made up for comedic purposes. It is one of the "jokes" promised in my subtitle. See if you can find the other one.

tent as long as I wasn't debunking dishonest attacks on Kerry by the Bush team. What they didn't realize was that this agreement had a loophole that you could drive a truck through. By debunking the dishonest attacks on Kerry by dishonest, semi-unofficial Bush surrogates like Fox's Sean Hannity, I could continue work on the chapter without losing my health insurance for not complying with my doctors' instructions. It would work fine, so long as Fischbein and especially Vajpayee didn't get wise to my scheme.

I know just where to start.

The fundamental goal of the GOP was to define Kerry as a flip-flopper. This wasn't a new tactic. Bush's father attacked Clinton as a "waffler" who was guilty of "flip-flops." Gore, as George W. explained in 2000, was a "serial exaggerator" who was doomed because voters "don't want flip-floppers as President of the United States." Now, the Republicans argued, the Democrats had done it again—they'd nominated another one of their flip-floppers.

As Jonathan Chait pointed out in an October 12, 2004, *New Republic* article, it would have been "quite a coincidence" if the Democrats had had such an "astonishing run of bad luck" to choose a string of nominees with such "dismal personal integrity." But it was no coincidence. In fact, it was the opposite of a coincidence. It was a result of the Bush family's love of Lee Atwater and his protégé Karl Rove.

Uh oh! Doctor's orders: no Rove. Nurse, OxyContin, stat!

Ahhhh. So much better. A guy could get hooked on this stuff.

Where was I? Oh, yes. Flip-flopper. You'll have to pardon me, I'm hopped up on hillbilly heroin.

No single man or woman accused John Kerry of flip-flopping more doggedly than Sean Hannity. Sean, who has a radio audience of some 8 million weekly listeners and a nightly TV audience of nearly 2 million, has a trademark technique: assemble a litany of dishonest scraps of partisan distortion on a particular topic, and employ it at every available opportunity. His Kerry flip-flop litany was a classic of the genre.

Here's an early version of it, quoted verbatim from Fox's March 25, 2004, *Sean Hannity Show*:

Here's a guy that supported gay marriage, now against it. Here's a guy that by my count has had six separate different unique positions on the war on Iraq. Here's a guy that voted for the $87 billion to fund the war before he voted against it. Here's a guy that was for the Patriot Act. Now against it. No Child Left Behind, for it, now against it. Here's a guy that supported— was against the death penalty for terrorists who kill Americans. Now he's for it. The only thing he seems consistent on is that, throughout the nineteen years he was in the Senate, he voted to raise taxes consistently 350 times.

What does that tell us about a man that has no core values or principles?

Now, I'm going to debunk these one by one. But let me tell you what I've learned about Sean Hannity. No matter how many times you debunk the man, no matter how many times his lies are exposed, he keeps on using them. He doesn't switch to new lies, as a minimally respectable hack like a Dick Morris or a Jonah Goldberg might. He doesn't even wink at the debunking by slipping a qualifier or two into his litany. So, I've come up with a new tactic. Instead of fighting his lies with truth and calling it a day, I have taken to fighting Sean Hannity's lies with lies about Sean Hannity.

So, here now, is a debunking of Hannity's patented, endlessly repeated "Kerry is a flip-flopper" litany, interspersed with vicious, unfounded lies about Sean Hannity himself.

HANNITY: Here's a guy that supported gay marriage, now against it.

This is a lie. Kerry's position has always been consistent on this. I disagree with him, but Kerry has always been against gay marriage. He is for civil unions. Hannity was taking Kerry's vote against the 1996 Defense of Marriage Act and deliberately misrepresenting it as a declaration in favor of gay marriage. Here's what Kerry said on the floor of the Senate about that vote:

> I will vote against this bill, **though I am not for same-sex marriage,** because I believe that this debate is fundamentally ugly, and it is fundamentally political, and it is fundamentally flawed. . . . The results of this bill will not be to preserve anything, but will serve to attack a group of people out of various motives and rationales, and certainly out of a lack of understanding and a lack of tolerance, and will only serve the purposes of the political season.

On *that*, I totally agree with him. In fact, it was beautifully put. So, Kerry had never flip-flopped on gay marriage. Sean Hannity was lying, and he knew he was lying.

Time to hit back with a lie about Sean Hannity. Remember, what you're about to read is not true. It's a lie.

But here's the thing. Sean Hannity blames 9/11 on the Jews. And not just any Jews. But Jews in the media. Can you believe that? It disgusts me. And not just because I'm in the media, but because I think it emboldens our enemies.

Remember. That was a lie.

> **HANNITY:** Here's a guy that by my count has had six separate different unique positions on the war on Iraq.

This was just stupid. Kerry's position on Iraq was totally consistent. In retrospect, a bad position, sure, but it was absolutely consistent. Yes, Kerry voted to authorize the President to use force against Iraq. But he voted for that in order for Bush to go to the U.N. and get the inspectors back into Iraq, which Bush lyingly said was the only way to avoid a war.

It sounds counterintuitive that Bush would want an authorization to use force in order to avoid war. But Bush claimed that that's what this was all about. Here's an exchange between Bush and a reporter from September 19, 2002, just before the vote in Congress:

> REPORTER: Mr. President, how important is it that that resolution give you an authorization of the use of force?
>
> BUSH: That will be part of the resolution, the authorization to use force. If you want to keep the peace, you've got to have the authorization to use force. This is a chance for Congress to indicate support. It's a chance for Congress to say, "We support the administration's ability to keep the peace." That's what this is all about.

On the eve of that vote, Kerry explained his position:

> As the President made clear earlier this week, "Approving this resolution does not mean that military action is imminent or unavoidable." It means "America speaks with one voice."
>
> Let me be clear, the vote I will give to the President is for one reason and one reason only: to disarm Iraq of weapons of mass destruction, if we cannot accomplish that objective through new, tough weapons inspections in joint concert with our allies.
>
> In giving the President this authority, I expect him to fulfill the commitments he has made to the American people in recent days—to work with the United Nations Security Council to adopt a new resolution setting out tough and immediate inspection requirements, and to act with our allies at our side if we have to disarm Saddam Hussein by force. If he fails to do so, I will be among the first to speak out.

So the vote for the resolution was not a vote for the war. And when the President did launch his attack, not as a last resort, or even a second-to-last resort, Kerry *did* speak out. For example, here's Kerry on CBS's *Face the Nation* on September 14, 2003:

> The President promised he would go to war as a matter of last resort. He didn't. The President promised he would build a coalition and work through the United Nations. He didn't. We're paying the price for the reckless way in which this president approached this. It's a failure of diplomacy, and today it's a failure of leadership.

Totally consistent.

As Marc Sandalow, Washington bureau chief of the *San Francisco Chronicle*, wrote on Thursday, September 23, 2004, after six-plus months of daily accusations of Iraq flip-floppery from Hannity and others, "An examination of Kerry's words in more than 200 speeches and statements, comments during candidate forums and answers to reporters' questions" showed that "Kerry has offered the same message ever since talk of attacking Iraq became a national conversation more than two years ago."

So there weren't, as Hannity asserted, "six separate different unique positions." There was only one position. And it wasn't unique. I held it myself.

Hannity was debunked over and over again, and yet he never wavered. It is time, therefore, for another lie about Hannity. This is even less true than the last one. Which wasn't true at all. It's been made up out of whole cloth. But it will shock you, just as it shocked me.

In 1993, utility workers repairing a gas line in the garden of Hannity's Los Angeles–area home found a buried human hand missing its ring finger. Hannity denied any knowledge of the hand, and it couldn't be conclusively linked to him. But questions remain.

Next.

> **HANNITY:** Here's a guy that voted for the $87 billion to fund the war before he voted against it.

This is correct, but it's not a flip-flop. Kerry voted *for* an amendment to the Iraqi appropriations bill that would have paid for the $87 billion by taking it out of the tax cut for those Americans making over $300,000 a year. Remember that never in the history of this country have we had tax cuts while we were at war. In fact, according to Paul Krugman, never in human history had *any* civilization cut taxes during a war.

Americans are always happy to sacrifice a little bit out of respect for those who are sacrificing everything. President Bush has a different view. He threatened to veto the money for the troops if it came from rich people by suspending a portion of their tax cut instead of the children of the troops, who will eventually wind up having to pay off the national debt. Kerry's amendment lost, 57–42. Then the Republican version of the $87 billion bill passed, 87–12.

So, in other words, the Republicans voted *against* the $87 billion before they voted *for* it. Nobody flip-flopped. It was just a difference of values. The very rich vs. the children of the troops. And every other American child, as well.

On this one, instead of telling a lie about Hannity, I'll simply tell you something true about him that is deliberately misleading. Here it is. As I reported in *Lies*, Hannity actually describes the act of "fisting" in his book *Let Freedom Ring*. It's on page 158 of the hardcover, right after the discussion of "ingesting semen in front of fourteen year olds." And I'm sorry to say that there is more than a little evidence that "fisting" is something of an obsession of Sean's. If you Google the words "Hannity" and "fisting," you'll get over 15,000 hits.

Remember, this was deliberately misleading. The quote from *Let Freedom Ring* is taken out of context. As for the fisting statistic—if you Google "Franken" and "fisting," for some reason you get 149,000 hits. Go figure.

Let's move on.

HANNITY: Here's a guy that was for the Patriot Act. Now against it.

Bullshit. Here's what Kerry said at Iowa State University on December 1, 2003:

> I voted for the Patriot Act right after September 11—convinced that—with a sunset clause—it was the right decision to make. It clearly wasn't a perfect bill—and it had a number of flaws—but this wasn't the time to haggle. It was the time to act.
>
> But George Bush and John Ashcroft abused the spirit of national action after the terrorist attacks. They have used the Patriot Act in ways that were never intended and for reasons that have nothing to do with terrorism. That's why, as President, I will propose new anti-terrorism laws that advance the War on Terror while ending the assault on our basic rights.

In other words, he supported parts of it, objected to parts of it, voted for it, and Bush abused it. Too nuanced for Sean? No. Sean is secretly very smart.

If you didn't catch it, that was the lie about Hannity to fight that particular Hannity lie.

HANNITY: No Child Left Behind, for it, now against it.

This is an easy one. On this issue, like all the others, Kerry is consistent and principled, and Hannity is dishonest. Kerry voted *for* the bill, which the President promised to fund. The President didn't fund it, which created unfunded mandates on states and school districts across the country. As a result, class sizes went up, after-school programs were dropped, teachers were fired, and children were left behind.

So, time for another lie about Hannity. Like the buried hand, this lie pertains to one of the many suspicious incidents in Sean's shadowy past.

In 1995, Hannity was named president and CEO of a Houston-area petting zoo doing business under the name "Goats and Beyond, LLC." In

1996, Hannity fled Houston under a cloud of accusations from local parents and representatives of the Texas Humane Society. Goats and Beyond paid out half a million dollars in sealed, out-of-court settlements, and shuttered its doors for good, selling the animals to a local tannery. Hannity has never commented publicly on the affair. Questions remain.

> **HANNITY:** Here's a guy that supported—was against the death penalty for terrorists who kill Americans. Now he's for it.

Actually, Sean's right on this one. Kerry was against the death penalty before 9/11. And now, after 9/11, he supports the death penalty for *terrorists*. Now, Bush, before 9/11, wanted to invade Iraq. And after it, he wanted to invade Iraq. So maybe he was more consistent. Kerry was affected viscerally by 9/11 and changed one of his views. But I'm not sure I'd call that a flip-flop.

But maybe Sean has an honest difference of opinion with me on this one, so I won't make up a lie about him. I'll just make up a difference of opinion.

I happen to think that whether or not you support the U.S. Postal Service, you should never pee in mailboxes while drunk. That's what I believe. Unlike Sean.

Last accusation.

> **HANNITY:** The only thing he seems consistent on is that, throughout the nineteen years he was in the Senate, he voted to raise taxes consistently 350 times.

This is a lie-apalooza. It is a distortion of a phony statistic put out by the Bush campaign that Kerry had voted 350 times for, quote, "higher taxes." That total included every vote against any tax cut, including crazy, irresponsible tax cuts that were overwhelmingly defeated by Democrats and Republicans alike. It included votes *for* tax cuts when someone else had proposed an even bigger tax cut. Where a bill contained more than one item, it counted each item separately. In two cases, one vote counted four times.

On Bush's list, there's only one actual tax *increase* that Kerry voted for, which incidentally is counted twice. It's his vote for Clinton's 1993 Deficit Reduction Act, which raised taxes on the top 1 percent and cut taxes on people at the bottom, and was followed by eight years of unprecedented growth. That was a real embarrassment, huh?

So Bush's statistic was absolutely, totally, and completely dishonest, while clinging to a fig leaf of defensibility. The phrase "higher taxes" was chosen with extreme care, just as Bush's references to Iraq and al Qaeda were chosen with extreme care. And the list was painstakingly constructed with the most delicate, though dishonest, craftsmanship. Something to be proud of.

But like the out-of-control, gleefully vicious four-year-old he once was, Hannity kicked down the sand castle. There's no way anyone could ever claim that Kerry voted to "raise taxes" 350 times. Bush's "higher taxes" statistic was a lie. Hannity's "raise taxes" statistic was a *LIE*. Hannity's a disgrace.

Speaking of disgrace, you won't *believe* the next lie about Hannity I'm about to unveil. And for good reason. It's not true. But if it were, it would be a career-ender. Hannity, a married man with children, actually forced his much younger female producer to stay on the phone with him as he detailed a disgusting sexual fantasy and masturbated. The fantasy involved taking her to the Caribbean and getting her drunk. Then, as she showered, touching her breasts and her genitals, first with a loofah mitt and then, inexplicably, with a falafel. The sordid tale came to light when the female producer sued him and released transcripts of the phone sex. Hannity, who never denied the specific allegations, settled the lawsuit, reportedly for millions of dollars.

Now, of course, you know this is just a lie I made up to fight Hannity's lie. You know it because any media personality who was caught doing something so sensationally reprehensible and, frankly, gross, would obviously have lost his job, rather than remaining one of the Fox News Channel's top two stars. Especially if it was someone who, like Hannity, portrays himself as such a defender of traditional values.

> **HANNITY:** What does that tell us about a man that has no core values or principles?

It tells us that the man who has no core values or principles is not, in fact, John Kerry. It is a man named Shawn.

I mean, Sean.

The truth is that John Kerry's long career in public life wasn't any more flip-floppy than the career of any politician who's had to debate and vote on complex issues in a complex and changing world—for example, our world. In fact, over twenty years in the Senate, Kerry arguably flip-flopped less than George W. Bush did in his first four years as president. Bush waffled on the Department of Homeland Security, the 9/11 Commission, federal intervention on same-sex marriage, whether the War on Terror is winnable, McCain-Feingold, regulating CO_2 emissions, nation-building, steel tariffs (against-for-against), the reasons for the Iraq War, and ushering in an era of personal responsibility. Can you believe he said he was *for* that in the 2000 election? I'm not making it up. Go back to the 2000 election and see what he said. The man who refused to admit a single mistake actually used to *campaign* on a platform of personal responsibility. Really.

At the same time, it's true that Kerry's image in the public mind was defined by a single, enormous flip-flop on an issue at the center of his, and our country's, life. After volunteering to fight in Vietnam and comporting himself with extraordinary valor, John Kerry flip-flopped—and came home to protest the war.

Looking back, it's possible to argue that Kerry took the most principled and courageous route. Despite misgivings about our policies, he volunteered out of a sense of patriotic obligation to serve his country. Once in Vietnam, he fought bravely and saved the lives of his men, but saw that the war was both wrong and unwinnable. When he came home, he weathered enormous criticism for speaking out on the basis of his experience and convictions. In the end, he played a small but significant role in bringing to a close one of America's darkest chapters.

And for that, the Swift Boat Vets could never forgive him and were willing to lie.

Compare Kerry's record to mine. During Vietnam, I was in college, enjoying my student deferment. The government wisely felt that in my case, military service was less important than completing my studies to prepare me for my chosen career: comedian. By the time I graduated, the draft was over and the coast was clear. In my defense, however, I protested against the war and thought not only that I should not have to go, but that nobody should.

So on a one to ten scale I give Kerry a ten and I give myself about a three.

What does George W. Bush get? Well, he thought it *was* a good idea for young American men to fight in Vietnam. He just didn't want to be one of them. So, on the same scale, I give him a two. ("One" is reserved for Nixon.)

Kerry's historic flip-flop probably cost him the election. But if he had the choice, I bet he'd do it again.

There. I feel better. Nothing like a good debunk of a lightweight like Sean Hannity. It's like picking low-hanging fruit, instead of scooping turds out of Karl Rove's cesspool. One makes you sick, while with the other you have fruit. And fruit is good for you. Right, Dr. Vajpayee?

> VAJPAYEE: That's right, Al. I recommend three to five servings of fresh fruits and vegetables a day.

> AL: You're so much more accommodating than Dr. Fischbein.

> VAJPAYEE: Oh, no. In his way, Dr. Fischbein is even more of a softy than I am.

AL: Anyway, I'm feeling so much better. I think I can get back to the "smear" chapter now.

VAJPAYEE: Very well. But if you feel queasy, debunk Regis.

AL: You don't really understand what I do, do you?

VAJPAYEE: No, I do not.

AL: Can I get some OxyContin for the road?

VAJPAYEE: No.

6 | With Friends Like Zell

To comprehensively debunk every lie and misleading attack the Bush campaign leveled against Kerry would yield a document longer than the U.S. tax code—the code that Bush has pledged to "simplify" but has in fact increased in length by roughly 30 percent.

In the spring of 2005, according to a *Washington Post* analysis of data from the Campaign Media Analysis Group, Bush ran 49,050 negative ads in the top one hundred media markets, compared to 13,336 from Kerry. 75 percent, or approximately three out of four, of Bush's ads were negative, as compared to 27 percent of Kerry's.

I know what you're thinking. Kerry didn't have negative things to say about Bush. But you're wrong. According to an unpublished study by Franken et al, there were 9.7 times as many bad things to say about Bush as there were about Kerry. For example, Bush lied us into war.

Don't misunderstand me. There's nothing inherently wrong with a negative ad. It's part of the rough-and-tumble of American politics. I myself sometimes use negativity in order to make a political point or just to defame Bill O'Reilly.

But there is something wrong with a negative ad that, in addition to being negative, lies. I'm not a big fan of lies. I object to them on principle.

This isn't an exercise in "gotcha" journalism, like my last book. No, I've debunked the preceding anti-Kerry smears, and will debunk a few more, in order to demonstrate an actual point. A point foreshadowed in the first chapter, "Election Day." Bush did not win a mandate for his policies. The country is not more conservative now than it was in the nineties or when Bush lost in 2000. In addition to the powerful specter of Bush's Little Black Dress, Kerry lost, in part, because the electorate was made to believe a raft of wildly untrue things about his character, his personal history, and his policies.

One of the best ways to minimize the power of such attacks is to say one thing about yourself and your opponent and stick to it. George "Vote for Me or Die" Bush did a helluva job on that score. So did Bill "It's the Economy, Stupid" Clinton. Another technique, pioneered by "Silent Cal" Coolidge in the little-remembered 1924 campaign, is to avoid saying anything at all. But Kerry didn't use either technique. Unfortunately, Kerry spoke not in sound bites, not even in sentences, but in paragraphs—richly textured paragraphs, paragraphs laden with dependent clauses, abstruse qualifications, and exotic punctuation, like semicolons; em-dashes—and even the occasional interbang. Why in God's name did he *do* that?!

He had been in the Senate, the world's greatest deliberative body, for twenty years. But that's not where it came from. No, the problem arose when he was very young—when he started to display an interest in the world around him and a tendency to think through complex problems in a thoughtful way. How the Democratic Party ever allowed itself to nominate such a person continues to mystify me. Still, he was our candidate.

As Kerry himself knew, the Bushies stood ready to pounce on anything that Kerry said—in public or private, even to himself—and fashion it into a crude shiv with which to stab him in the back, neck, and face. That's why, when he sat down with Matt Bai of *The New York Times Magazine* to discuss his foreign policy views, Kerry seemed to regard the interview as, Bai wrote, "an invitation to do himself harm."

But once Kerry got going, he opened up and made the mistake of saying something that was perfectly reasonable but also, in the context of a campaign against an utterly shameless liar, dangerously misquotable. Read what Bai wrote, and see if you can find the word that the Bush smear artists zeroed in on:

> When I asked Kerry what it would take for Americans to feel safe again, he displayed a much less apocalyptic worldview. "We have to get back to the place we were, where terrorists are not the focus of our lives, but they're a nuisance," Kerry said. "As a former law-enforcement person, I know we're never going to end prostitution. We're never going to end illegal gambling. But we're going to reduce it, organized crime, to a level where it isn't on the rise. It isn't threatening people's lives every day, and fundamentally, it's something that you continue to fight, but it's not threatening the fabric of your life."

If you chose anything other than "nuisance," you obviously don't have what it takes to rise through the ranks of the Republican hate machine. I'm sorry. But it's better that I tell you now than your having to find out the hard way. The way I did.

If, on the other hand, you guessed that the Bushies pounced on "nuisance," I have bad news for you as well. It doesn't necessarily mean you're ready to play with the big boys. It probably just means you watched television or listened to the radio some time after October 10. Because Team Bush went nuts with the "nuisance" business.

It took the Bush campaign a total of zero days to announce that they were going to use the "nuisance" line as the basis of a campaign ad ("terrorism—a nuisance?!").[1] It took Bush one additional day to incorporate an attack on Kerry's nuisance line in his stump speech. And in less than the seven minutes that it took President Bush to read *The Pet Goat* that fateful day three years before, the right-wing media swarm had engulfed the nation's airwaves in a cloud of distortion.

Bill O'Reilly was taking a well-deserved break on October 11, so Fox News anchor Tony Snow was filling in on the *Factor*. "This morning," Snow crowed, "the President pounced on a quote in Sunday's *New York Times Magazine* where Senator Kerry called terrorists a nuisance." When O'Reilly returned, he must have been furious. Because Snow had broken the cardinal rule of the No Spin Zone: no spinning.

Sean Hannity, who doesn't bother pretending he has such a rule, out-uglied Snow by a Fox News mile:

> He is saying—these are his words, this is his little debate he's had
> with himself—the fact that three thousand of our fellow citizens
> were slaughtered on 9/11—we're supposed to believe that these
> terrorists are only a mere nuisance. Just a nuisance.

Hannity, as usual, was just cribbing from his father-figure Rush Limbaugh, who had spent the afternoon telling his audience that the nuisance quote meant, "John Kerry really doesn't think three thousand Americans dead in one day is that big a deal."

By the end of the campaign, voters had so internalized this smear that the vice president could score a huge round of laughter and applause by growling, "The American people understand there's nothing nuisance-like,

---

[1] Here's the full transcript of the ad:

ANNOUNCER: First, Kerry said defeating terrorism was really more about law enforcement and intelligence than a strong military operation. More about law enforcement than a strong military? Now Kerry says, "We have to get back to the place where terrorists are a nuisance like gambling and prostitution . . . we're never going to end them." Terrorism—a nuisance? How can Kerry protect us when he doesn't understand the threat?

BUSH: I'm George W. Bush and I approve this message.

if you will, about the problems we're having to deal with today." Which in ordinary circumstances would have barely qualified as a point, let alone a crowd-pleaser.

"Nuisance" was just one of a series of shameless decontextualizations used to portray Kerry as a clueless nancy who would rather windsurf down the Seine than confront the terrorist menace head-on. Terms like "sensitive" and "global test" were deployed against Kerry with even less explanation of their original context than I am providing in this sentence, which is now coming to a close.

These attacks worked on two levels. The obvious level was the literal. If Kerry thought terrorism was just a nuisance, then he was obviously the wrong man to lead the fight against it. But there was another level. The *sub*text of the constant attacks on Kerry's toughness was that the Bush team was tough and Kerry wasn't. It's what blogger Joshua Micah Marshall called the Republicans' Bitch-Slap Theory of Electoral Politics. By slapping Kerry around continuously, the President was sending America the message that "Kerry is my bitch." Kerry, by focusing on his positive, nuanced agenda (including a modest, but eminently sensible health care plan that involved the word "reinsurance"), rather than fighting back with equal or greater ferocity, was whispering the opposite message: "I am Bush's bitch." That's not a very "war president" kind of thing to whisper.

Uh oh. John and Teresa are back. I sure hope they don't see that last paragraph.

Hi, John. Hi, Teresa. How was New Hampshire? An extraordinary state? Yes, I agree. "Won't take it for granite"? Ha, ha, ha. No, no, I understand. You won it in 2004, but nevertheless you won't take it for granted in 2008. Yes. I know. New Hampshire's the granite state. Thank you, Teresa.

Oh, the book? It's going fine. I was just talking about how the campaign focused on a positive message. Yes, that was a mistake. That's what I was saying. Right. I wouldn't hire Shrum again either. No, not even for less money. I just wouldn't hire him at all. Huh? Oh. Hmmm. Uh, *sure* you should run again. Wow. That'd be great. How many books did you guys say you were going to buy?

Whew. They've left. Off to dinner at the French Embassy. I'm glad they didn't look over my shoulder and read the "I am Bush's bitch" line. I want that to be a surprise.

The point is, every good candidate should have a positive agenda. But you also have to fight back. Let me illustrate what I'm saying with a hip cultural reference. As anyone who has seen *The Karate Kid* knows, being a sweet friendly heartthrob like Ralph Macchio isn't enough if you want to win the other guy's girl (Electoral College—played here by the beautiful Elisabeth Shue). If you want to kiss Elisabeth Shue, you have to know the Way of the Fist: Strike First. Strike Hard. No Mercy.

Wait, that's the bad guy's formula. That's Rove. What you really have to know is what Mr. Miyagi told Daniel-*san*: "Man who catch fly with chopstick accomplish anything." I think that means you have to be incredibly nimble.

Also, you have to know the crane kick. And that's where Kerry came up short. In politics, you can never turn the other cheek. Especially when you're fighting the Christian right.

Nothing demonstrates the "viciousness gap" between the Bush and the Kerry campaigns better than their respective national conventions.

In Boston, the Democrats made the horrible mistake of responding to a very ironic attack from the Bush team, the claim that Democrats had nothing to offer but "partisan anger." Instead of hitting back with the obvious countercharge that, no, it's Republicans who were the party of partisan anger, the Democrats decided to internalize the message of their abuser and try to be nicer.

The Republicans, on the other hand, ran a convention so partisan and angry that its fundamental dishonesty passed nearly unremarked.

Even though Democrats almost to a man believed that President Bush was an unrivaled horror show who was driving the nation off a cliff, it was easy to watch the Democratic Convention and conclude that the Democrats thought everything was hunky-dory in America, and that their only motivation was the sunny belief that their nominee could do an even better job than the incumbent.

This was no accident. In fact, it was the result of uncharacteristic message discipline on the part of the Democrats. Below the stage at Boston's Fleet Center, an elite team of wordsmiths had the thankless job of "cleansing" the speeches before they reached the teleprompter. Here's how someone who worked in the speechwriting office described it to me, on the condition that I not reveal his or her name:

> One of our primary responsibilities was to take out negative comments. We were very concerned about casting the party in a positive light. If there was a line like "Bush has overseen a cataclysmic downturn in the economy and is running the country into the ground," we would have to change it to something like "Kerry will strengthen our economy and put the country on the right track." We'd flip all of the attacks into positive messages. Specifically, we didn't mention George Bush by name. I'd be surprised if there were a single speech that went into the teleprompter that had the President's name in it. Some speakers said it, but they were going off-message. We weren't even allowed to say "White House." I remember somebody asking about that, and being told to write "some in Washington."

I asked him or her (okay, it's a "him") how he felt when he saw the unflaggingly venomous Republican Convention.

> Boy, I hope we didn't fuck up. That was my reaction.

But fuck up they had. After the Democratic Convention, Kerry's standing in the polls went up by 4 percent, the smallest post-convention bounce in the history of the *Newsweek* poll. Compare that to Bush's bounce of 13 percent.

Part of the difference was that, as I definitively proved previously, the

Republican Convention left the voting public literally terror-stricken. But fear was only half the equation. At the same time they were being scared witless, they were being told that Kerry wanted to gut the military and give the enemy (the French) command over whatever remained. Fear + Smear = 13 percent.

If Giuliani won the Mortality Salience Award, then the Palm d'Smear went to the Republican Convention's keynote speaker, Georgia Senator Zell Miller. Miller, technically a Democrat, gave the lie to the stereotype that Democrats can't be evil, vicious, lying fascists.

Looking like an enraged rooster pecking furiously away at the eyeball of the weakest chicken in the pecking order, Miller unrolled a litany of charges that, if taken together—and, crucially, if believed—backed up his contention that "for more than twenty years, on every one of the great issues of freedom and security, John Kerry has been more wrong, more weak, and more wobbly than any other national figure."

It was tough talk. But it was especially startling to those of us who had been present at Georgia's Jefferson-Jackson Dinner on March 1, 2001, when Miller introduced Kerry with a somewhat different tone: "My job tonight is an easy one: to present to you one of this nation's authentic heroes, one of this party's best-known and greatest leaders—and a good friend."

And what was Zell's good friend known for? In 2001, Zell Miller minced no words. "**John has worked to strengthen our military,** reform public education, boost the economy, and protect the environment."

In truth, I didn't go to that dinner. I just went to Zell Miller's website. Which, at the time of Zell's barn burner at the Garden, still carried the text of Miller's comments on that magical Georgia night.

But back to the Republican National Convention. Miller's case wasn't just hateful because it was full of hate. It was also hateful because it was full of lies. Lies about his good friend who had worked to strengthen our military.

> Listing all the weapon systems that Senator Kerry tried his best to shut down sounds like an auctioneer selling off our national security—but Americans need to know the facts.

"Tried his best to shut down." Hmm. "Facts." *Hmm.*

> The B-1 bomber, that Senator Kerry opposed, dropped 40 percent of the bombs in the first six months of Enduring Freedom.

Ah, the B-1. Kerry had opposed the B-1? He'd tried his best to shut it down? Funny way of shutting it down: In 2002, Kerry voted $160 million for the B-1 Bomber Defense System Upgrade.

> The B-2 bomber, that Senator Kerry opposed, delivered air strikes against the Taliban in Afghanistan and Hussein's command post in Iraq.

Kerry's tireless efforts to shut down the B-2 bomber had involved voting for more than $16 billion in defense authorizations for it. If Kerry was really passionate about shutting down the B-2 bomber, he should have taken a page from Dick Cheney, who was far more successful at opposing it when he was secretary of defense. It was Cheney who canceled the B-2 bomber program after twenty planes had been built, even though the Air Force said it needed 132. But did Miller attack Cheney? No! And he was the next speaker! What a perfect opportunity, and Miller blew it.

In fact, if Miller had wanted to, he could have really ripped Cheney a new one. Check out this litany from Miller:

> The **F-15 Eagles**, that Senator Kerry opposed, flew cover over our nation's capital and this very city after 9/11. The modernized **F-14D**, that Senator Kerry opposed, delivered missile strikes against Tora Bora. The **Apache helicopter**, that Senator Kerry opposed, took out those Republican Guard tanks in Kuwait in the Gulf War.

Now compare that litany to this excerpt from the 1990 testimony before the Defense Subcommittee of the Senate Appropriations Committee by then–Secretary of Defense Dick Cheney:

This is just a list of some of the programs that I've recommended termination: the V-22 Osprey, the **F-14D,** the Army Helicopter Improvement Program, Phoenix missile, **F-15E,** the **Apache helicopter,** the M1 tank, et cetera. ["Et cetera" his.]

Was Dick Cheney trying to gut our military? No. The Cold War had ended, and there was this thing called the "peace dividend." Cheney was just doing what Zell Miller would have done if *he* had been defense secretary, which is to choose which weapons systems would be most useful in the post–Cold War world, and get rid of the others.

Miller was confronted by this inconvenient fact on CNN that very night, in what many consider Judy Woodruff and Wolf Blitzer's finest moment.

> **WOODRUFF:** But do you simply reject the idea that Vice President Cheney, as Wolf said and as we know from the record, also voted against some of these systems?
>
> **MILLER:** I don't think Cheney voted against these.
>
> **BLITZER:** No, but he opposed some of them when he was the defense secretary, and sometimes he was overruled by the Congress because he was concerned, he was worried that the defense of the United States could be better served by some other weapons systems, not specifically those. I'm specifically referring to the B-2 and the F-14 Tomcat.
>
> **MILLER:** I'm talking about John Kerry's record. I'll let Dick Cheney, the vice president, answer those charges. He knows what happened in the Department of Defense years ago. I don't know that.

Of course you don't, Zell. Your brain has been melted by rage.

As for Kerry, there *is* a technical sense in which he had voted against all of those systems. He had also voted *for* all of them. Flip-flops? No. Let me explain.

All of the attempts to "shut down" weapons systems cited by Miller referred to votes on defense appropriations bills that contained every single dollar of defense spending for an entire year. Three of Miller's examples (the B-1, the B-2, and the F-15) referred to a single vote on Senate Bill S. 3189 on October 15, 1990.

I admit it. That day, John Forbes Kerry—along with five Republicans—cast a "nay" vote on S. 3189. That meant he "voted against" every weapons system, every toilet, every fiber in every sheet of toilet paper that the military was slated to buy in 1991. There was not a vote on each specific weapons system.

Miller could have argued just as honestly that Kerry had tried his best to shut down the entire military, toilet paper and all. But while the delegates on the convention floor would have believed it, those at home might have scratched their heads and said, "Hey, that can't be true." And they would have been right.

Why did Kerry cast that fateful vote against S. 3189? I don't know. But I assume it's the same reason John McCain voted with Kerry against the 1996 conference report on the Defense Appropriations Bill, the vote that inspired Miller to say Kerry wanted to kill the Apache helicopter. Here's what John McCain said on May 12, 2004 on *The Sean Hannity Show*, taking a break from stumping for Bush in order to momentarily defend Kerry:

> **MCCAIN:** *I* would be accused of voting against numerous weapon systems, because *I* voted against defense appropriations bills, because they're loaded down with pork. And they're obscene today with all of the pork-barrel spending and multitrillion-dollar deficits. I'll probably vote against the Defense Appropriations Bill *this* year.

Why would McCain have bothered to defend Kerry on this point?

MCCAIN: I was also subjected to allegations of being against things like breast cancer research, which was on a defense appropriations bill.

He was talking about the Rove-donor-financed smear job from the 2000 primary campaign. Hannity responded with uncharacteristic decency:

HANNITY: I remember. That's not fair. I understand.

(By the next day, Hannity had regained his composure and indecency enough to go back to claiming that Kerry had "voted against every major weapons system.")

In other years, Kerry did vote "aye," which means "yes." If you want to play Zell Miller's game—and why not?—then you can truthfully say that Kerry had voted for $4.4 trillion in military spending over the years. But you didn't hear that from Zell Miller. Instead, you heard:

> This is the man who wants to be the commander in chief of our
> U.S. Armed Forces? U.S. forces armed with what? *Spitballs?!*

And then you heard a huge roar from the Hate Pit at Madison Square Garden.

There were plenty of other lies in Miller's speech that night, but do we really need to go through them?

I'd prefer to think back to a different Zell Miller. Here's what the same man, if he can be called the same man, told a very different Madison Square Garden crowd when he delivered the keynote speech at the 1992 Democratic National Convention:

> For twelve dark years the Republicans have dealt in cynicism
> and skepticism. They've mastered the art of division and diver-
> sion, and they have robbed us of our hope.

Screw you, Zell. Really. Honest.

Disgusted with Zell's speech and Cheney's follow-up, which did little to improve my mood, I headed over to Tavern on the Green to party with the California delegation to the Republican Convention. You might not expect that I would seek comfort in that particular environ. But my pal Darryl Worley, a jingoistic but bighearted country star whom I had bonded with on a USO Tour to Iraq, was providing the night's entertainment and had hooked up some VIP passes for my staff, my wife, Franni, and me.

Dancing with my wife to Darryl's down-home, twangy melodies, the ugliness of the evening's speeches melted away. As Darryl's lead guitarist, Soir, was pickin', we were grinnin'. Everybody in the place was grinnin'. Sean Hannity came up and put his arm around me. I'm not kidding. It was like that.

My twenty-three-year-old producer, Ben Wikler, danced with the second-most-beautiful girl in the place (after Franni—who is not a girl, but a woman). Impressed by Ben's fancy footwork on the dance floor and his rugged good looks, the California Republican beauty seemed to want to make more of the evening. Ben, however, demurred. Not because he's gay, as so many good-looking dancers are, but because he was thinking about his girlfriend, Beth, who is even more beautiful than the Republican lass (although, in my opinion, still a hairsbreadth short of Franni).[2] All in all, it was the kind of bipartisan night that brought back memories of the kinder, gentler days of the Ford administration.

The next evening, as I waded into the crowd on the convention floor to deliver my final evening of field reports for Air America Radio, I ran into that same stunningly beautiful Republican young woman. She gave me a smile that looked like the sun rising over the ocean (much like my wife's smile—though thirty years younger). We got to talking about the differences between Republicans and Democrats, and I had an idea. I asked her

---

[2] I sure hope Ben and Beth stay together.

to make me a promise. When she got home to California, would she get on the Internet and watch the keynote speeches of the two party conventions? Zell Miller's and Barack Obama's. She said she would.

You might have picked up from this chapter that I wish that the Democratic Convention had had a somewhat harder edge to it. Not a dishonest, contemptible Zell Miller 2004 edge, but a genuine, hard-hitting Zell Miller 1992 edge. I think it's possible to fight hard without selling your soul. Sometimes you can gain your soul by fighting for what you believe in. So, if I had been in charge of the messaging for the Democratic Convention, instead of whoever the hell *was* in charge, I would have changed a lot of those speeches. But I wouldn't have changed a word of Barack Obama's.

Here's the part of Obama's speech that made me proudest, not just of my party, but of my country:

> Alongside our famous individualism, there's another ingredient in the American saga. A belief that we are connected as one people. If there's a child on the South Side of Chicago who can't read, that matters to me, even if it's not my child. If there's a senior citizen somewhere who can't pay for her prescription and has to choose between medicine and the rent, that makes my life poorer, even if it's not my grandmother. If there's an Arab-American family being rounded up without benefit of an attorney or due process, that threatens my civil liberties. It's that fundamental belief—I am my brother's keeper, I am my sister's keeper—that makes this country work. It's what allows us to pursue our individual dreams, yet still come together as a single American family. "*E pluribus unum.*" Out of many, one.
>
> Yet even as we speak, there are those who are preparing to divide us, the spin masters and negative ad peddlers who embrace the politics of anything goes. Well, I say to them tonight, there's not a liberal America and a conservative America— there's the United States of America. There's not a black America

and white America and Latino America and Asian America; there's the United States of America. The pundits like to slice-and-dice our country into Red States and Blue States; Red States for Republicans, Blue States for Democrats. But I've got news for them, too. We worship an awesome God in the Blue States, and we don't like federal agents poking around our libraries in the Red States. We coach Little League in the Blue States and have gay friends in the Red States. There are patriots who opposed the war in Iraq and patriots who supported it. We are one people, all of us pledging allegiance to the Stars and Stripes, all of us defending the United States of America.

I hope someday to see that young lady again and find out if she kept her promise. And if she did, I'd like to raise a glass with her to a more united America, an America where books like this one aren't necessary, but still sell millions of copies.

But if she didn't keep her promise, she's just another typical Republican.

7 How Bush Won: Queers

As much as I like and admire John Kerry, I have to admit he made some pretty tone-deaf, even boneheaded mistakes in the 2004 campaign. Why on earth, for example, would he pay good money to generate automated calls to African-American voters in Michigan claiming that voting for him would help legalize gay marriage? Here's what the calls said, according to the *Detroit Free Press*:

> When you vote this Tuesday, remember to legalize gay marriage by supporting John Kerry. It's what we all want. It's a basic Democratic principle.

I don't know what numbskull got the idea that the best way to use campaign funds was to make these robo-calls. Especially to people who were probably going to vote for Kerry already, but who, sophisticated polling had shown, were particularly hostile to gay marriage. And why do it the weekend before the election? Talk about shooting yourself in the foot!

It was almost as dumb as the automated phone calls telling Michigan Democrats that their polling places had changed when they really hadn't. That's just crazy!

But believe it or not, those robo-calls weren't the Kerry team's biggest blunder of the campaign season. That had to be Kerry's moronic pledge to *ban* the Bible. The Bible! The holiest book not just of Judaism, but of Christianity as well. Why offend almost everyone in the country?!

The Bush camp wasted no time in capitalizing on *that* misstep. Here's the flyer the Republican National Committee sent to religious voters in the swing states of Arkansas and West Virginia:

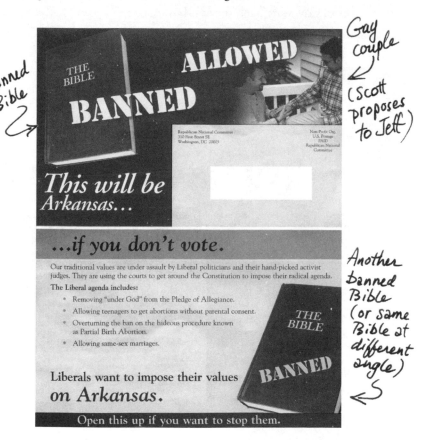

A mailing from the Republican National Committee.

Notice how the RNC picked up on the gay marriage theme, too. Kerry just played into their hands by wanting to ban the Bible and by supporting gay marriage. It's hard to think of anything that would alienate traditional religious voters more. My goodness!

But Kerry wasn't content to use just phone calls and mailings to communicate his radical, secularist, homosexual agenda to religious voters. No, he went so far as to actually pay openly gay AIDS activists—*from San Francisco!*—to mince up and down lines of black voters in Fort Lauderdale carrying colorful signs touting the Kerry-Edwards team's support for gay adoption. And couldn't he at least have stopped them from yelling, "Vote for Kerry, Support Gay Marriage!" over and over again? I mean, that's so gay!

It's almost too stupid to be believed, but here's a photo:

Republicans pose as San Francisco gay activists
outside a Fort Lauderdale polling place.

The dumbest part about all of this is that Kerry didn't even support gay marriage. As you know, Kerry has had a consistent, if in my view misguided, opposition to equal marriage rights for all Americans. He supports civil unions for same-sex couples, but not full-fledged marriage. And yet here he was pouring all this time and money and gay people into waving his gay agenda in front of his socially conservative black supporters.

Unless—wait. It's just occurred to me.

Could it be that these purportedly gay demonstrators from San Francisco were actually Republicans from Florida trying to peel off some African-American Kerry votes at the last moment? And would that explain why these demonstrators turned and ran when a couple of Democrats started filming them?

Hmm.

Come to think of it, I followed the campaign pretty closely, and I don't remember *ever* hearing Kerry call for the Bible to be banned. In fact, he's an observant Catholic. Could the Republicans have made up the Bible-ban thing?

If so, then maybe the *Bush* campaign had financed those crazy African-American robo-calls, even though they denied it.

I guess we'll never know the real story. We'll never know whether it was a series of inexplicable, suicidal mistakes by the Kerry team, or a systematic dirty-tricks campaign by Republicans eager to use religion and homophobia to divide America. But we do know that, since the beginning of their first term as president, George W. Bush, Dick Cheney, and Karl Rove mounted a concerted, relentless effort to recapture the 4 million religious conservative voters who, according to Rove, had not turned out in 2000. Some observers claim that this effort was the key to the election. I, and even more importantly, the data, disagree. As it so happens, the religious right's turnout went up about the same amount as everyone else's. But that doesn't forgive Bush, Cheney, and Rove's incredibly shameless and cynical abuse of sincere religious faith. Only God can do that. Ironic.

From the earliest days of the first Bush-Cheney-Rove administration, the White House held regular conference calls with people like James Dobson from Focus on the Family, Chuck Colson of Prison Fellowship and the Watergate cover-up, and Reverend Richard Land of the Southern

Baptist Convention. Per their instructions, White House policymakers would sometimes take breaks from lining the pockets of extremely wealthy cronies in order to pander to fundamentalist voters by cutting off aid to family planning groups in desperately poor countries, restricting stem cell research, and ensuring that a "partial-birth abortion" ban being considered by Congress would not include an exception for the health of the mother.

Rove also courted the Christian conservative vote more directly, by funneling money to churches. One plank of Bush's 2000 "compassionate conservative" platform was fighting poverty by supporting faith-based initiatives. John DiIulio, Bush's first director of the Office of Faith-Based and Community Initiatives, resigned once he realized that the program's focus was on politics rather than on actually helping people. But DiIulio's successor, Jim Towey, had no such qualms. Towey oversaw the distribution of over a billion dollars to carefully selected religious groups. Thanks to his efforts and the tireless work of congressional Republicans, it is impossible to account for almost all of that money, but we do know that two thirds of Towey's trips during 2004 were to battleground states. When the *Los Angeles Times* confronted him about this, Towey defended his travel schedule with what I call a non-denial acknowledgment: "If you look at where the battleground states are, it's where the action is in the faith-based initiative." Right. Exactly.

Towey also differed from DiIulio in that he was willing to go on the offense against "the secular extremists" hell-bent on "creating a godless orthodoxy," as he put it in a speech at the taxpayer-sponsored White House National Conference on Faith-Based and Community Initiatives. And he told the Christian conservative magazine *World*, "I would expect that Senator Kerry, if he was elected, would stick the Faith-Based Initiative in the Smithsonian."

Most Democrats have no problem with churches, synagogues, and, to a lesser extent, mosques, receiving federal money to provide services to the needy. In fact, the feds have been funding faith-based charities since the Revolutionary War. The group Catholic Charities, which does heroic work, has been getting money from the federal government for over a hundred years—almost as long as there have been Catholics. Kerry, a Catholic himself, had laid out plans to expand the faith-based initiative into the type of poverty-fighting machine that John DiIulio had originally signed on for. So despite Towey's warnings, Kerry would never have sent Bush's Faith-Based Initiative to the Smithsonian, except as part of a special exhibition on rank political patronage.

It is actually illegal for tax-exempt religious organizations to engage in partisan political activity. But that didn't stop the Bush-Cheney campaign from encouraging clergy in battleground states to do their civic duty. In Pennsylvania, for example, ministers received this e-mail from a Bush-Cheney staffer.

Subject: Lead Your Congregation for President Bush

Dear ---- :

The Bush-Cheney '04 national headquarters in Virginia has asked us to identify 1600 "Friendly Congregations" in Pennsylvania where voters friendly to President Bush might gather on a regular basis. In each of these friendly congregations, we would like to identify a volunteer coordinator who can help distribute general information to other supporters. If you are interested, please email Luke Bernstein at LBernstein@GeorgeWBush.com your name, address, phone number and place of worship.

Thanks, Luke

Paid for by Bush-Cheney '04, Inc.

Jesus Christ! And *this* from a *Bernstein*?!

Look. Churches are always going to be involved in social justice issues, on one side or the other. Just ask Dr. Martin Luther King, Jr. (for) or Dr. Jerry Falwell (against). And some congregations certainly have a political bent, such as Our Lady of Gun Control in Bayside, Queens. But this was ridiculous. Even the campaign's allies thought the White House had gone too far, considering the state of the law at the time.

There was only one solution. Change the law.

In early June 2004, Republicans in the House Ways and Means Committee added an amendment to H.R. 4520, the American Job Creation Act of 2004 (which cut corporate taxes, thereby creating jobs for people who gild bathroom fixtures), that would allow churches to commit three (count 'em, three) "unintentional violations" of legal restrictions on political activities each year without losing their tax-exempt status. I call that the "four strikes and you're out" law. Even more exciting, clergy would now be allowed to endorse candidates, as long as they made clear they were acting as individuals and not on behalf of their religious organizations.

Thankfully, when even the Southern Baptist Convention said the Republicans were getting a little too cute, the "Safe Harbor for Churches" amendment died a quiet death.

It seems that not every pastor got the word about section 692 of H.R. 4520. In the foothills of North Carolina's Great Smoky Mountains, the Reverend Chan Chandler decreed in October '04 that any East Waynesville Baptist Church congregant planning to vote for John Kerry should either leave the church or repent. After the election, the good reverend made good on his threat and kicked nine Democratic sheep out of his flock. Unfortunately for him, and fortunately for lovers of religious freedom everywhere, about forty other flock members turned out not to be sheep at all, but rather stubborn goats, who resigned in protest. Ultimately, Reverend Chandler himself was forced to resign, and now manages a Republicans-only Tastee-Freez in nearby Hazelwood.

Kerry, of course, was not a Baptist. So he couldn't have been thrown out of the East Waynesville Baptist Church for supporting himself. But the Roman Catholic archbishop of St. Louis, Raymond Burke, knew the next best thing. He forbade Kerry from taking communion in his diocese.

What had Kerry done to deserve such punishment? Had he molested hundreds of children? Had he covered up the crimes of other child-molesting senators and reassigned them to other states where they could continue preying on the young, rather than bringing them to justice? Or perhaps as governor of Texachusetts he had overseen the executions of 152 of God's children, including some who were mentally retarded and probably a few who were innocent?

No. His crime was that he had the same position on abortion rights as other Catholic politicians like Rudolph Giuliani, Arnold Schwarzenegger, Maine Senator Susan Collins, Alaska Senator Lisa Murkowski, New York Governor George Pataki, and then–Homeland Security Secretary Tom Ridge. All were personally opposed to abortion, but didn't agree with Oklahoma Senator Tom Coburn, who believes abortion doctors should be executed.[1] Instead, they agreed with notable Southern Baptist sinner William Jefferson Clinton and scholarly Jew Al Franken, who believe that abortions should be safe, legal, and rare.

Giuliani, Schwarzenegger, Collins, Murkowski, Pataki, and Ridge did differ from Kerry in one key respect—they were all Republicans. For some reason, Archbishop Burke had no problem with pro-choice Republicans partaking of the body and blood of their Savior.

Neither did the most shameless members of the right-wing press. But Kerry was an affront to G-d H-ms-lf. C-l Th-m-s—excuse me. Cal Thomas, writing on the right-wing opinion site Townhall.com, proclaimed that "Kerry has a choice: either 'resign' as a Catholic, or withdraw from the presidential race." He was joined by the *National Review*'s William F. Buckley and L. Brent Bozell of the Media Research Center.

Sean Hannity, unsurprisingly, weighed in as well. "I choose to be a Catholic," he explained in a discussion of whether Kerry should receive communion, "but that's the point. They set the rules. And if you don't like them you can ask them to change it or you can go to another church."

---

[1] "I favor the death penalty for abortionists and others who take life." Tom Coburn to the Associated Press, "Coburn Different Kind of Political Cat," July 9, 2004. Here's another great thing about Coburn. In 1997, he condemned NBC for its prime-time airing of *Schindler's List*, saying it took network programming to "an all-time low" by exposing children to, among other things, "vile language, full frontal nudity and irresponsible sexual activity."

Since Sean describes himself as "a big death penalty supporter," I can only assume he has left the Catholic Church for something a little more bloodthirsty.

None of these pundits mentioned that only 28 percent of American Catholics believe abortion should be illegal. Nor did they rail against the avowedly pro-choice Catholic "public figures" who happened to be Republicans. It wasn't just that no Republicans had ever been put in this position. Until John Kerry, no Democrat had ever faced it either. As CBS News reported on April 6, 2004, "The denial of communion to a Catholic eminent politician would be unprecedented."

So why Kerry? Kerry was the first Catholic nominee since John Fitzgerald Kennedy, who faced concerns that, as a bootlicking papist, he was in thrall to the Vatican and would do its bidding by, for instance, relocating the White House to Vatican City. But ten years after Kennedy took one in the squash, the Supreme Court ruled in *Roe v. Wade* that women had the right to make decisions about their own reproductive systems.

It wasn't enough to browbeat pro-choice Democrats for being pro-choice. In order to divide Americans enough to conquer them, the right had to convince the public that Democrats just *hate* pro-life people.

There is one piece of evidence to support this claim, and it pops up like a dandelion in every election cycle. It's called the "Bob Casey Wasn't Allowed to Speak at the 1992 Democratic Convention Because He's Pro-Life" myth. In the summer of 2004, everyone from Bill O'Reilly to Chris Matthews touted the story of the brave, pro-life Pennsylvania governor who lost the right to speak because he wouldn't toe the party line on the rights of the unborn. Like other myths, such as the one about alligators in New York sewers, this myth isn't true. The real reason Casey didn't speak at the Democratic Convention in 1992 is, get this, because he wouldn't endorse the Democratic candidate for President of the United States.

Counterintelligence operative Robert Novak learned this the hard way when he tried to use the Bob Casey myth in an argument with someone who actually knew something, eyewitness Paul Begala. From the June 28, 2004, *Crossfire*:

> **NOVAK:** I would say that the difference between Republicans and Democrats is, Republicans let all kinds of people in. Your party, like your friend, the former governor of Pennsylvania, Casey, wouldn't even let him speak because he was pro-life.
>
> **BEGALA:** No, sir. I was there. It's a point of personal privilege. I was there. He was my client. We did not let him speak because he would not endorse the ticket. Nobody gets to speak at any convention unless they support the candidate for president. That's the only—
>
> **NOVAK:** He wouldn't speak because he was pro-life.
>
> **BEGALA:** That's not true, Bob. I was there. I helped make that decision. And you did not. This, I know firsthand.

You didn't see many anti-Bush speeches at the Republican National Convention, did you? Neither did I. Why? Because the Republicans aren't morons. As James Carville put it to *The New Republic*'s Michael Crowley, "You'd have to be idiotic to give a speaking role to a person who hadn't even endorsed you."

If you still think Democrats try to muzzle pro-life speakers, take a look at the list of people who *did* speak at the 1992 Convention. As Crowley noted, the podium was graced by "a slew of pro-life Democrats, including Chicago Mayor Richard M. Daley, Jr., Senators John Breaux and Howell Heflin, and five governors." And pro-life speakers, from Breaux to Harry Reid, have graced every Democratic Convention stage since then. So, please, if you ever hear anyone repeat the "Bob Casey Wasn't Allowed to Speak at the 1992 Democratic Convention Because He's Pro-Life" myth, do me a favor. Hit him over the head with a pan.

Nobody likes getting an abortion. Except, perhaps, rape victims. It's just that pro-choice people know that sometimes women get pregnant when they aren't ready to have a child. Nobody enjoys unwanted pregnancies either. Which is why Democrats support access to birth control and comprehensive sex education that promotes abstinence but also provides accurate information about contraception. Because of policies like those, in the eight Clinton years that followed the convention where Bob Casey was prevented from speaking because he wouldn't endorse the ticket, abortions went down every single year.

Most pro-life Americans are absolutely sincere about their beliefs. Not just pro-life Democrats like Senate Minority Leader Harry Reid, but also pro-life Republicans like *Wheel of Fortune* host Pat Sajak. I respect their convictions. But sometimes I just get the feeling that the pro-life movement is being used by politicians who don't have the best interests of America's fetuses in mind.

In the thirty-plus years since *Roe v. Wade,* reproductive freedom has been more explosive than any other issue in the culture wars. That is, until 2004. As Gary Bauer told *The New York Times,* gay marriage is "the new abortion." Bauer meant that, like abortion, equal marriage rights were a culturally powerful issue being decided by judicial fiat. But if Karl Rove had said it, he would have meant it in the "Xbox is the new PlayStation" sense. It was a heavy, sharp, new wedge with which to divide America. Gay marriage had fabulous potential.

Uncharacteristically, Rove was a little behind the curve on same-sex marriage. After all, in 2000, he had let his candidate say that gay marriage was an issue best left to the states. But when the Massachusetts Supreme Court ruled that gay people, being people, should have the right to marry not just people of the opposite sex, but people they actually loved, all hell broke loose. Grassroots homophobes from coast to coast, but mainly between the coasts, started organizing state ballot initiatives and voter turnout drives in order to defend the sanctity of marriage from the Pink Menace rapidly sashaying their way.

Anti-gay activists were already primed to explode. On June 26, 2003, the Supreme Court had ruled in *Lawrence v. Texas* that consensual homosexual sex wasn't just widespread, it was *legal*. Can you imagine that? So when the Massachusetts decision arrived on February 6, 2004, and, six days later, San Francisco mayor Gavin Newsom started marrying off homosexuals on the steps of City Hall, it was clear to slippery-slopers that it wouldn't be long before a guy married a chicken. (Pennsylvania Senator Rick Santorum took the less alarmist position that we were headed only for "man-on-child, man-on-dog" state-sanctioned relationships, both of which, for the record, Rick and I oppose. And, Rick, if I get to the Senate, let's do a bill on this one. Just you and me, buddy. Cosponsors of the Franken-Santorum—hell, the Santorum-Franken Man-Dog Marriage Act.)

On February 24, 2004, President George W. Bush announced the most flamboyant flip-flop of his presidency. Suddenly, equal marriage rights weren't a state issue after all. What was needed was a new amendment to the Constitution of the United States. Something that he could be for, and Kerry against. Perfect. The White House was out in front, leading the charge once again. The charge against bad culture things.

Like Rove, I myself was a little behind the curve on this one. As I said frequently on my radio show, I just didn't understand how two gay people getting married was a threat to the marriages of people like myself. Was I going to walk down the street, see two men with wedding rings, and tell my wife of twenty-nine years, "Hey, that looks great. Maybe I could marry a guy who likes football, watch the game with him, and then come home and have sex with you"? Every time Franni heard this, she'd call the station and tell me I didn't understand the whole concept. But I kept insisting I did.

I also said that the biggest threat to marriage was divorce, and that there should be a three-strikes-you're-out rule. Rush Limbaugh shouldn't be allowed to marry again. Newt Gingrich? Sorry. You're stuck with the congressional staffer that you chose as your third and, if I had my way, final wife.

I even crafted a negative ad, based on my woeful misunderstanding of the gay marriage controversy:

> George W. Bush wants to amend our Constitution to make it illegal for gays to marry. But evidently, he has no problem with *terrorists* getting married. Even now, terrorist couples are plotting to sanctify their love for each other in holy matrimony— and then blow up the Holland Tunnel. Call George W. Bush. Tell him that America can't afford a president who is soft on terrorist marriage. Because unlike gays . . . terrorists can breed.
>
> Paid for by the Committee to Distract You from Real Issues.

The ad did make a good point. And then made sure you got the point with the tagline. But what I didn't understand was that, for the religious right, gay marriage wasn't about marriage. It was about gay.

Like everyone in show business, I know gay people. Did you know that there are a lot of gay people in hair and makeup? And in costume design? There are. And in all the other areas of the business as well. Even some of the female impersonators are gay. And every gay person I know feels strongly that they didn't "choose" their sexual orientation. Rather, they came to realize something about themselves that had been true about them all along.

But how would they know?

As Russell Shorto described in his June 19, 2005, *New York Times Magazine* cover story, anti–gay marriage activists have a different view. According to Shorto, these activists "deny that homosexuality is inherent. It can't be, because that would mean God had created some people who are damned from birth, morally blackened. This really is the inescapable root of the whole issue."

So if you're not born gay, how do you become gay? Seems like an odd choice to make in a society where sodomy laws were only struck down a few months ago. But the Family Research Council (run by Tony Perkins, one of the sometime participants on the White House Christian-right conference calls) settled the matter in its book, *Getting It Straight: What the Research Shows About Homosexuality*. Right in Chapter One, "What Causes Homosexuality," we learn that homosexuality is not natural or genetic, but springs from early experiences in the home, such as child abuse.

Did Lynne and Dick Cheney abuse their gay daughter, Mary? Of course not.

Did conservative matriarch Phyllis Schlafly and her husband abuse their gay son, John? Perhaps.

Did Alan Keyes and his wife abuse their gay daughter, Maya? Absolutely. If you count exposing her to Alan's insane anti-gay tirades.

Did anyone in the White House leadership actually agree with the FRC's perverted view of homosexuality, and disagree with the American Medical Association, the American Psychiatric Association, and the American Academy of Pediatrics? I really doubt it. But that didn't stop them from throwing bone after bone to the bone-craving Christian activists pushing anti–gay marriage ballot initiatives in eleven states.

Every one of those initiatives passed. And Bush got his 4 million additional evangelical votes. Combine those facts with the "moral values" 22 percent exit poll factoid[2] and you can see why so many analysts thought the election was a triumph for the religious right.

This view was immediately bolstered by certain interested parties, such as leaders of the religious right who wanted to make sure that the White House knew whom it owed.

No one was more excited than Bob Jones III, president of Bob Jones

---

[2] I'm using "factoid" here in its original and proper sense. Most people think that a factoid is an interesting little fact. It's not. According to the *American Heritage Dictionary*, a factoid is, in actuality, a "piece of unverified or inaccurate information that is presented in the press as factual and that is then accepted as true because of frequent repetition." Ironically, the wrong meaning of the word "factoid" has come into common usage because of frequent repetition.

University. In a public letter to the newly elected president, Jones laid out his hopes and prayers for Bush's second term:

> Undoubtedly, you will have opportunity to appoint many conservative judges and exercise forceful leadership with the Congress in passing legislation that is defined by Biblical norm regarding the family, sexuality, sanctity of life, religious freedom, freedom of speech, and limited government.

Oh, and one other thing:

> Don't equivocate. Put your agenda on the front burner and let it boil. You owe the liberals nothing. They despise you because they despise your Christ.

Gulp.

Thing is, I know a lot of liberals and not one of them despises Christ. Personally, I like Christ. I don't worship him, but as my rabbi told us when I was a kid, Jesus was a great prophet who had wonderful ideas—none of them new.

So, I bear no ill will toward anyone's Christ, and particularly not Bush's. It was Jesus, after all, who helped Dubya stop drinking. As bad as things are now, can you imagine how much worse a fix we'd be in if Bush were still hitting the bottle, slurring his way through another morale-boosting speech to the troops or staggering around a G8 summit? Thank you, Jesus.

But Jones III and I don't just disagree on whether I despise Christ. We also part company on the question of who elected Bush and why. In his letter, Jones writes, "In your reelection [sic][3] God has graciously granted America—though she doesn't deserve it—a reprieve from the agenda of

---

[3]Bush wasn't "elected" in 2000. Thus, he was "elected" to his second term, not "reelected," and is entitled to run again in 2008. That's the downside of holding this position.

paganism." According to all the exit polls *I've* seen, paganism had little or nothing to do with the outcome of the election.[4]

Also—and this is probably the more important point—Bush's victory was *not* a resounding triumph of the religious right. Yes, Bush got more votes from self-identified evangelical Christians than he did in 2000. But he *and* Kerry got more votes from all kinds of places. Bush got 11.5 million more votes than he did in 2000. Kerry got 8 million more than Gore. And, in fact, Bush's vote share increased more among people who rarely or never go to church (3–4 percent) than among people who go to church one or more times a week (1 percent). And it's not just me saying that. It's Emory University political scientist Alan Abramowitz, whom you've never heard of.[5]

More specifically, there are some serious problems with the idea that Kerry got reamed because of the gay marriage issue.

Here's another political scientist you've never heard of. Stephen Ansolabehere. And another one: Charles Stewart III. You might think you have heard of him, because a Charlie Stuart killed his wife in Boston back in 1989 and blamed it on a black guy. But that was a different Charles Stuart entirely.

Coincidentally, Stewart and Ansolabehere also live in the Boston area, since both are political science professors at MIT. The two of them make a compelling case that the eleven anti–gay marriage ballot initiatives didn't help Bush at all, and possibly worked against him. Only four of them were in battleground states: Arkansas, Michigan, Ohio, and Oregon. By my calculations, Bush won in precisely one half of those four states. But in classic MIT fashion, Stewart and Ansolabehere dug deeper. They found that,

[4]That is because pagans are what's called a "structural" component of the vote, which goes in predictable proportions to Democrats, Republicans, and, even more, the Libertarian, Green, and Natural Law parties.

[5]Here's another little wrinkle. The Fourth National Survey of Religion and Politics conducted by the Ray C. Bliss Institute of Applied Politics at the University of Akron determined that Kerry took 82 percent of the vote among atheists and agnostics. Which I suppose makes sense, although you'd think agnostics would be swing voters.

comparing 2000 to 2004, Bush improved less in battleground states with anti–gay marriage referenda than he did in battleground states without them.

You'd think those conclusions would be enough for any scholar. But not for Stewart and Ansolabehere. They didn't settle for just the battleground states. They looked at the change from 2000 to 2004 in *all* the states with anti–gay marriage initiatives, and compared that to the change in all the states without them—not just at the state level, but at the county level. Sounds like a lot of work, I know. But this is all these guys do. They don't have real jobs, like you or me. Well, like you.

What they found was remarkable. In states *with* the initiatives, red counties got redder and blue counties got bluer, with a net advantage of 2.6 percent for Kerry. Whereas in states *without* the referenda, Bush gained about 3 percent overall. So the initiatives seemed to polarize people, and actually *hurt* Bush. Isn't that something? Bush being *hurt* by a divided America? That's the kind of counterintuitive result that puts the "T" in MIT.

Did millions of Christian conservatives turn out to vote on social issues like abortion, gay marriage, and Bible banning? Sure. Is this anything new? Not really. The alliance of religious conservatives with the Republican elite was signed in blood back in 1980, when Ronald Reagan was swept into office in part thanks to televangelists like James Robison, Jerry Falwell, and Ayatollah Khomeini. It was a triumph for the conservative movement. Paul Weyrich, founding president of the Heritage Foundation, explained what happened:

> The conservative movement, up to that point, was essentially an intellectual movement. It had some very powerful thinkers, but it didn't have many troops. And as Stalin said of the Pope, "Where are his divisions?" Well, we didn't have many divisions. When these folks became active, all of a sudden the conservative movement had lots of divisions. We were able to move literally

millions of people. And this is something that we had literally no ability to do prior to that time.

So there was nothing new about the Christian conservative vote, unless you count the depths of the shamelessness with which it was wooed by Rove and company. The religious man-on-dog-and-pony show simply brought out the base. The fear-mongering terrified the middle. And the smear campaign convinced just enough of the terrified that Kerry couldn't protect them. That's how a terrible, unpopular president, a president who had misled his country into war and failed to produce a single net job by Election Day, a Republican facing an extraordinarily united Democratic mobilization, managed to eke out a record-breakingly narrow victory. And then claim a mandate.

As historians like myself understand, that's the true story of 2004. But the ground troops of the religious right were fed a very different line.

They were told that Bush owed his victory to them, and them alone. Richard Land, the Southern Baptist leader from those White House conference calls, put it simply: "The faith factor was the difference in this election."

Another conference call participant, James Dobson,[6] pinned the tail directly on the party symbolized by the donkey:

> As is now apparent, those who appealed to the unelected and unaccountable courts to legalize same-sex "marriages" had miscalculated and overreached. Ultimately, Democrats paid a price for it. I am among those who believe the President would not have won reelection if it had not been for the power of this issue to drive conservative voters to the polls.

[6]As it so happens, I ran into Dr. Dobson at the 2005 White House Correspondents Dinner, where we were both guests of ABC News. "It must be great to always know the absolute truth," I said to him admiringly. "It's such a burden for the rest of us." Dobson got the joke but immediately launched into a vivid, gory description of a late-term abortion procedure.

The values voters had spoken. And now it was time for the values voters to get some value for their votes. It was payback time—or else. Dobson laid it out to *The New York Times*:

> I believe that the Bush administration now needs to be more aggressive in pursuing those values, and if they don't do it I believe they will pay a price in four years.

As the *Times* reported on November 4, Dobson and his 1.2 million followers weren't alone in calling in their marker:

> Austin Ruse, president of the conservative Catholic Culture of Life Foundation, suggested that if Chief Justice William H. Rehnquist steps down, Mr. Bush could begin to repay his social conservative backers by naming Justice Antonin Scalia to replace him. "We'd love to see Scalia in that spot, and I think we have earned it," Mr. Ruse said.

Oddly, it fell to Chuck "When You've Got Them by the Balls, Their Hearts and Minds Will Follow" Colson to urge restraint:

> I am tired of reading articles about evangelicals voting for Bush because they want to "get something" from him, and I disassociate myself from anyone who says, "Now we voted for you, it's payback time. Give us our due." That's what special interest groups do, and we're not a special interest group.

But Colson's sage counsel was drowned out, as the Christian generals who thought they'd won the culture war rushed in to claim the spoils.

In the Oval Office, in the halls of Congress, and in the oxygenated bubble at the bottom of Karl Rove's cesspool where the real decisions are made, the conventional wisdom congealed instantly, like a blood clot. The right believed the country had moved to the right. They believed Dobson, not Colson, and believed there'd be hell to pay if they failed to cater to the demands of Dobson's Christian soldiers.

Republican leaders believed that if there came a time when they were called upon to demonstrate absolute, unquestioning, extra-constitutional fealty to their theocratic allies, they would have no choice but to do so, and to do so with the utmost enthusiasm—no matter what.

Even if, in the President's case, it meant interrupting a vacation.

Such a time would come soon. It would make household names of Terri Schiavo, Tom DeLay, and Bill Frist. It would spark a nation's interest in living wills, durable powers of attorney for health care, and the legal distinctions between those two documents. But perhaps even more importantly, it would come to symbolize Republican overreach—and fuel a mainstream backlash that would discredit Dobson's delirious dream of domination. Bush's pretensions to a mandate would be brushed away like so many cobwebs in the path of a bulldozer.

They thought the Bible had made them omnipotent.

But God had other plans.

8 | Al Franken Talks About God

I'm Jewish. So, I suppose I'm not really in much of a position to argue that conservatives have hijacked Christianity. And I haven't read the New Testament from cover to cover. But from what I understand, if you cut out all the passages in the Bible where Jesus talks about the poor, about helping out the least among us—if you cut out every one of those passages, you'd have the perfect container to smuggle Rush Limbaugh's drugs in.

My views about God come from my Dad. He died twelve years ago, of lung cancer. Which brings me to a funny story.

Dad died at home. My brother and I both came back to Minnesota to be with him and Mom for what turned out to be the last three weeks of his life. About a week before Dad died, we got a call from Rabbi Black, who asked me if he could come over and talk to him. I thought about it for a moment and told the rabbi that I didn't think so. Dad knew he was dying. He knew we knew he was dying. But we never discussed it as such, and I just didn't want Dad to have to talk about his death unless he brought it up himself.

A couple days later Rabbi Black called again. Could he come over and comfort my mother? Well, Mom was a total wreck by then, and if someone was capable of giving her any comfort, it would certainly have been a relief for me and my brother. Sure, Rabbi. So Rabbi Black came over and sat in our living room with the three of us for however long, and I don't remember a thing he said, other than: "Would it be okay if I could see your father?" The thought instantly crossed my mind that the comforting Mom bit was just a way for the rabbi to get his foot in the door to get at Dad. But I felt guilty immediately for even thinking that. I was kind of a wreck myself.

I told the rabbi I'd check with my Dad and went down the hall to his bedroom. By now, Dad was down to about seventy-five pounds and extremely weak. But he was still totally on the ball. I said to him, "Dad, Rabbi Black is here and he was wondering if he could talk to you."

It took Dad a moment to gather his breath and say, "Well, I don't really know him." Rabbi Black was new to the temple. Then with a shrug in his frail voice, Dad said, "But if he feels it will do him some good . . ."

I laughed really hard. And Dad smiled. A happy, satisfied smile, because his son had given him the best gift you could receive in our house. I had laughed at his joke.

I went back to the living room and told Rabbi Black that Dad would see him. The rabbi spent about a half hour with Dad, who died five days later. Rabbi Black presided over Dad's memorial, where I told the "if he feels it will do him some good" story. Everyone laughed, especially Rabbi Black.

It wasn't until a few months ago that I heard the rest of the story. I was in Albuquerque, New Mexico, where Rabbi Black now has a congregation. Our radio show was touring the Southwest, and I invited the rabbi to be part of the audience. Before the show, we sat in a small office at the National Hispanic Cultural Center, and I asked Rabbi Black how his talk with my Dad had gone. The rabbi smiled. "Oh, he tried to make me feel comfortable."

That was my Dad.

Joe Franken was born in 1908 in New York City to immigrant parents. His dad, my grandfather, Otto Franken, died of tuberculosis when Dad was sixteen. So Dad went to work and didn't finish high school. He never had much of a career—Dad was a printing salesman for the last thirty years of his working life—but everyone liked Joe Franken. He and Mom were married fifty-three years. They bickered sometimes—maybe more than sometimes—but were completely devoted to each other. Mom pretty much fell apart after he died.

Neither of my folks was particularly observant, but my Dad liked going to temple. Mainly, for him, it was a social thing. He was an usher, and he loved the music and the sermons. Rabbi Shapiro, the rabbi he knew, spoke from the *bema* about Jewish religious philosophy and the requirement that Jews not only *be* just but that we *do* justice.

Unlike Mom, Dad was comfortable talking with me about religion and God. He believed in God, but not as an old man with a long white beard sitting in Heaven. In many ways, Dad's view of God was like our Founding Fathers'. Not Abraham, Isaac, and Jacob. Thomas Jefferson, John Adams, and James Madison, who were not really Christians so much as Deists.

To Dad, the Bible—meaning the Old Testament—was not to be taken literally. Woman evolved along with man through natural selection. Not from Adam's rib. The work of God could be found, as our Founders believed, in Nature.

Dad told me that he believed Nature, which to him included humankind, to be so beautiful, so magnificent, that there had to be something behind it all. That was it. That was Dad's idea of God: something behind it all. It was no more or less complicated than that.

For Dad the rest of religion lay in the ethical teachings of Judaism and, to the extent he had absorbed them, of any other faith, Western, Eastern, or whatever. Again, not so different from our Founders. In their famous correspondence at the end of their lives, Adams and Jefferson wrote a lot about religion. When Adams concluded that his personal creed was "contained in four short words, 'Be just and good,' " Jefferson replied, "The result of our fifty or sixty years of religious reading, in the four words, 'Be just and good,' is that in which all our inquiries must end."

So if your definition of traditional American religious values starts with the Founders, you could say my Jewish father's values were as traditional as they get. Jefferson, of course, had sex with a slave, which Dad would have disapproved of. Mainly on the slavery front.

My conception of God is pretty much the same as Dad's. And like him, I respect other people's religious beliefs. I know they derive tremendous inspiration, joy, and solace from their faith. I also expect others to respect my beliefs. That's also a traditional American value.

I consider myself a very fortunate person, most of all because I've been extremely lucky in my family life. Even though my wife and I had not been totally abstinent before getting married, we will be celebrating our thirtieth wedding anniversary a few weeks before this book is published. How have I managed to stay married for thirty years, many of them happy? I credit fear. My fear of being alone. Also, there's Franni's willingness to tolerate me.

And, of course, we're a family. I'm not a big one for prayer. Unless you consider counting your blessings as praying. I am grateful every day for my two unbelievably great kids. Please indulge me in a moment of fatherly pride here. Both my kids are smart, happy, funny, and kind. Those of you who listen to my radio show know I brag way too much on my daughter Thomasin and the fact that she teaches third grade at an inner-city public school in the Bronx. She hates when I do it and always asks me to stop, which makes me even more proud of how modest she is. She didn't get that from me.

My son is Joe, after my Dad. Here's another point of pride. At Joe's high school they give out one prize to a graduating senior. There are no academic awards, no valedictorian, just the Billy Farrell Award, named for a particularly beloved student who died in a car accident a number of years ago. Essentially, it's the Mensch of the Class Award. You know I'm telling you this because the school presented Joe with the honor.

Of course, I credit his Mom. Mostly. You see, when Joe was about eight years old, he was over at another kid's house and the kid's mom asked Joe why he was such a nice guy. Joe said, "I think it has something to do with my grandfather."

Is Dad in Heaven looking down, giving that smile he gave me when I laughed at his joke? I have no clue. Actually, I really doubt it. But I know he's a part of me. And a part of everyone who loved him.

I think somewhere in there is God.

Book Two

Seeds of Collapse

9 "A Great Political Issue"

Al Gore has had a lot of gloomy days in the last five years. But even by his extremely high standards, December 26, 2004, was a standout. On that day an undersea earthquake sent a shock wave through the Indian Ocean, triggering a massive tsunami that claimed more than 150,000 lives.

It was an unspeakable tragedy for everyone. But for Gore, the horror was compounded by the knowledge that a huge amount of the suffering could have been prevented if, not so many years before, Republicans in Congress had been able to set aside partisanship and let him carry out his plan for a Global Disaster Information Network. Had his system been put in place, ocean-bottom earthquake detectors would have alerted scientists at a monitoring hub that a tsunami was on the way. The scientists in turn would have activated an international alarm system, warning officials in Asian coastal areas to immediately begin evacuation. As Gore's national security adviser, Leon Fuerth, explained in a rueful *New York Times* op-ed two weeks after the disaster, "Tens of thousands of people might have been able to flee to higher ground."

Gore had begun working with a variety of government agencies on this project during the second Clinton administration. Some might claim he was angling for the Indonesian ex-pat vote, but I think it was because he cared about human life. Gore has always had that weakness. And if there's one thing that Republicans know how to exploit, it's weakness. They knew that Gore was planning to run for president, and they didn't want him to be able to point to any "accomplishments," so they killed the project's funding. Today, the Global Disaster Information Network survives as little more than a professional society for people in the depressing, though crucial, field of disaster management.

The killing of the GDIN is a perfect example of the thing I hate most about Washington: The "I will stop you from doing good because I don't want you to get credit" thing. That's why Jimmy Carter's perpetual motion machine never saw the light of day.

The tsunami struck the northern coast of Sumatra at around 8 A.M. local time on December 26. But it was still Christmas Day in Crawford, Texas, where George W. Bush was taking the first well-deserved vacation of his presidency. Amid the worldwide outpouring of grief, sympathy, and pledges of help, Bush would not comment publicly on the terrible catastrophe for a full three days. Even by December 28, as international aid agencies scrambled to prevent further loss of life and a stunned world began to grasp the magnitude of the unfolding horror, the President did not speak, preferring instead to go bicycling and clear brush on his ranch, and perhaps write Christmas thank-you notes. Those concerned about America's collapsed standing in the world began to grumble that the President was missing a rare opportunity to engender some goodwill by showing that he was not indifferent to the suffering of non-Americans.

A White House official responded to this criticism by attacking Bill Clinton. Bush, he said, "didn't want to make a symbolic statement about 'We feel your pain.' "

No one missed the reference. As the *Washington Post* reported, "Many Bush aides believe Clinton was too quick to head for the cameras to hold forth on tragedies with his trademark empathy."

That's good old Dubya for you. Never one to make a show.

Four months later, back again in Crawford, President Bush faced another crisis. This crisis was arguably less earthshaking than the Asian tsunami. For example, instead of countless unexpected deaths and the destabilization of an entire region, it involved a single family's dispute over the fate of one irreversibly brain-damaged, persistently vegetative woman in Florida. But the President's response to this crisis was very different. In his response, as well as the response of Congress and the right-wing press, can be seen all the elements of dishonesty, hypocrisy, extremism, and corruption that I believe will lead to the complete and utter destruction of the Republican Party within one year and one month of the publication of this book.

Although I think that much of the *response* to the Schiavo case was ugly and richly deserving of scorn and ridicule, I don't want to make light of what was a very real tragedy. In 1989, twenty-six year-old Terri Schiavo collapsed and stopped breathing, depriving her brain of oxygen for a prolonged period. Although doctors were able to restore her heartbeat, there is no credible evidence that she ever regained consciousness. But her family didn't give up on her. In 1991, her husband and legal guardian, Michael Schiavo, began studying nursing so he could "learn more how to take care of Terri." Michael would become a respiratory therapist and emergency room nurse. Terri's parents, Robert and Mary Schindler, also poured themselves into caring for their daughter, hoping that she would recover.

In 1998, Michael, convinced that there was no hope for Terri, filed a petition to discontinue her life support. The Schindlers fought back in court. The ensuing seven-year legal battle became a flashpoint for the right-to-life movement. Now, in March of 2005, a Florida state circuit court judge had ruled that Michael Schiavo had the right to ask that his wife's feeding tube be removed. The Schindlers appealed, but no other

Florida court would take the case, and the feeding tube was removed. But hope was not lost. Over the years, some powerful people had taken up the Schindlers' cause. And those powerful friends had some chits to cash in.

On March 20, the day before Palm Sunday, Senate Bill 686, which transferred jurisdiction of the Schiavo case to federal court, was passed unanimously by a narrow three-vote margin. I'm not contradicting myself. It was a voice vote, and only three senators—Frist (R-TN), Martinez (R-FL), and Santorum (R-PA)—voted. Can they do that? Yes. Yes, they can.

Late, late that night, Tom DeLay's House of Representatives passed the same bill 203–58. All that was needed now for the bill to gain the force of law was the signature of the President of the United States. But he wasn't in Washington. He was in Crawford. There were only two legal ways for the President to sign the bill. Either the bill had to go to the President— boring!—or the President could go to the bill.[1]

This time, unlike after the tsunami, the President felt the need to make a symbolic statement to show the Schindlers and their supporters that he felt their pain. And so, cutting a precious vacation short for the first and, he hoped, the last time, Mr. Bush went to Washington.

The President immediately received plaudits for his political canniness. Richard Cizik, chief lobbyist for the National Association of Evangelicals, explained why: "Look, this is a symbolic move, for sure. It's his willingness to interrupt his vacation to make a statement." Cizik said it "would have been acceptable" for Bush to sign the bill at his ranch, "but this President seizes opportunities when they come his way. That's what makes him a good politician."

Richard Cizik and George W. Bush weren't the only Washington power players who thought the Schiavo bill was great politics. So did Brian Darling, the author of an unsigned memo that had circulated the previous week among Republicans on the Senate floor. "This is a great political issue," Dar-

---

[1] Actually, now that I think about it, there was a third option. The President and the bill could have both gone to a third location, perhaps halfway in between—say, Arnold Air Force Base in Tullahoma, Tennessee. That way, he could have signed the bill as much as an hour earlier, and cheered up some airmen while he was at it.

ling wrote anonymously. "This is a tough issue for Democrats." And just as importantly, it would satisfy the holders of the infamous chits. "The pro-life base will be excited that the Senate is debating this important issue."

Though the pro-life base did indeed find the issue "exciting," it quickly became apparent that most other Americans found it "disgusting." In a CBS News poll taken March 21 and 22, 82 percent of Americans thought that Congress and the President "should stay out of" the Schiavo matter, while only 13 percent said they should be involved.

Also, only 13 percent of Americans thought that "Congress passed this bill because they really care about what happens in this case," while 74 percent thought that they passed it "to advance a political agenda." A mysterious 1 percent answered "neither." Oh, and in that same poll, 26 percent of respondents said they thought of themselves as evangelical or born-again Christians. So, at best, the Republicans were getting just *half* of the evangelicals on this one.

That poll must have been a shock to those in Washington who had shared Brian Darling's assessment of the political dividends to be had in exploiting the Schiavo tragedy. What had seemed like a sure bet was coming up snake eyes. It was time to kick up some dust.

Target number one: Brian Darling's anonymous memo. It must have been news stories about the memo, not the frantic Congressional posturing and Bush's midnight flight, that convinced Americans that Congress was just advancing a political agenda. And so, logically, the memo must have been a hoax.

Right-wing bloggers kicked it off. PowerLineBlog.com, which *TIME* magazine had dubbed "Blog of the Year" for its role in bringing down Dan Rather, attacked the memo's authenticity under the suggestive headline: "IS THIS THE BIGGEST HOAX SINCE THE 60 MINUTES STORY?" As evidence, PowerLine's John Hinderaker assembled these shocking revelations:

1. The memo wasn't signed.
2. The memo wasn't on official letterhead.

3. The memo mixed talking points ("this legislation ensures that individuals like Terri Schiavo are guaranteed the same legal protections as convicted murderers like Ted Bundy") and strategy points ("Senator Nelson of Florida has already refused to become a co-sponsor").

See? Had to be a Democratic dirty trick. In fact, Hinderaker wrote,

It does not sound like something written by a conservative; it sounds like a liberal fantasy of how conservatives talk. . . . What conservative would write that the case of a woman condemned to death by starvation is "a great political issue"?

That was a good question. Brian Darling is a garden-variety Republican hack of the *Floridium* genus. His previous fifteen minutes of fame had occurred during the 2000 Florida recount battle, when he earned the respect of his peers by invalidating nine Gore ballots in Miami–Dade County. More recently, he'd worked with some former Tom DeLay staffers at a Washington lobbying shop, as well as moonlighting as a "media bias monitor" in an off-the-books arrangement with Ken Tomlinson, the GOP operative whom Bush had installed as the head of the Corporation for Public Broadcasting. So, that's what kind of conservative would write that. An incredibly well-connected one.

When he wrote the anonymous memo, Darling was serving his country as a staffer for Florida freshman Senator Mel Martinez. Perhaps aware of his boss's habit of blaming his staffers for the over-the-top ugliness that seemed to stream forth from his campaigns,[2] Darling kept his mouth shut

---

[2] During the 2004 Senate primary campaign, Florida Republicans received a flyer from Martinez accusing his opponent, Bill McCollum, of being "the new darling of the homosexual extremists." After defeating McCollum, Martinez apologized and blamed the flyer on "a couple of young turks" on his campaign staff. In the general election, Martinez did it again. After his campaign sent out a news release calling the federal agents who had removed Elian Gonzalez "armed thugs" that had "allow[ed]" Fidel Castro to have his way," Martinez again blamed his overzealous staff. We may never know who made these mistakes, but it certainly wasn't Mel Martinez.

during the weeks-long "fake memo" fake scandal ginned up by his kins-men in the right-wing media.

In the days and weeks that followed, Brit Hume, Tucker Carlson, and even Rush Limbaugh all cast doubt on the memo's authenticity, develop-ing Hinderaker's already airtight case by citing such further evidence of its phoniness as "creepy phrases" and "misspellings."

The funniest new piece of evidence deployed against the memo was that it closely mirrored the previously acknowledged work of Republican Senator Mel Martinez. Here's Fred Barnes in the *Weekly Standard*:

> True, a few paragraphs were of Republican origin. They had been lifted, word for word, from a Martinez press release outlin-ing the provisions of his legislative proposal, "The Incapacitated Person's Legal Protection Act." This was the inoffensive part of the memo. The offensive part—it didn't come from Martinez—left the strong impression that Republicans are callous and cyn-ical in their attempt to save Schiavo's life, ill-motivated in the extreme.

Republicans? Callous, cynical, ill-motivated in the extreme? The memo had to be a fraud!

Soon the mainstream media had been suckered into reporting on the "controversy." *Washington Post* media critic Howard Kurtz puzzled that "while there is no hard evidence that the memo is fake, there are several strange things about it, including the basic fact that no one seems to know who wrote it." When Brian Darling read that line in the *Post* that morning, he probably sprayed his coffee in that funny way they do in comedy movies.

And Rush? Well, he was Rush. As hard as the others might try, no one could match Limbaugh's perfectly executed triple axel. Here he is on March 24:

> It was forged! The memo was made up by Democrat staffers. . . .
> So it is clear that the Democrats wanted to politicize this

and make the Republicans look like *they* were politicizing Terri Schiavo, and pandering. Why would the Democrats do this? Because they're scared of this issue.

And he lands it!

Of course, when Darling was finally exposed on April 7 and forced to resign, there was no wave of resignations from the right-wing media, though Tucker Carlson's show was soon canceled for other reasons.

While the right-wing media were trying to prove that Republicans weren't trying to politicize the Schiavo case, House Majority Leader Tom DeLay was focused on a different aspect of the story. The politics.

Tom DeLay, as you may remember, was in a lot of hot water over what some people call "ethics violations." He had recently been reprimanded three times by the House Ethics Committee, and the media were beginning to realize that DeLay might not be just a little bit corrupt, but very, very corrupt. Even the unblinkingly partisan *Wall Street Journal* editorial page would write that DeLay had "an odor" to him, an "unsavory whiff" of Beltway corruption that "sooner or later [would] sweep him out" of office if he didn't reform.

To DeLay, Schiavo was literally a godsend—the kind of explosive hot-button issue that could instantly swing the spotlight away from his accelerating implosion. On March 18, DeLay told the Family Research Council:

> I tell you, ladies and gentlemen, one thing that God has brought to us is Terri Schiavo, to elevate the visibility of what's going on in America that Americans would be so barbaric as to pull a feeding tube out of a person that is lucid and starve them to death for two weeks. I mean, in America, that's going to happen if we don't win that fight. So it's bigger than any one of us, and we have to do everything that is in our power to save Terri Schiavo and anybody else that may be in this kind of position.

And let me just finish with this. This is exactly the issue that's going on in America, of attacks against the conservative movement, against me and against many others. The point is, the other side has figured out how to win and defeat the conservative movement.

So, to Tom DeLay, the Schiavo case wasn't so much about Terri Schiavo as about Tom DeLay. And he was determined to make the most of it. Where other Republicans confined themselves to vague generalities about the possibility that Terri was aware of her surroundings, DeLay felt no compunctions about making a case that was both laughably and tragically false on its face. The *St. Petersburg Times*, reporting on March 21 on DeLay's leadership in the Schiavo matter, quoted his argument for reinserting the feeding tube:

> She talks and she laughs and she expresses likes and discomforts.
> It won't take a miracle to help Terri Schiavo. It will only take the
> medical care and therapy that patients require.

In other words, given proper treatment, there was no reason Terri Schiavo couldn't live out her lifelong dream of being a Rockette.

Then again, DeLay wasn't a doctor. Senate Majority Leader Bill Frist, on the other hand, was not just a doctor, he was a heart transplant surgeon of the first order. As the Senate's only physician,[3] he bore a special responsibility to choose his words carefully.

Frist took this responsibility seriously. Only a few months before, he had attacked his colleague, Senator John Edwards, for claiming that stem cell research could lead to cures for people like the just-deceased Christopher Reeve. In a conference call with reporters organized by the Bush-Cheney campaign, Frist had blasted Edwards's claims as "crass,"

---

[3] Besides Tom Coburn, who, as previously discussed, is a nut.

"shameful," "dishonest," and "cruel." "It's giving false hope to people," the doctor-senator charged, "and I can tell you as a physician who's treated scores of thousands of patients that you don't give them false hope."

It was that kind of scrupulous regard for medical ethics that lent his words special weight when Frist took to the Senate floor on March 17 to discuss the Schiavo case. He didn't want anyone to misunderstand how seriously he took this matter.

> From my standpoint as a physician, I would be very careful before I would come to the floor and say this, that the facts upon which this case were based are inadequate. To be able to make a diagnosis of persistent vegetative state—which is not brain dead; it is not coma; it is a specific diagnosis and typically takes multiple examinations over a period of time because you are looking for responsiveness—I have looked at the video footage. Based on the footage provided to me, which was part of the facts of the case, she does respond.

The video Frist was describing was drawn from hours and hours of footage that the Schindlers had edited together to highlight the moments when Terri's random actions seemed to correspond with external stimuli. I'm sure the grief-stricken Schindlers believed their daughter really was responding. But of all people, Frist should have known that families sometimes have "false hope."

In fairness, Frist was not giving Terri Schiavo false hope. She was in a persistent vegetative state. She was as incapable of false hope as she was of real hope. Or, for that matter, blinking on command.

Months later, Schiavo's autopsy would confirm that her brain damage had been massive and totally irreversible. Rather than owning up to his senatorial malpractice, Frist committed the ultimate sin and lied to Matt Lauer in this amusing exchange on the June 16 *Today Show*:

LAUER: You were on the floor of the Senate at that time, not only as a senator, but a doctor, and in talking about Ms. Schiavo, you said, quoting you now, "She does respond." End quote. Were you wrong in your diagnosis?

FRIST: Well, first of all, I never made a diagnosis. I think it's very important that we saw the autopsy today. It does give us the definitive information that we did not have at that point in time. And that's why I think it is big news that she had totally irreversible brain damage, and we now have that information. All we were arguing for on the floor of the Senate was to get an accurate diagnosis before you withdraw a feeding tube from a live person . . .

LAUER: . . . but when you stand on the floor and you said, "She does respond," are you at all worried that you led some senators . . .

FRIST: No, I never said that. I never said she responded. I said—and I reviewed the court videotapes—the same ones the other doctors reviewed—and I questioned, "Is her diagnosis correct?"

It's hard to see how someone so careful about his standing as a physician would forget making such an emotionally charged statement. It made me doubt the wisdom of his latest legislative initiative, S. 687, known as the FristCam Act, which would place a video camera in every one of America's 4,226 intensive care units. The FristCams would pan the ICUs, and Frist would give each patient a thumbs-up or a thumbs-down, depending on his assessment of their condition. According to Frist's chief of staff, the Majority Leader would be able to make life-or-death medical decisions for tens of thousands of American families, even while signing correspondence or calling potential donors.

Let's face it. The Schiavo case did not bring out the best in people. On the right, you had shameless abuse of medical "expertise" and flagrant exploitation of a family's tragedy. On the left, it was even worse. Over in the culture of death, the "pull-the-tube people" were becoming increasingly "red-fanged and ravenous." This according to Peggy Noonan, whose March 24 *Wall Street Journal* column was titled, "In Love with Death: the Bizarre Passion of the Pull-the-Tube People."

Her argument was based on a fundamental, and almost certainly deliberate, misconception about the nature of the debate. For a vast majority of Americans, the real principle at stake in the Schiavo matter was whether Congress and the President should override the medical decisions of individual families. Because so many Americans had experienced similar tragedies in their own lives, they knew in their gut that this was painful enough as a private matter.

But for people protesting outside the clinic, it wasn't about the appropriate limits of federal power. It was about whether to save a living, breathing, laughing, talking, thinking human being from judicially sanctioned murder. That gave the Peggy Noonans of the world an opening to attack Democrats.

"Why are they so committed to this woman's death?" she asked. Peggy, let me answer your question with a question of my own. If in the middle of the whole thing, Terri's husband, Michael, had said, "I may have remembered her wishes wrong—put the tube back in," do you honestly think any of "the pull-the-tube people" would have screamed, "No! Kill her anyway! Kill her! *Kill her!*"? Is that what you think, Peggy?

It must have been what she thought, because otherwise there was no explanation for how she ended that column. By comparing us tube-yankers to Nazis.

> When a society comes to believe that human life is not inherently worth living, it is a slippery slope to the gas chamber. You wind up on a low road that twists past Columbine and leads

toward Auschwitz. Today that road runs through Pinellas Park, Fla.

Wow. She is *awful*, isn't she?

Rush Limbaugh, always ready to give his political opponents the benefit of the doubt, had a more charitable explanation for why liberals wanted Terri Schiavo to die:

> A question for those of you who are our friends on the left. Just answer honestly to yourself. How many of you want Terri Schiavo to die simply because some Christian conservatives want her to live?

So we weren't Nazis after all. We were just sickos.

Bay Buchanan gave CNN's *Inside Politics* a third explanation, one that cut a little closer to the bone. "There's only one reason that they want this person to die, and that's because they've decided this woman is the property of her husband," bayed Bay. "I ask you, where are the feminists?" But, alas, the feminists were nowhere to be found. They were all watching *Sex and the City* and eating ice cream straight out of the carton at Betty Friedan's place. That's how bad it's gotten.

Perhaps the most honest response to the phantom phenomenon of death-crazed secular liberals came from Bill O'Reilly. "I don't know why some of these left-wing columnists want this woman to die," he wondered aloud to his tiny radio audience. "Nobody can explain that to me."[4]

As good as Republicans are at spreading lies about whole groups of people, they really shine when they go after the character of their enemies

---

[4]A week later, after Terri Schiavo had died, O'Reilly offered a heretofore unconsidered basis for opposing the withdrawal of the feeding tube: "One of the most powerful arguments against the way Terri Schiavo died is that you couldn't do it to an animal in America. You'd be charged with a crime."

One obvious reason that this argument didn't gain much purchase is that anyone keeping a vegetative dog on a feeding tube would probably be either arrested or institutionalized.

individually. And no one was asking for a beating more than Michael Schiavo. Yes, he had gotten his nursing degree, but after years building his life around the care of his irreversibly unconscious wife, he had begun, with the Schindlers' blessing, to begin dating again. Eventually, he moved in with another woman and fathered two children, though he didn't technically divorce Terri.

This "alternative lifestyle" called Michael's motivations into question. What was the real reason he wanted to pull the tube?

On his MSNBC show, *Scarborough Country,* Joe Scarborough featured interviews with a guest who said Michael was "pulling a huge hoax simply to kill his wife."

Tom DeLay let his disgust for Michael boil over at a press conference. "I don't have a whole lot of respect for a man that has treated this woman in this way," he growled. "What kind of man is he? . . . Unless she has specifically written instructions in her hand, with her signature, I don't care what her husband says."

Soon after, Alan Colmes, Sean Hannity's goofy sidekick on Fox's *The Sean Hannity Show,* asked virtue czar Bill Bennett about DeLay's comments.

> COLMES: This is the party that wants to preserve the institution of marriage. They want to amend the Constitution. They have Tom DeLay saying, "I don't care what her husband thinks"? Do you think that's appropriate?
>
> BENNETT: I don't think we particularly care about preserving marriages like that, frankly. That's not a good—
>
> COLMES: Oh, please.
>
> BENNETT: "Oh, please" yourself. That's not a good marriage. That's a bad marriage.
>
> COLMES: We don't know that.
>
> BENNETT: Oh, I think we do.

Some of us might think that a bad marriage is when you lose $8 million gambling and don't tell your wife. (Bennett went so far as to tell casinos not to call him at his home number.) But I'm not going to presume anything. It would be wrong to judge someone else's marriage, Bill. I'm not going to judge yours any more than I'd judge any of Rush Limbaugh's three marriages, or his prospects for a fourth.

Meanwhile, thanks to the heroic intervention of the Congress and President Bush, *Schindler v. Schiavo* was finally working its way through the federal courts. Which is to say, federal court after federal court was declining to hear the case. When U.S. District Judge James Whittemore, a Clinton appointee, issued the first federal ruling on behalf of Michael Schiavo, the right raised a hue and cry over the activist judicial tyrants who defied not only the will of the people and the demands of morality, but also the brand-new law of the land.

Curiously, the right's fury remained fixated on Whittemore even as a series of conservative judges declined multiple opportunities to overrule him, or even to criticize him in a dissenting opinion. Even William Pryor, Jr., the ultra-right-wing 11th Circuit judge whom Bush had snuck in with a recess appointment after he was successfully and rightfully filibustered, remained stolidly silent when his chance came to champion the cause of the Schindlers. Only when the case was turned down by the Supreme Court did the right turn its fury to a new target—Associate Justice Anthony Kennedy.

Already, Kennedy had incurred the wrath of right-thinking pro-life conservatives by casting the tie-breaking vote in *Roper v. Simmons,* outlawing the death penalty for people who committed their capital crimes while still minors. The right, who, like Tom Coburn, supported killing baby killers as well as baby-killers, was most incensed by Kennedy's acknowledgment of "the overwhelming weight of international opinion against the juvenile death penalty." Somehow, foreigners had infiltrated our highest court. World government was clearly just around the corner. As Tom DeLay would thunder on Fox News Radio:

> We've got Justice Kennedy writing decisions based upon inter-
> national law, not the Constitution of the United States. That's
> just outrageous.

He was right. Thomas Jefferson's call for "a decent respect to the opin-
ions of mankind" appeared in the Declaration of Independence, not the
Constitution. But that wasn't Kennedy's only unforgivable sin, according
to DeLay:

> And not only that, he said in session that he does his own
> research on the Internet. That is just incredibly outrageous.

I must admit that we at *The Al Franken Show* puzzled over that one for
almost eleven minutes until we concluded that DeLay must believe that
the Internet is composed entirely of porn.

By the time Kennedy issued the Supreme Court's second refusal to
consider the case (with no dissent from Scalia, Rehnquist, or Thomas),
Schindler v. Schiavo had been reviewed by more than three dozen judges
and justices on the state and federal level in the course of seven years of
adjudication.

By now, Americans weren't just disgusted by it, they were sick of it.
And above all, they were sick of Congress. If nobody in the country had
had any real problems, perhaps they would have forgiven their legislators
for dropping everything to pursue this macabre charade. But between rising gas prices, the health care crisis, crumbling schools, war, and for those
who remembered, the now-forgotten threat of terrorism, it was hard to
conclude that Congress and the President had the same priorities as the
people who hired them. And their poll ratings were sinking faster than a
mini-sub going to explore the Titanic. In mid-March, at the height of
the Schiavo frenzy, Congress enjoyed a 34 percent approval rating. No
national poll had them cracking 40 percent during the month of April.
By May 23, after the "nuclear option" fight over the Senate filibuster, only

17 percent of Americans answered "yes" when asked if Congress "shares your priorities."

Health care, in particular, consistently ranks as a top priority for most Americans. Poll after poll has found that Americans favor universal health coverage by a two-to-one margin. Conservative Republican politicians also see health care as a crucial issue, but in a different way. They want to ease the suffering of insurance companies. Perhaps because the health insurance industry gives them so much money and because trial lawyers who defend injured patients tend to give money to Democrats, Karl Rove decided long ago that "tort reform" should be near the top of the Republican agenda, even higher than the development and deployment of Robust Nuclear Earth Penetrators, popularly known as "bunker busters." And Tom DeLay and Bill Frist have been right there with Rove. Never mind that much of Terri Schiavo's medical care had been financed by medical malpractice awards whose value would have been slashed if DeLay, Frist, and Rove had had their way.

As I said above, many Americans have faced wrenching decisions not so different from the one faced by Michael Schiavo. On March 27, the *Los Angeles Times* wrote about another family's private tragedy—one in which, as in the Schiavo case, Tom DeLay played an important role. But a much less controversial one. In 1988, DeLay, along with his mother, his aunt, and the rest of the family, decided not to take extraordinary measures to prolong the life of Tom's father, Charles Ray DeLay. Charles had been critically injured in a freak accident when his home-built backyard tram jumped the track and slammed into a tree. (More about this in my next book.) According to Tom's aunt JoAnne, doctors told the family that Charles would "basically be a vegetable."

"Tom knew—we all knew—his father wouldn't have wanted to live that way," Tom's mother, Maxine DeLay, told the *Times*. The family decided not to connect Charles to a dialysis machine, and he passed away on December 14, 1988, with his family by his side.

In marked contrast to the Schiavo case, Tom DeLay never accused the

DeLay family of "an act of barbarism," "medical terrorism," "murder," or "homicide." He did, however, join his family's lawsuit against the maker and the distributor of a faulty coupling that had contributed to the accident. The lawsuit was settled in 1993 for $250,000, and Tom signed over his portion to his mother.

Three years later, DeLay cosponsored a bill to override state product liability laws like the one cited in *DeLay v. Midcap Bearing Corp. and Lovejoy Inc.*, part of his career-long campaign to defend corporations from "predatory, self-serving litigation" brought by trial lawyers who "get fat off the pain" of plaintiffs and the "hard work" of defendants. These "frivolous, parasitic lawsuits" had to stop.

Thankfully, President Clinton vetoed the bill. He said it "tilts against American families and would deprive them of the ability to recover fully when they are injured by a defective product," like a home-built backyard tram.

A million questions must be running through your head after reading this chapter. Were Tom DeLay and his allies in Congress and the White House as hypocritical as it seemed? Did they really care about the fate of Theresa Marie Schiavo? Or did Brian Darling and 82 percent of America have it right—that this was just about advancing a political agenda? About paying off the grassroots activists that they thought had won them the election?

Did they actually care about anything other than staying in power? Were they sincere about their commitment to a culture of life even when the cameras weren't rolling? Or were they, for all their bluster about the sanctity of the unborn and the unconscious, just hypocrites—big, fat hypocrites who, if the price were right, wouldn't hesitate to sell out every principle they claimed to be fighting for?

My research indicates that the answers are, respectively: yes, no, yes, yes, no, no—and, on that last question, more than you could ever, ever imagine.

10 The Tom DeLay Saipan Sex Tour and Jack Abramoff Casino Getaway

I need a break.

Making jokes about Terri Schiavo is one of the hardest things I have to do as a humorist. And I bet you could use a breather, too. Not from my "entertaining and powerful" book (reviewers, take note), but from the avalanche of political sludge set off by the falling snowflake of the Schiavo tragedy. So let's take a trip, somewhere warm. But not to a foreign country where people don't share our American values and might try to cheat us when we purchase a souvenir. No, let's go to one of the less-traveled byways in America: the remote South Pacific island of Saipan.

You may have heard of Saipan from its key role in the Greatest Generation's victory over Japan in World War II.[1] In June of 1944, 3,100 U.S. Marines died in the desperate eleven-day battle for the island, giving their lives to defend America's freedom and American values. Saipan became a staging ground for B-29 bomber runs against Tokyo. After the war ended

[1] Japan had started a preemptive war against us, which in those days was strictly verboten.

with mysterious abruptness on August 14, 1945, Saipan became a United Nations trust territory, administered by the United States. By 1986, Saipan and its neighbors became the American Commonwealth of the Northern Mariana Islands, and their indigenous peoples were granted U.S. citizenship.

These days, Saipan is a tourist destination renowned for its turquoise waters, balmy breezes, white-sand beaches, and hiking and snorkeling. And golf.

But this island paradise is no island paradise. While most U.S. laws apply in the Commonwealth of the Northern Mariana Islands, local entrepreneurs won a few key exemptions in the areas of labor standards and immigration laws. Even with a minimum wage of $1.35[2] an hour, and loopholes that allowed factory owners to import desperately poor guest workers from China, the Philippines, Indonesia, and elsewhere, garments manufactured in Saipan could still be labeled "Made In USA."

For all-American clothing manufacturers like the Gap, Liz Claiborne, Wal-Mart, Old Navy, JCPenney, Ralph Lauren, Abercrombie and Fitch, Brooks Brothers, and, appropriately, Banana Republic, Saipan was a secret haven from annoying American labor laws. But facing constant threats from do-gooder, anti-sweatshop busybodies on the mainland that could force Wal-Mart to pay American wages for the manufacture of its American flag T-shirts, Saipan's garment factory owners needed powerful allies in Washington.

Fortunately for them, in 1994, just as Democrats in Congress and the Clinton White House were closing in on Saipan's sweatshops, the Gingrich Revolution swept a new crop of business-friendly Republicans to power. Saipan's elite would turn to two emerging heavy hitters: former exterminator and born-again ex–party boy Tom DeLay, the incoming House majority whip, and a new and handsome face on the Washington

[2]The CNMI minimum wage has grown from $1.35 in 1979 to a whopping $3.15 an hour today.

scene: the hard-charging Orthodox Jewish lobbyist Jack Abramoff, who had spent the better part of his last ten years battling Communism. In Hollywood. As the producer of the 1989 Dolph Lundgren film *Red Scorpion*, Abramoff had ignored the then-fashionable anti-apartheid views of the civilized world by filming his action-adventure epic in South Africa–occupied Namibia and by using extras and military vehicles provided by his friends in the apartheid regime.

When the sequel, *Red Scorpion 2*, failed to garner even the tepid response of *Red Scorpion 1*, Abramoff was out of ideas. There would be no *Red Scorpion 3*. Fortunately, on the Saturday after the 1994 elections, the phone rang. Abramoff was being recruited by the prestigious Washington lobbying and law shop Preston Gates Ellis. It wasn't that they were big fans of the *Red Scorpion* series. No, they were fans of Abramoff's close ties to conservative power brokers like Grover Norquist and Christian Coalition Executive Director Ralph Reed, both of whom had served under him when he chaired the College Republican National Committee from 1981 to 1985. He was also friends with Tom DeLay.

The second Battle of Saipan was about to begin. On one side, you had Liz Claiborne, Brooks Brothers, JCPenney, Tom DeLay, and Jack Abramoff. And on the other, you had a few principled leaders in Congress and some officials in Clinton's Interior Department. At stake: thousands of powerless workers trapped in a system of horrific sweatshops, de facto slavery, and a practice not normally associated with the religious right: forced prostitution.

I broke this story myself, in the spring of 2005. As I reported on my radio show, Brian Ross of ABC News' *20/20* had traveled to Saipan with a camera crew in 1998. There, he found the very conditions that I reported to my radio audience and that you're going to read about now. Ross's *20/20* story and his 1999 follow-up provided the basis for my own investigation, which consisted of watching tapes of his reports and then reading some other documents in the public record. I'm proud to say that if it weren't for my enterprising work as a journalist, no American would have ever heard about Ross's landmark exposé, except those who saw it on network television or heard about it elsewhere.

Barbara Walters, as usual, demanded the opening lines—even though she, like me, had not done any of the actual reporting:

> **WALTERS:** Tonight, we take you to a tiny American island, a gem where the beaches are gorgeous, the palm trees sway, but an outrage against common decency and American values is going on in the shadow of the American flag.

Way to set the scene, Barbara. Let's go to the real journalist, shall we? Brian Ross found factories . . .

> **ROSS:** . . . jammed full of low-cost workers brought in from China, putting in fourteen-hour days, under often miserable conditions, making clothes under contract for the American market.

So far, not so bad. Just run-of-the-mill exploitation of powerless workers. Did Brian Ross have anything more specific?

> **ROSS:** Workers are kept in crowded, often rat-infested labor barracks. Of course, some are better than others. But at this one, the toilets didn't work, the showers barely worked, and the water was contaminated.

Picky, picky, picky. Time was when people would be *grateful* to have a job where they had to drink contaminated water. It's called an entry-level job. Used to have one myself. I was a caddy. I had to buy my own soda.

Then Brian Ross spoke with Eric Gregoire, a Catholic Church human rights worker.

ROSS: Authorities say [garment workers] essentially have become indentured servants, a practice outlawed in America at the same time as slavery.

GREGOIRE: I've seen people locked in barracks, locked behind barbed wire.

Okay. It's a bad job. I get it. But these women have bootstraps, don't they? They're in America! They may be locked inside a fetid, even toxic hellhole, but if they're lucky enough to have a window, they can look out through the barbed wire and see the Stars and Stripes swaying in the balmy tropical breeze. This is the land of opportunity. After all, that's why they came. They could get a management position, or maybe even some-day start a sweatshop of their own. I mean, they're working fourteen hours a day, seven days a week. How long could it take?

ROSS: The women have to pay government officials in China fees of as much as $6,000 or $7,000 to even get jobs on Saipan, putting them deep in debt and beholden to both fac-tory bosses and the officials back in China.

Oh. So, they're basically screwed, then.

And not just figuratively. As Ross reported, many young women who paid their family's life savings for "good jobs in America" ended up instead as involuntary sex slaves servicing government officials, sailors on shore leave, and Japanese businessmen.

KATRINA (through translator): Once there was a customer that bit my breast. But the boss told us the customer is always right.

ROSS (voice-over): Many of the women who work here are only teenagers. Many underage, like Katrina, not her real name, who was fourteen when she was recruited from the Philippines.

KATRINA (through translator): It was my first time to dance naked, and I was ashamed.

ROSS (voice-over): Katrina told federal investigators that she signed this official Saipan government affidavit, thinking she was going to be a waitress, and ended up forced into live sex acts onstage.

Pretty disgusting. Hideously disgusting. If you ask me, this is a clear case where the customer is definitely not always right.

Why wasn't anyone in Washington doing anything about it? Because a certain congressman wouldn't let them.

Saipan's labor practices had been raising concerns in D.C. since the eighties. California Congressman George Miller first convened a hearing on Saipan's garment industry in 1992. By 1997, the Clinton administration was calling for American worker protections to extend to the CNMI. By March of 1998, when the *20/20* piece ran, the issue was coming to a head. Miller released a report describing in detail how the involuntary prostitutes faced "threats that they or other members of their families would be killed if they prematurely returned to China." But even when a Senate committee conducted its own hearing, nothing seemed to happen in the House.

That's because Congressman Tom DeLay and lobbyist Jack Abramoff were winning the battle.

As in World War II, the key to winning the second Battle of Saipan was an invasion. This time, it was an invasion of members of Congress, congressional staffers, and right-wing opinion leaders. The eighty-plus conservative junketeers didn't stay in barbed wire–fenced labor barracks, but rather in the luxurious beachfront Hyatt Regency Saipan, where they enjoyed fourteen manicured acres of tropical gardens, afternoon cocktails at the Splash Pool Bar, and Las Vegas–style entertainment at the SandCastle Saipan. And golf. Their every expense was covered, per Abramoff's arrangements, by the generous members of the Saipan Garment Manufacturers Association and the CNMI government.

"Suddenly," Marshall Wittmann, a former Christian Coalition official, later explained, "the Mariana Islands became one of the critical conservative causes of the mid-nineties."

Leading the pack was the number three Republican official in the House. Tom DeLay, his wife, his daughter, and several aides enjoyed an all-expense-paid Christmas vacation to Saipan in 1997. At a lavish New Year's Eve dinner thrown in his honor, DeLay sang for his supper, toasting his hosts and promising to fight to preserve the Saipan manufacturers' way of life. Brian Ross, reporting exclusively for *20/20* and *The Al Franken Show*, caught him on tape.

> **DELAY:** You are a shining light for what is happening in the Republican Party, and you represent everything that is good about what we're trying to do in America and in leading the world in the free market system.

Let me quote that again.

> **DELAY:** You are a shining light for what is happening in the Republican Party.

One such shining light was Willie Tan, whose particularly sweaty sweatshop had a history of, among other problems, contaminated water that made workers sick.

> **ROSS (voice-over):** When Steve Galster of Global Survival Network went undercover posing as a garment executive, he heard all about Congressman DeLay from the Mr. Big of Saipan garment manufacturers—this man, Willie Tan. Tan claims he is close to DeLay and boasted of the assurances he

said the congressman had given him that the proposed laws on Saipan would be killed.

TAN: Do you know what Tom told me? He said, "Willie, if they elect me majority whip, I make the schedule of the Congress, and I'm not going to put it on the schedule." So Tom told me, "Forget it, Willie. No chance."

When DeLay's office was contacted for that report, you might have expected some fancy footwork. But no.

ROSS (voice-over): A spokesperson for DeLay says it's no secret he opposes the legislation.

DeLay was as good as his word. Even when Republican Senator Frank Murkowski returned from Saipan "appalled" and succeeded in passing a bill through the Senate, DeLay killed it in the House. It never even got a vote.

Odd that DeLay would fight to preserve a system involving forced child prostitution. After all, he was in the middle of cementing his reputation as the champion of the Christian right. As he told the *Washington Post* two years later, his goal in life was building a more "God-centered" nation, because "our entire system is built on the Judeo-Christian ethic."

If DeLay was the Christian, his friend Jack Abramoff was the Judeo. And although he didn't celebrate Christmas, he was in Saipan for the holiday in 1998 as well, probably for a late Hanukkah. DeLay toasted him, too:

DELAY: When one of my closest and dearest friends, Jack Abramoff, your most able representative in Washington, D.C., invited me to the islands, I wanted to see firsthand the free market success and the progress and reform you have made.

Abramoff was not representing Saipan for free. All told, he received $7 million—almost twice what *Red Scorpion* made at the box office. Jack Abramoff had clearly found his calling.

It was the Abramoff connection that brought the Saipan story to my attention in the spring of 2005. Tom DeLay wasn't the only Republican heavyweight facing charges of corruption during the time of the Schiavo controversy. Sure, DeLay had been reprimanded three times in 2004 by the House Ethics Committee. But Abramoff was in even worse trouble. He had used his personal credit card to pay for luxurious hotels and lavish dinners during Tom DeLay's $120,000 fact-finding mission to St. Andrews Links in Scotland,[3] which was illegal.

Also, he had bilked a number of Native American tribes to the tune of $82 million. Let's leave sunny Saipan for a moment, and walk a mile in Jack Abramoff's moccasins.

Eighty-two million dollars is a lot of money. Even for those filthy rich Indians, who have always lorded their wealth over the rest of us. Well, not necessarily *always*. And not *all* Indians. For example, Native Americans have a life expectancy of 70.6 years, compared to 77.3 years for whites, and a quarter live below the poverty line. But there are a few who have done reasonably well for themselves over the last twenty years because of something called "gaming," which is the gambling industry's term for "gambling."

It was these Indians that Jack Abramoff set his sights on. Some of them were getting their casinos shut down by busybody bureaucrats. He offered to help them out. Other Indians wanted to get bureaucrats to shut down the casinos of neighboring tribes in order to drive out the competition. Jack offered to help them, too. Sometimes, he was able to do both at once, with competing tribes. If that sounds like it might be a conflict of interest, then you don't know "Casino Jack" Abramoff. Jack, you see, was interested in one thing: making money.

---

[3] Fact: The third hole at St. Andrews has a sharp dogleg to the right. Fact: Angus is the best caddy, but he has a temper. Fact: Road Hole Bunker at the seventeenth is impossible to hit out of. Fact: Angus tells the best dirty jokes. Fact: Dirty joke about priest and nun golfing is funniest of Angus's jokes. Fact: Don't tell joke to beer cart girl.

Abramoff didn't work alone, just like I don't work alone. I have a staff of researchers and producers that make sure that all my facts and figures are on the level. In the same way, Abramoff had a partner named Michael Scanlon, a former Tom DeLay aide, who made sure that they made as much money as possible off the Indians.

Jack and Mike liked to write each other e-mails. Lots of people use e-mail. It's very convenient. Just today, I sent an e-mail to my publisher asking them to take a little bit off my chin in the cover photo. But some e-mails just shouldn't be sent. Especially e-mails about the types of things that might provoke massive investigations from multiple subpoena-brandishing federal agencies—things like stealing money from Indians.

The Senate Indian Affairs Committee, chaired by John McCain, conducted one such investigation, and posted many of the incriminating e-mails on its website. If you look hard enough, even the untrained eye is able to detect a certain lack of respect in the way Abramoff and Scanlon discussed their Native American clients.

For example, look at the phrasing in this February 7, 2002, e-mail from Abramoff to Scanlon regarding the billing on a contract with Mississippi's Choctaw tribe:

```
We need to get some $ from those monkeys!!!!
```

Or this April 11, 2002, message, again from Abramoff, pertaining to the Saginaw Chippewa of Michigan:

```
These mofos are the stupidest idiots in the land for
sure.
```

The Chippewa, in particular, seemed to inspire a certain bluntness in Casino Jack. Here's an interchange from December 17 and 18, 2001, in which Abramoff described his hope that the Saginaw Chippewa Tribal Council would vote to retain his services:

```
3:51 P.M., Abramoff: Can you smell money?!?!?!
```

(Abramoff was not afraid to use a little extra punctuation to get his message across.)

```
4:11 P.M., Scanlon: Did we win it?

4:56 P.M., Abramoff: The f-ing troglodytes didn't vote
on you today.

5:52 P.M., Scanlon: These knuckleheads are never going
to do it.

6:09 P.M., Abramoff: Yes they will.

7:16 P.M., Scanlon: What's a troglodyte?

7:12 A.M. the next morning, Abramoff: What am I, a dic-
tionary? It's a lower form of existence, basically.
```

Though Scanlon might seem younger and dumber than Abramoff in this interchange, you'll note that he is somewhat more restrained. That might be because Scanlon had been burned by inartfully worded electronic mail before.

In 1998, when Scanlon was running the Clinton impeachment "war room" in his capacity as Tom DeLay's communications director, he fired off a missive that turned into something of an embarrassment when it was reported in the *Washington Post*. Watching President Clinton testify to a grand jury on television, Scanlon ruminated on the most prudent way to deal with a wounded political adversary.

```
This whole thing about not kicking someone when
they are down is BS—Not only do you kick him—You
kick him until he passes out—then beat him over the
head with a baseball bat—then roll him up in an old
```

```
rug—and throw him off a cliff into the pounding surf
below!!!!!
```

When that e-mail hit the papers, even some Republicans were embarrassed. But amid the kerfuffle, or maybe *because* of the kerfuffle, "Abraham Jackoff" (as he was known in high school)[4] was impressed. He talked the young, not-fully-formed Scanlon into joining his lobbying and law firm, Preston Gates. Besides nabbing a rising star, the hire helped cement Abramoff's extremely profitable relationship with Tom DeLay.

As *Newsweek*'s Michael Isikoff would report: "For years, nobody on Washington's K-Street corridor was closer to DeLay than Abramoff." Michael Scanlon wasn't the first DeLay aide to enjoy the fruits of that friendship, but he was almost certainly the one who got the most fruit. As Abramoff put it in yet another e-mail to Scanlon, an uncharacteristically nonracist one:

```
You are a great partner. What I love about our part-
nership is that when one of us is down, the other
is there. We're going to make $ for years together.
```

And Scanlon felt the same way:

```
You got it, boss.
```

It almost makes you like them. If only they weren't making all of that $ by ripping people off.

And no one got ripped off worse than the Tigua.

In 1993, the tiny and impoverished Tigua tribe opened the Speaking Rock Casino on the dusty east side of El Paso, Texas. Interestingly, the rest

---

[4]Timothy Noah, who went to high school with Abramoff, wrote in *Slate* about how he coined the nickname.

of El Paso was built on land that had been taken from the Tigua, which is one reason why they became so tiny and impoverished.

Now, you might be opposed to Indian gaming. Perhaps you object to all gambling on religious grounds or for sociological reasons. Or maybe you've lost a lot of money at a blackjack table. Or maybe you're an Italian casino owner with ties to organized crime, and you don't like the competition. Or maybe you just don't like Indians. People oppose Indian gaming for all kinds of reasons, some good, some bad.

But it's worth pointing out that the Tigua used their casino money to create jobs with good wages and health insurance, build decent housing, and provide college scholarships for their children. As Lori Rivera, a former supervisor in the casino cashier's office, who grew up in a one-room mud shack without running water or electricity, told a *New York Times* reporter: "Before the casino, most Tigua kids didn't stay in school because they were so poor they couldn't afford shoes, and they were embarrassed." Once the casino opened, "Everything was going really well."

That is, until Texas Governor George W. Bush entered the picture. One of the planks of his 1998 reelection campaign was opposition to casino gambling generally, and the Speaking Rock Casino specifically. When Bush won, he sent Attorney General John Cornyn, who later became a U.S. senator, to go after the Tigua's casino.

But when Cornyn filed suit in 1999, he had more than Bush on his side. He also had the benefit of a statewide PR, lobbying, and grassroots campaign organized by Ralph Reed, the formidable former executive director of the Christian Coalition.

Reed wasn't fighting the Tigua merely out of the goodness of his heart. He had lots of other reasons. Four point two million reasons. Each one, a crisp dollar bill.

The money came from the Louisiana Coushatta, who operated an extremely profitable tribal casino along the Texas border and wanted to shut down competition in neighboring states. Reed had hooked up with the Coushatta through his old friend Casino Jack. Abramoff and Scanlon were in charge of a whole range of operations for the Coushatta, who ultimately paid them a cool $32 million. So they could afford to throw a little money Reed's way.

Besides, Reed had delivered for Casino Jack before. In 1999, Abramoff had arranged for Reed to help his pals in the Mississippi Choctaw, the richest and most successful gambling tribe in the country, to block a proposal for a state-sponsored lottery and video poker in nearby Alabama. In exchange for $1.3 million, Reed produced radio ads featuring James Dobson, organized phone banks, and printed church bulletin inserts.

Reed, Abramoff, and Scanlon were playing a tricky game. The pastors they enlisted in their anti-gambling campaign would have been furious if they had known their church bulletin inserts were being financed by casino money. That's why Abramoff and Reed took great care to obscure the money's origin. For the Choctaw account, the main money laundry was the tax-exempt Americans for Tax Reform, run by their old College Republicans friend Grover Norquist, the take-no-prisoners Republican power broker who once told the *Denver Post*, "Bipartisanship is another name for date-rape."[5] The Choctaw money went through Norquist to groups like the Alabama Christian Coalition, which has a policy of refusing money even indirectly connected to gambling. As the Senate Indian Affairs Committee would later find, this setup had the added benefit of allowing Abramoff and Scanlon to pad the accounts, ripping off millions of extra dollars from the "monkeys." All in all, it was a great system.

So Reed was a natural for the Coushatta's campaign to shut down the Tigua casino. They would work through the churches to whip up moral

[5] Abramoff (College Republican National Committee chair, 1981–85), Norquist (CRNC executive director, 1981–83), and Reed (ED, 1983–85) were following in the footsteps of Karl Rove, who had been ED from 1970 to 1972 and national chairman from 1973 to 1974. Vast-right-wing-conspiracy trivia buffs might also be interested to know that Bush I henchman Lee Atwater managed Rove's first campaign for chairman.

outrage against Indian gambling in Texas—at the behest of Indian gambling interests in Louisiana.

This time, instead of laundering the money through Norquist, they set up a not-for-profit "think tank" called the American International Center. The AIC's sole reason for existing was to hide the source of Reed's Indian money from his evangelical Christian pawns, but that's not what they said on the website. Visitors to the AIC's home on the Internet read that the organization's mission was to "influence global paradigms in an increasingly complex world."

As the Senate Indian Affairs Committee would later discover, the prestigious AIC was run by two uniquely qualified boyhood friends of Scanlon's: yoga instructor Brian Mann and former lifeguard David Grosh. Grosh testified that Scanlon had asked him, "Do you want to be the head of an international corporation?" and he had responded, "Sure." Then, Grosh told Committee Chairman John McCain, "I asked him what I had to do, and he said 'Nothing,' so that sounded pretty good to me."

Grosh influenced global paradigms out of the basement of his house. For his trouble, he received $2500 and tickets to a Washington Capitals–Pittsburgh Penguins hockey game. The NHL later folded.

I'd like to take a moment to recount Grosh's opening statement to McCain's committee. In its entirety.

> I'm embarrassed and disgusted to be a part of this whole thing.
> The Lakota Indians have a word, *wasichu*, which aptly describes
> all of us right now.

That was it. *Wasichu*, by the way, means "he who steals the fat." Truer words had never been spoken by a former lifeguard who ran an international think tank.

Reed's efforts to, as he wrote to Abramoff, "get our pastors riled up" gave Cornyn the political cover he needed to continue his anti-Tigua crusade. On February 11, 2002, Cornyn won his case, and a federal judge demanded that the Speaking Rock Casino shut its doors.

Perhaps if the Tigua had hired Casino Jack, things would have been different. As Abramoff ruefully wrote that day to Reed:

```
I wish those moronic Tiguas were smarter in their
political contributions. I'd love us to get our mitts
on that moolah!! Oh well, stupid folks get wiped out.
```

Oh, well.

Unbeknownst to Reed, Abramoff *was* working to get his mitts on that moolah. Anticipating that the court would close the casino, Abramoff had already approached the Tigua about working on their behalf to reopen it. The Tigua, you see, didn't know that Casino Jack had just been working the other side—and Abramoff neglected to tell them. Five days before the court's decision, everything was falling into place. Abramoff e-mailed Scanlon with his usual infectious enthusiasm:

```
I'm on the phone with Tigua. Fire up the jet baby,
we're going to El Paso!
```

Scanlon replied,

```
I want all their money!!!
```

Abramoff felt good,

```
Yawzah!!
```

That's how he spelled it. "Yawzah."

Four days later, the jet was indeed fired up. Abramoff arrived in El Paso and presented the Tigua with an ingenious plan. Not ingenious because it would help them reopen their casino, but ingenious because it would get all their money. Promising to rectify the "gross indignity perpetrated by the Texas state authorities" (that he had engineered), Abramoff assured the Tigua that he had already lined up "a couple of Senators willing to ram this through." Not only that, but Abramoff and his law firm would accept no fee and work pro bono.

Of course, the Tigua would need a good PR firm. Luckily for them, Abramoff knew the best guy in the business. A guy named Michael Scanlon. Scanlon was expensive, sure, but Abramoff had heard that he was worth every penny of the $4.2 million it would cost to retain him.

To the Tigua's delight, Scanlon was indeed interested in taking on their case. It didn't take long for him to come up with a plan for a PR blitz with the catchy name "Operation: Open Doors."

On February 19, as the Tigua tribal council prepared to vote on O.O.D., the *El Paso Times* ran a story headlined "450 Casino Employees Officially Terminated." Scanlon sent Abramoff the story, with the note:

```
This is on the front page of todays paper while they
will be voting on our plan!
```

Abramoff wrote back:

```
Is life great or what!!!
```

I know this will shock you, but even though Abramoff *said* he was working pro bono, Scanlon sent him $2.1 million, coincidentally exactly half the take.

The Tigua weren't done paying yet. There were members of Congress to impress. Abramoff had promised the Tigua that Bob Ney, the Republican chairman of the House Administration Committee, would sneak an amendment that would reopen Speaking Rock into a completely unrelated bill. But first, the Tigua would have to contribute $32,000 to Ney's political action committee.

Oh, and Ney wanted to play golf. In Scotland. You know, at St.

Andrews, just like DeLay got to. Another fact-finding tour. That would cost $100,000-plus, because Ney wouldn't want to play golf all alone.

When Ney asked for the trip in June, he had every intention of helping the Tigua get their casino reopened. Why wouldn't he? He was going to get his golf trip, and his PAC would be $32,000 richer. Abramoff had assured Ney that Senator Chris Dodd, the Connecticut Democrat, would handle the Senate side of the equation by sneaking the Tigua provision into the Help America Vote Act. Perfect. The only problem was that when Ney met with Dodd on July 25, he discovered that the Connecticut senator had absolutely no clue what he was talking about. Abramoff and Scanlon, it seemed, hadn't been straight with, well, anybody. There was no way the Speaking Rock Casino was going to be reopened.

Nevertheless, Ney took the golf trip to Scotland. In his defense, at the time of the trip it was clear to Ney that the bill would never go through, so he wasn't really taking a bribe from the Tigua. He was just ripping them off.

The fact-finding trip was fun. Ney brought his chief of staff, plus two good friends: Jack Abramoff and Ralph Reed.[6]

Needless to say, the Speaking Rock Casino's doors stayed shuttered. But the story has a happy ending. Sort of. Once it became clear that they'd been screwed, the Tigua reached a settlement with Abramoff's law firm and got half their $4.2 million back.

Although we know a great deal about the lying, cheating, and scamming that Abramoff engineered in the back rooms of that El Paso casino, there are no doubt tales of his skullduggery that will never see the light of day. If only Speaking Rock could talk.

But enough about American Indians. It's kind of depressing. No one in America has it worse than they do. Unless they're locked in labor barracks and/or brothels in Saipan. It turns out that neither the beaches of Saipan

---

[6]Fact: Ralph Reed takes a lot of mulligans. Fact: Abramoff hits from ladies' tee. Fact: Maybe I can trick the Indians into buying me a new set of golf clubs. Fact: Reed's supposedly dirty joke not really very dirty at all.

nor the blackjack tables of El Paso are really the perfect place for our vacation from Terri Schiavo.

You know, sometimes the best vacations are the ones you take right in your own backyard. Let's head back to the Big Apple. Maybe catch a Broadway show. Or attend a star-studded media event for the Reporters Committee for Freedom of the Press.

That's exactly where I bumped into Brian Ross. He was looking good, still trim and fit despite years of legendary overeating.[7] As he wolfed down a massive dollop of bread pudding, I told him that I'd been telling my audience about his Saipan investigation.

"Pretty ugly, eh?" I said.

"Yeah, especially the forced abortions."

I thought I'd misheard him because his mouth was full. "You mean the forced prostitution, yeah," I said. "It's amazing that a guy like Tom DeLay—"

"No, no. Forced *abortion*. The forced prostitution was in my second report. The thing that still gets me is the forced *abortion*."

Every journalist makes mistakes. And I'm no exception. Turns out I'd only done half my homework. Instead of watching *both* of Ross's reports, I had merely read the transcript of one of them. Fortunately, my years of training had prepared me for this very moment. I knew just what to do.

"Brian, could I get the tapes of those two reports?"

Those were the magic words. A day later, I received a package containing a videocassette. On that cassette was the smoking gun. Two episodes of *20/20*, detailing everything my listeners, and now my readers, needed to know.

In this book, I've described some pretty revolting stuff. But in terms of sheer hypocrisy, it is hard to match Tom DeLay's defense of a system that involved forcing young women to get abortions in order to keep their jobs.

[7] According to my anonymous source, *The Truth About Hillary* author Ed Klein.

In his *20/20* report, Ross interviewed Allan Stayman, who ran the office in the Interior Department that oversaw the Northern Mariana Islands.

> **STAYMAN:** We have now documented the fact that management coerces female workers who become pregnant into having abortions.

Ross didn't take Allan Stayman's word for it. He talked to Tu Tao May, a Chinese woman who had made Ralph Lauren Polo brand T-shirts in a Saipan sweatshop.

> **MAY (through translator):** When I told them I was pregnant, they tell me to have an abortion.

When she refused, she was fired.

> **ROSS:** Will you get your job back, then?
>
> **MAY:** Cannot.

Ross also interviewed Eric Gregoire, the Catholic human rights worker who had talked about the barbed wire surrounding the labor barracks.

> **GREGOIRE:** With eleven thousand Chinese workers here, I have never seen a Chinese garment factory worker have a baby in my entire four years on Saipan.

Pretty sick. Even for Tom DeLay and Jack Abramoff. It made me wonder how a guy like DeLay, who reportedly spends hours a week in church praying to his pro-life God, can sleep at night.

Is it possible that he just lies to himself? Hard to say. But the *Galveston*

Daily News did offer a clue, which is that he has no problem lying to everybody else.

When their reporter interviewed DeLay for a May 15, 2005, story, the majority leader called the allegations against the sweatshop owners "totally false," "incredible lies" told by "the left," which was "trying to destroy what was going on in the Marianas Islands." And he knew all this, he told Marty Schladen of the *Daily News,* because he had investigated it himself.

> We met with people who were making these kinds of allegations, including the Catholic Church, and asked them to show us even one story that was brought up by the George Millers of the world,[8] and they could not produce one story, or one individual to prove their allegation. I saw it for what it was: the left wanting to impose federal bureaucracy on the economy of the Marianas Islands, and shut down what was going on there. They will say and do anything.

Of course, there were plenty of stories and plenty of individuals who backed up the allegations. Besides "Katrina" and Tu Tao May, there were the 150 victims in the ten involuntary servitude cases brought by the Clinton Justice Department at the end of the nineties.

In one case, for example, Soon Oh Kwon, president of Kwon Enterprises, pled guilty in U.S. District Court to bringing Chinese women to Saipan on contracts to become waitresses, and then forcing them to have sex with patrons at his karaoke club, K's Hideaway.

As for DeLay's contention that only the "left" was attacking the conditions in Saipan, it's worth remembering that it was Alaska Senator Frank Murkowski, a conservative Republican, who led the charge in the Senate

---

[8]George Miller, remember, is the California Democrat who has fought for labor protections in Saipan throughout his congressional career.

to clean up the sweatshops and sex shops on the island. It's also worth mentioning that DeLay blocked an actual fact-finding trip to Saipan that had been planned by Representative Peter Hoekstra, Republican of Michigan, by threatening Hoekstra with the loss of his subcommittee chairmanship. A former aide told the *National Journal*, "We were under very strict orders not to deal with the Marianas. . . . Hoekstra was told to lay off the Marianas." Hoekstra was "absolutely beside himself," the aide added. "He was livid."

So this wasn't a left-wing plot to socialize a bastion of free enterprise. This was about corruption trumping principle. Principles like "don't enslave people" or "don't force women to have abortions."

Although the Saipan episode does call DeLay's "pro-life" credentials into question, at least he was being consistent on the issue of "choice." On the mainland, Tom DeLay doesn't want women to be able to choose to have an abortion. On Saipan, he thinks it's okay if they can't choose *not* to.

For Tom DeLay, this wasn't about human lives. This was about golf trips. It was about his nearest and dearest friend, Jack Abramoff, getting millions of dollars. For these old buddies, government wasn't about serving the public, it wasn't about freedom or democracy, it wasn't even about sticking up for ideological principles. It was about personal gain. Living high off the unspeakable misery of the poor and the powerless.

Republicans. They're not all like that. But more of them should know that this is what their leaders are about. After all, as Tom DeLay said to the Saipan slave drivers:

> You are a shining light for what is happening in the Republican Party.

Saipan and the Tigua are just the tip of the iceberg. In almost every aspect of government—from energy to military contracting to environmental protection to health care—you find the exact same kind of cynical looting and betrayal of the public good.

These people should not be running our country. They should be in prison. Or forced to work at K's Hideaway, singing "Knock Three Times on the Ceiling If You Want Me" while taking it in the caboose from a Japanese businessman.

Enough vacation. Back to work.

11 | Social Security: Franni vs. Bush

Ⱘn January 25, 2001, just five days after the inauguration of a new president under disputed circumstances, Federal Reserve Chair Alan Greenspan testified to the Senate Budget Committee about the new challenges posed by the country's incredibly and unexpectedly sunny fiscal outlook. After eight years of Clinton-style fiscal discipline and economic growth, the era of big deficits was over, and we were running surpluses like nobody's business. Greenspan was excited.

> The most recent projections from the OMB [Office of Management and Budget] indicate that, if current policies remain in place, the total unified surplus will reach $800 billion in fiscal year 2011.

It was hard to believe how good things were. But the numbers were solid. Greenspan painted a picture of abundance with what was, for him, an almost frothy enthusiasm.

In almost any creditable baseline scenario, short of a major and prolonged economic contraction, the full benefits of debt reduction are now achieved before the end of this decade— a prospect that did not seem likely only a year or even six months ago.

In other words, our collective ass was in ice cream. The rules of the game had suddenly changed. Even after making every school in the country a palace; even after spending hundreds of billions on the Star Wars program, maybe even enough to achieve one successful test; even after providing health care to every man, woman, child, and pet in America— and abroad—even after all these things, we'd still have money to burn. We could even afford an enormous, humongous tax cut for the wealthy. In the rest of his speech, Greenspan warned about the dangers of having *too much* money, of paying off the national debt too quickly.

Too much money. That was our problem four and a half years ago.

Since then, thanks to the leadership of President George W. Bush, we have entirely averted that problem. Some might even argue that we've gone too far in the other direction. Instead of drowning in black ink, the government has had to borrow more than 2 trillion dollars.

That gives you some idea why we might not want to make huge, fundamental decisions based upon long-term economic forecasts. If Alan Greenspan can be that far off in four and a half years, try to imagine the size of the margin of error when George W. Bush tells you what to expect in, say, 2042.

Of course, after Greenspan's testimony, a number of unforeseen events changed the fiscal landscape. Things like 9/11, the war in Iraq, Bush's general incompetence, and, most of all, Bush's dogged insistence on a series of increasingly unaffordable tax cuts for the rich. My point is that there may be some unforeseeable circumstances between now and 2042. What are they? When will they happen? It's tough to say with any certainty. That's my point.

One thing that has proved very resilient to unforeseen circumstances is

Social Security. Social Security survived World War II, the Cold War, Vietnam, the sexual revolution, oil shocks, stagflation, and the demise of Kozmo.com, which used to deliver snacks to people's apartments in less than an hour with no delivery charge. No matter what America and the world could throw at it, Social Security just kept on ticking, sending out checks to delighted seniors, people with disabilities, and widows and orphans. Today, Social Security provides more than half the income for most of America's senior citizens. If it disappeared tomorrow, the poverty rate among senior citizens would jump from 8.7 percent to 46.8 percent. By almost all accounts, Social Security was the greatest achievement of the New Deal, and perhaps the greatest achievement of any kind in human history.

But after winning the 2004 election, George W. Bush decided that he had some "political capital" to spend, and he was going to spend it to "save" Social Security. Why did it need saving? Because there was a crisis looming. In 2042, a mere thirty-seven years hence, Social Security would be "bankrupt," "flat broke," and would have to, if the very conservative projections of the Social Security Administration were precisely on target, cut future projected benefits by 27 percent. (Of course, benefits will grow every year until then, so that even after the cut, they'd still be higher than they are today.)

The solution to this crisis? Driving a stake through the heart of the program by transforming it from a system of shared protection from, as Roosevelt put it, "the hazards and vicissitudes of life" into a glorified IRA. Plus cutting benefits.

Incidentally, this would be a windfall for Bush's friends in the money management business.

I know it all sounds like some kind of crazy dream. But earlier this very year (assuming you're reading this in 2005), Bush and his friends actually tried to begin privatizing Social Security. What they did, why they did it, and how we beat them is more than just a satisfying bedtime story for young Democrats. It shows how today's Republicans have an extreme agenda that has nothing to do with the public interest, how there's no way to sell that agenda with anything approaching honesty, and how, once people find out what the hell they're really trying to do, their "new ideas" are exposed as "bad ideas" that "fail."

Why did Bush choose to spend his capital on Social Security? After all, there are plenty of problems facing America. What made this more important than, say, armoring the Humvees of our fighting men and women in Iraq? As far as I can tell, there are two possibilities. Either Bush chose to "save" Social Security for the reasons that he repeatedly put forward. Or, he chose it because of reasons he *didn't* put forward.

If it was for the reasons he *did* put forward, then we don't have to speculate about any hidden reasons. That would save time. Not to mention what a relief it would be to know the President was dealing in good faith with the American people. So let's look at those reasons first.

The biggest reason of all was that Social Security was in crisis. The President explained the "looming danger" in his weekly radio address on December 11, 2004:

> In the year 2018, for the first time ever, Social Security will pay out more in benefits than the government collects in payroll taxes. And once that line into the red has been crossed, the shortfalls will grow larger with each passing year. By the time today's workers in their mid-twenties begin to retire, the system will be bankrupt, unless we act to save it. A crisis in Social Security can be averted, if we in government take our responsibilities seriously.

So that was the crisis: There would more money going out of the Social Security Trust Fund than coming in. Starting in 2018. That was only thirteen years away! That wasn't as scary as the mushroom cloud he used to sell his last phony crisis, but still—pretty scary.

So what was his solution? Private accounts. Instead of paying money into the Trust Fund, you'd be able to put it into a private investment account. Crisis averted. But wait. If we put less money into the Trust Fund, how does that ensure that the Trust Fund will have more money? Hmm.

Didn't make sense to me. But then again, I'm not an economist. I picked up the phone and called Peter Orszag, the Joseph A. Pechman Senior Fellow in Economic Studies at the Brookings Institution. "Bush says the Social Security Trust Fund will start losing money in 2018. But," I asked Peter, "when will it start losing money under *his* plan?"

"Depends on when the plan starts," Peter said.

"Let's say it starts right away."

"In that case," Peter told me, "outflows from the Trust Fund would exceed inflows starting in 2006."

"So, next year?"

"Yeah."

Okay. So the year the Trust Fund started shrinking would actually be *way sooner* if Bush "fixed" it. So *that* couldn't have been the problem Bush was trying to solve. It must have been more of a long-term problem. That's when I remembered Bush's other argument. On December 9, 2004, the President talked to reporters gathered at the Oval Office. In this instance, as you will soon see, he was talking to a reporter named "Steve."

> I think what's really important in the discussions is to understand the size of the problem. And that is we are faced with a present value of unfunded liabilities of about $11 trillion. What's important, Steve, is before we begin any discussion is to understand the scope of the problem.

My God. Eleven *trillion* dollars. Where would we get that kind of money? I mean, that really was a crisis. And I kept hearing the number over and over. From Vice President Dick Cheney. From Treasury Secretary John Snow. On right-wing radio, it was hard to hear any other number.

Where did that number come from? Well, it came from the Social Security Administration. Bush's Social Security Administration. And the number, $11 trillion, represented the total Social Security shortfall, adjusted for inflation, from now until the year Infinity.

That's right. The year Infinity. Not the year 2018. Not the year 3018. Not the year 3,000,018. No. The year ∞.

That kind of put it in a different perspective. If you think about it, $11 trillion over infinity years is *nothing*. Think about it. Over the first 11 trillion years, that's just one inflation-adjusted dollar a year. Easy. After that, it's nothing. You're done. What exactly was the problem?

Why would Bush's Social Security Administration come up with such a number? I mean, unless it was to mislead people. As it turned out, the American Academy of Actuaries, of which (full disclosure) I am not a member, had a similar concern. Taking aim at the projection out to the "infinite horizon," they wrote a letter to the Social Security Advisory Board saying that it could "mislead" people into "believing that the program is in far worse financial condition than is actually indicated."

A reporter asked Treasury Secretary Snow about this very matter.

REPORTER: You emphasized in your opening statement the $11.1 trillion unfunded liability over the infinite horizon.

SNOW: Right.

REPORTER: You began publishing that number in 2003, and after you published it, in 2004, the American Academy of Actuaries wrote you a letter and said that the number was misleading.

But the reporter wasn't done. He had a more specific point to make.

REPORTER: And I understand that in coming up with that number, you extend longevity to 150 years and keep the retirement age at 67. Now, doesn't that provide a misleading number for the American people?

Hold on a sec. In order to get *that* number, $11 trillion over *infinity* years, they had to assume that people would live to an average age of 150, but still retire at 67. That's an eighty-three-year retirement. They're never gonna get to that without stem cell research.

Snow did the honorable thing and passed the buck to the Social Security actuary who'd been told to work with those assumptions.

> **SNOW:** They're his numbers. He's the actuary. I'm not an actuary. I have great respect for actuaries.

One reaction to the "crisis" of an unaffordable eighty-three-year retirement would be to raise the retirement age to a more reasonable, say, 110. But this wouldn't have to be done immediately. You could wait until, maybe, oh, the year 2,000,005.

Or you could take the Bush approach: privatize and slash benefits.

So let's face it. The $11 trillion shortfall could not possibly have been the actual motivation behind Bush's Social Security crusade. Or more properly, *jihad*.

Of course, that doesn't mean there wasn't *any* projected shortfall. Depending on whose assumptions you trust—and you'll remember from Alan Greenspan how precise these things can turn out to be—the Trust Fund will contain zero dollars in 2042 (Social Security Administration) or 2052 (Congressional Budget Office). At that point, the money that comes in from workers paying their payroll taxes will be the only source of money for Social Security benefit checks. As I've said, the pessimists over at SSA tell you that at that point the government would have to cut benefits by 27 percent. The slightly less pessimistic, but still far from irrationally exuberant, wonks at the CBO contend that benefits would be cut by 19 percent.

But either way, there is a projected shortfall. That's what people are talking about when they talk about the solvency problem. And it's not new. Solvency problems in Social Security, much bigger ones, have been dealt with before. As Mark Weisbrot, economist for the liberal Center for Economic and Policy Research, has written:

> Social Security is currently more financially sound than it has been throughout most of its entire history. To cover any short-falls that may occur over the next 75 years would require less than we came up with in each of the decades of the 1950s, 60s, 70s, or 80s.

There is literally an infinite number of ways to deal with the projected solvency issue. Especially over the infinite horizon. One way is to, as Bush has proposed, lock in cuts to future benefits. But that doesn't seem like a solution to the problem of maybe having to cut benefits down the road. A more elegant solution might be to simply wait and see what happens. In their projections, the Social Security Trustees assume that the economy will only grow at a sluggish 1.8 percent a year. But the last time the economy was that bad for any length of time was during the Great Depression. From 1961 to 2001, the average growth rate was 3.4 percent a year. It's good to be cautious when planning for retirement, but it's not like we're gonna get extra stupid over the next four decades and let the economy sputter out. I'm optimistic. I think we can grow at 2 percent, or maybe even 2.3 percent a year. I pulled those numbers out of my ass.

See, every year, the Social Security Administration makes three fore-casts: an optimistic projection, a pessimistic projection, and an interme-diate projection. The press takes a Goldilocks approach and assumes that the intermediate projection is just right. But David Langer, an indepen-dent actuary, has spent the last ten years picking through those projec-tions, and he's noticed something of a pattern. So far, at least—and this could change, it's good to be cautious—the optimistic projection has been right on the money.

When Bush says the Trust Fund will go flat broke in 2042, he's using the intermediate projection. But guess what the optimistic projection says? It says we'll have much more money in the Trust Fund *then* than we have *today*. In other words, it's very possible that we have nothing to solve.

But let's say you want to play it safe and use the intermediate projection. You still have plenty of options for ways to achieve solvency. The most popular one is to raise the cap on income subject to the payroll tax, known as FICA, after the Federal Insurance Contributions Act. Right now, the cap is at $90,000, meaning that if you make $180,000, you pay FICA on only half your income. Everyone earning *under* $90,000 pays payroll taxes on every dollar they make, which is why a majority of Americans pay more than half their federal taxes in payroll taxes.

Polls consistently find that more than two thirds of Americans favor getting rid of the cap entirely. Another strategy is to raise the cap to $120,000, or $150,000. I've been proposing something called "The Al Franken Donut Hole," which is too complicated to describe anywhere but in a footnote.[1] Representative David Obey of Wisconsin has proposed reinstating the estate tax and using that to help pay for any shortfall. You could also gradually raise the retirement age. Or the Social Security Administration could invest part of the Trust Fund in stocks, rather than treasury bonds, which would introduce a little bit of risk, but that risk would be shared by everyone, and the administrative costs would be almost nothing.

There aren't many moving parts in Social Security. It's not like

---

[1] Here's the idea. You raise the cap to $120,000. Then you don't pay any more payroll taxes until you get to $500,000. Why? I don't know, it just seems fairer somehow. The gap from $120,000 to $500,000 is the "Donut Hole." Now, I don't mind if you change the numbers around; they're pretty arbitrary. But here's why I like this idea. Imagine the Al Franken Donut Hole were adopted, and it saved Social Security into the infinite horizon. Then, maybe, 12 trillion years from now, people would say "You know who saved Social Security? Al Franken. It was that Donut Hole idea of his. Thank God for Al Franken. Because of him, we had the resources to put down the Robot Uprising back in 4,449,288,573,223 A.D."

Medicare, which is a nightmare.[2] Two reasonable senators of good faith, one Republican and one Democrat, could sit down and solve the solvency problem in five minutes.

If we have nothing to solve but solvency itself, we have nothing to fear.

But in every speech where Bush talks about solvency, he talks about private accounts. Here's a clue that Bush isn't on the level. The private accounts would do *nothing* to solve the solvency issue. Nothing. Nada. Not a cent. No help. At all.

And the Bush administration has, albeit reluctantly, admitted it. In a February 2 background briefing, an anonymous Bush administration official addressed the issue directly. "In a long-term sense," he said, "the personal accounts would have a net neutral effect on the fiscal situation of Social Security and on the federal government."

When a reporter asked the anonymous official whether that meant "it would be fair to describe the personal accounts by themselves as having no effect whatsoever on the solvency issue," he—or she—responded that "that's a fair inference."

In fact, while private accounts were "net neutral" in the long term (sixty-plus years), they were "net horrible" in the short term as far as solvency was concerned. Every dollar paid into a private account would be a dollar *not* paid into the Social Security Trust Fund. Over the first twenty years, the federal treasury would have to borrow an extra $5.3 trillion to cover the costs of private accounts.

Of course, that $5.3 trillion would be subject to what Albert Einstein called "the most powerful force in the universe": compound interest. Bush's plan was for your children, your children's children, and probably *their* children and their children's children to pay down all of that interest.

For this and other reasons, Democrats in Congress announced that they would be happy to negotiate a plan for Social Security, as long as

---

[2] And which is way, way less solvent than Social Security. The ridiculously unreliable infinite shortfall for Medicare is $65.4 trillion, six times worse than the one for Social Security. But you don't hear Bush talking about *that*.

private accounts were taken off the table. But Bush dismissed the offer out of hand. And then kept on denouncing Democrats for being the party of obstruction.

Maybe Bush's motivation for private accounts was rooted in something more profound. Of all the reasons he gave for taking on Social Security, there was one that seemed philosophically distinct from the humdrum concerns about benefits and solvency. At the same time as he was warning about the dangerous shortfall in the Trust Fund, he was also claiming that there was no Social Security Trust Fund at all.

That came as a surprise to the millions of working baby boomers who have been paying high payroll taxes from every paycheck in order to build up a reserve big enough to handle their retirement. As of 2004, according to the Social Security Trust Fund's website,[3] America's hardworking workers had squirreled away $1.64 trillion in the Trust Fund. But the President wasn't buying it. Not one bit.

To illustrate his point about the Trust Fund's nonexistence, the President spent some taxpayer money to take a trip to the Bureau of the Public Debt in Parkersburg, West Virginia, where a tour guide showed him the actual filing cabinet full of paper notes representing the bonds in which the Trust Fund is invested. Then the President went outside and reported on his findings:

> There is no "trust fund," just IOUs that I saw firsthand, that future generations will pay—will pay for either in higher taxes, or reduced benefits, or cuts to other critical government programs.

Bush used vivid imagery to drive home his point about the IOUs:

> They're stacked in a filing cabinet. Imagine—the retirement security for future generations is sitting in a filing cabinet.

---

[3]If you want to look at it, go to *www.ssa.gov/OACT/ProgData/funds.html.* It's very reassuring.

Those "IOUs" were actually what you and I call U.S. Treasury bonds, the safest investment on the planet. Or so I had thought. But now Bush was saying they were worthless, because "there is no 'trust fund.'" This might have spooked the Chinese and Japanese governments that have kindly paid for our trade deficits by buying up treasury bonds by the hundreds of billions. It also might have spooked the ghosts of the members of Congress and state legislatures who, in 1868, adopted the Fourteenth Amendment to the United States Constitution. Its fourth section kind of frowns on anyone, let alone the President, casting doubt on the full faith and credit of the United States. As ratified:

> The validity of the public debt of the United States, authorized by law, including debts incurred for payment of pensions and bounties for services in suppressing insurrection or rebellion, shall not be questioned.

Bush is lucky that he had a Republican Congress, or he almost certainly would have been impeached and imprisoned.

It's hard to understand how Bush might have arrived at the weird idea that the Trust Fund was worthless, but the right-wing media were right there with him. Republican pundits everywhere joined in the slander of the United States Treasury. Conservative columnist Charles Krauthammer went so far as to write, "These pieces of paper might be useful for rolling cigars. They will not fund your retirement." And as I've only recently learned, this line of thinking isn't new. In a 1999 pamphlet, the Heritage Foundation wrote that the Trust Fund "contains no genuine assets, only government bonds."

What were they all talking about? If you really want to understand their perspective, I do know one way to do it. I've arranged for my publisher to apply a drop of LSD to the upper right-hand corner of this page. Just rip off the page number and put it on your tongue. Now wait about twenty minutes.

Okay, ready? Are you tripping?

You're gonna be fine, dude. Big Al is here to walk you through it. Okay.

Take out your wallet, man. Now pull out a bill. Look at the face. Is it Lincoln? Is it Washington? Both? Actually, dude, it doesn't matter which one it is.

He's talking to you. He's saying, "Hey, man. I'm worthless. I'm just a fuckin' piece of paper, dude. You can't redeem me for gold, or silver, or nothin'. I mean, just think about it. All I am is a piece of paper."

You see? Bonds are just like dollar bills, dude. They're pieces of paper. And if the government decides not to pay, you're screwed, man. Totally screwed. Totally.

Sucks to be you, man.

That's what Bush was saying.

Was the President doing acid? It's hard to reach any other conclusion. Because three weeks later, Bush gave a prime-time press conference to announce his Social Security benefit cuts (under the comforting moniker "progressive indexation"). As usual, he warned that within a few decades, "Social Security will be bankrupt," a concept that makes sense only if you accept the existence of a trust fund with actual money in it. Then he did a 180, claiming that the Trust Fund was just "file cabinets full of IOUs" and thus worthless. But then, turning another 180 degrees to complete a full 360, he announced that owners of private Social Security accounts would be able to invest their money in something that would give them a real sense of security:

> I propose that one investment option consist entirely of treasury bonds, which are backed by the full faith and credit of the United States government.

Man, he must have been *flyin'*.

Besides solvency and Bush's metaphysical problems with the Trust Fund, there was one more argument against the Social Security status quo—one that raised the biggest red flag that the President was being more than a little disingenuous. Social Security needed to be overhauled, he said, because it was unfair to black people.

One is tempted to give Bush credit for his newly discovered interest in the problems of African-Americans. Until, that is, one learns the details. As it turns out, although blacks do have many problems in George W. Bush's America (for example, in some major cities, black men have an unemployment rate of over 50 percent), the fairness of Social Security isn't one of them.

Bush laid out the problem at a staged "Conversation on Social Security Reform" on a January morning in our nation's capital. This part of the staged conversation was with Bob McFadden, a health care consultant who happened to be African-American.

> **BUSH:** African-American males die sooner than other males do, which means the system is inherently unfair to a certain group of people. And that needs to be fixed. (Applause.)

> **MCFADDEN:** I agree, Mr. President, because from the minimal research that I've done, the average African-American male life expectancy is sixty-nine. And I may be off a little bit. But if you're telling me that it's sixty-nine, and the age is going to go to sixty-seven, you do the math. (Laughter.)

> **BUSH:** Right.

The math was easy. But Karl Rove didn't want to leave anything to chance.

> **MCFADDEN:** That's two years. (Laughter.)

> **BUSH:** Glad you came. Thanks.

McFadden had done his job: giving voice to the inescapable conclusion that the average black male would receive Social Security for only two years. But while numbers themselves do not lie, the Republicans who use them often do.

What McFadden hadn't discovered in his "minimal research" was that the numbers that he had been instructed to parrot came from a 1998 report by the extremely untrustworthy Heritage Foundation, a right-wing think tank not known for its leadership in the civil rights arena. That particular study had been cited by a Social Security actuary for "major errors in the methodology" and "incorrect or inappropriate assumptions." In fact, as the actuary pointed out, "the non-white population actually enjoys the same or better expected rates of return from Social Security than for the white population."

How was Heritage so wrong? Well, while errors in methodology and incorrect or inappropriate assumptions are seldom considered funny, the Heritage ones are fall-down, pee-in-your-pants hilarious.

First of all, the study assumed that every African-American man would live to *exactly* sixty-nine years of age, and then drop dead. No child died for lack of medical attention, no young black man died in an industrial accident or from neighborhood violence, no wise old black man rocked in a rocking chair on his porch with his great-grandchildren on his knee. It was work work work, pay into Social Security, retire at sixty-seven, collect benefits for two years, and then keel over. No exceptions.

Sure, it made the math easier. And it would remove some of the guesswork from estate planning. But it's slightly unrealistic. As Nipsey Russell, the eighty-one-year-old "poet laureate" of black comedy, said when I showed him the report:

> It shocked us both,
> My wife and me,
> That I've been dead
> Since '93.

This assumption did a lot of heavy lifting for the Heritage Foundation. It meant that every black man paid into Social Security for forty-six years and drew benefits for only two years. But Heritage ignored the fact that black males, like white males, die at every age, from 0 to, according to Treasury Secretary John Snow, 150. Black men who reach sixty-seven have a life expectancy of seventy-nine. That doesn't mean that they *all* die at seventy-nine. It's just an average. It means that, on average, black male retirees will receive Social Security benefits for twelve years—not two.

And here's another thing that Heritage fudged. Social Security doesn't just pay retirement benefits. It also pays disability and survivor benefits. And because of the enormous racial inequality in this country, African-Americans are much more likely than whites to receive both. Of all African-Americans who receive Social Security benefits of any kind, 47 percent receive either disability or survivor benefits. The number for whites is 28 percent. So, leaving out disability and survivor benefits would skew things a bit, don't ya think? Well, guess what? Somehow the Einsteins over at Heritage forgot to include them. By accident? On purpose? Who knows?

And that's not all. African-American men earn, on average, about $25,000 a year. That's a lot less than the average white guy. I think it has something to do with the legacy of slavery. Anyway, Social Security's benefits are progressive, which means that the less you earn, the bigger your benefits are, relative to your income.

That's why, in 2003, the nonpartisan Government Accountability Office found that "in the aggregate, blacks and Hispanics have higher disability rates and lower lifetime earnings, and thus receive greater benefits relative to taxes than whites."

Which is quite a contradiction to the Heritage Foundation's finding that "low-income African-American males realize particularly dismal rates of return from Social Security." And that's why I described the Heritage Foundation as "extremely untrustworthy."

So it's not just that Bush's argument that Social Security needed to be changed because "the system is inherently unfair" to blacks was demonstrably false. No, it's worse than that. Blacks do better than whites under Social Security *because* they get the short end of the stick in so many other ways. But Bush wasn't addressing any of those problems. He was just looking for another excuse to privatize Social Security. But it was nice of him to inject race into the debate.

None of the reasons Bush gave for taking on Social Security could survive critical scrutiny, or even comedic scrutiny. But if none of those reasons were the reason, what was the reason? Why, in God's name, was Bush so intent on using his hard-earned capital to introduce private accounts to Social Security? And why were Republicans lining up to support him?

I was hoping to avoid this. But it looks like we are now forced to turn to the aforementioned hidden reasons.

I think the basic reason Bush and company tried to privatize Social Security is simple. Conservative Republicans hate government. They hate the idea that the people can join together to use the government to solve their problems. Social Security is the biggest and most successful example of how public policy can provide a safety net where everyone shares the risk and everyone shares the reward. If they could unravel that, then anything was possible. Everyone could be left to fend for themselves. That's their vision of the "Ownership Society." Which is code for the "On-Your-Own Society."

At least, that's my gut. But one thing I've learned in this life is you gotta give people the benefit of the doubt. Maybe I'm wrong. Maybe, as they kept saying, they really did want to "strengthen" Social Security, and even though their arguments didn't make sense, their hearts were in the right place. Maybe they just got some bad intelligence.

But as much as I've learned to give people the benefit of the doubt, I've also learned to look for leaked memos. And wouldn't you know that in January of 2005, a memo was indeed leaked to *The Wall Street Journal*. It was a strategy memo written by Karl Rove's deputy, one Peter H. Wehner:

> For the first time in six decades, the Social Security battle is one
> we can win—and in doing so, we can help transform the politi-
> cal and philosophical landscape of the country.

Hmm. Six decades. Funny, Bush had never mentioned a six-decade
battle over Social Security. Let's see. What was the right trying to do to
Social Security six decades ago? Oh yes. Get rid of it! Back to Wehner:

> I don't need to tell you that this will be one of the most impor-
> tant conservative undertakings of modern times. If we succeed
> in reforming Social Security, it will rank as one of the most sig-
> nificant conservative governing achievements ever. The scope
> and scale of this endeavor are hard to overestimate.

"Conservative." Who do many Republicans consider to be the father of
the modern conservative movement? Barry Goldwater. What was Barry
Goldwater's position on Social Security? Destroy it! "Perhaps Social Security should be abolished," he mused during his 1964 presidential campaign.

In 1978, George W. Bush was running for Congress in Midland, Texas.
Social Security was facing a fiscal shortfall much worse than the one it
faces today. And candidate Bush's solution? No surprise, guys: Privatize.
Gary Ott of the *Plainview Daily Herald* recollected that Bush told him that
Social Security would go bust in ten years unless people were given a
chance to invest the money themselves.

Bush wasn't the only Republican with designs on Social Security.
When Reagan was elected in 1980 with help from the Ayatollah Khomeini, anti–Social Security forces saw their big chance. David Stockman,
Reagan's director of the Office of Management and Budget, called Social
Security "closet Socialism" and a "giant Ponzi scheme." He said disability
benefits were "a powerful temptation to the shiftless" and, with Reagan's
confused approval, tried to take a meat-ax to the program.

In less than a week, the Senate, in thrall to the shiftless interests, voted

96–0 against the package, and in the House, Speaker Tip O'Neill accused the GOP of trying "to balance the budget on the backs of the elderly." The next year, twenty-six incumbent Republicans lost their seats. It was a total rout.

The year after that, a surprisingly responsible bipartisan commission chaired by a younger, wiser Alan Greenspan recommended a body of major reforms that preserved the basic structure of the program and ensured its long-term viability. Part of their grand plan was to build up an enormous trust fund so that when the baby boomers retired, Social Security would be ready.

Nothing could have pissed off the privatizers more. In light of Social Security's overwhelming popularity, it was clear that they needed a new master strategy, something more long-range and devious. For inspiration they turned to an unlikely source: Vladimir Ilyich Ulyanov Lenin. That's right. The father of the Russian Revolution.

In an article in the journal of the libertarian Cato Institute, Stuart Butler, the Heritage Foundation's director of domestic policy studies, teamed up with Peter Germanis, a Heritage policy analyst. Although Heritage was notoriously unreliable when it came to factual arguments, it was also fiendishly clever when it came to right-wing scheming. Their piece, "Achieving a 'Leninist' Strategy," was a case in point.

By "Leninist," Butler and Germanis didn't mean "Communist." Far from it. It was only Lenin's tactical brilliance that they hoped to emulate. As they wrote:

> Lenin believed that capitalism was doomed by its inherent contradictions, and would inevitably collapse. But just to be on the safe side, he sought to mobilize the working class, in alliance with other key elements in political society, both to hasten the collapse and to ensure that the result conformed with his interpretation of the proletarian state. Unlike many other socialists at the time, Lenin recognized that fundamental change is contingent both upon a movement's ability to create a focused political

coalition and upon its success in isolating and weakening its opponents.

As we contemplate basic reform of the Social Security system, we would do well to draw a few lessons from the Leninist strategy.

What was the "basic reform" that the neo-Leninists were advocating in the Cato journal? Well, in this article, they were supporting a plan devised by one Peter Ferrara. At its heart was an IRA-like "private pension plan." A private pension that would replace Social Security once and for all.

Butler and Germanis's Leninist blueprint would directly inform President Bush's political strategy twenty-one years later. Let's start with the "isolating and weakening" component.

> Our reform strategy involves what one might crudely call guerrilla warfare against both the current Social Security system and the coalition that supports it.

And who would be in this coalition?

> The sine qua non of any successful Social Security reform strategy must be an assurance to those already retired or nearing retirement that their benefits will be paid in full.

Why not pay *everyone's* benefits in full, instead of just old people's? What makes seniors so special?

> From a purely political standpoint, it should be remembered that the elderly represent a very powerful and vocal interest group.

Oh. I'm catching on. The elderly are an interest group. And if you can buy them off, then you can isolate and weaken the young!

Any plan to change the system must therefore be neutral or (better still) clearly advantageous to senior citizens. By accepting this principle, we may succeed in neutralizing the most powerful element of the coalition that opposes structural reform.

Smart, right? Let's fast forward to April 5, 2005. In the very speech where President George W. Bush denounced the filing cabinets holding the Social Security Trust Fund's treasury bonds, he paused for a moment to address the concerns of an especially important segment of American society:

> On my trips around this country I have made it as clear as I possibly can that the government will keep its promise to those who have retired or near retirement. And that's very important for a lot of people to hear. I understand how important the Social Security check is to a lot of our citizens. A lot of people depend on that Social Security check.

In case that wasn't crystal clear, the President laid it out as plainly as he could:

> I'm here to tell you those who've retired are going to get their check. Those who are near retirement are going to get their check. (Applause.) The system will not change in any way for people who have been born prior to 1950. And I'm going to keep saying it over and over again.

On that final point, and that point alone, the President was as good as his word. He would repeat this at every fake town hall meeting, fake economic summit, and pre-scripted "Social Security Conversation" for the rest of the spring. He repeated it so much that even Bush, a man known for constantly repeating his talking points, felt the need to remark on the extent of the repetition. Here he is on May 24 just outside of Rochester, New York:

> If you've retired, you don't have anything to worry about—third time I've said that. (Laughter.) I'll probably say it three more times. See, in my line of work you got to keep repeating things over and over and over again for the truth to sink in, to kind of catapult the propaganda. (Applause.)

But as clever as they were, Stuart Butler, Peter Germanis, George W. Bush, and even Karl Rove were not as smart as Lenin. What Lenin might have told them is that people tend to divide along class lines rather than by generation. So while wealthy bankers might support Social Security privatization, the grandparents of regular working folks might not bite, even if they themselves were guaranteed their full benefits.

The polls bore Lenin out. As Bush's "60 Stops in 60 Days" Social Security tour wore on, his plan become less and less popular in every age group. After only two weeks on the road, it was becoming clear that things weren't going according to plan. Only 37 percent of those over sixty-five supported private accounts, even though polling indicated they knew their own benefit checks weren't in danger. Jonathan Weisman gave an illustrative example in his March 15 *Washington Post* story, "Skepticism of Bush's Social Security Plan Is Growing":

> At 69, Gene Wallace knows the White House's proposal would have no impact on his Social Security check, but if Bush believes that will silence the Republican mayor of Coldwater, Mich., Wallace grumbled, "he's all wet."
>
> "I'm a parent as well as a grandparent. Somewhere along the line, they are going to be eligible for retirement assistance," he said, with all the energy he could muster three weeks after

open-heart surgery. "It's everybody's concern what happens to this country."

See? Some Republicans are okay. But let's get back to Butler and Germanis's evil Leninist plot. There must be some aspect of it that worked out as planned. Remember: They not only wanted to isolate and weaken the opponents of privatization, they also wanted to "create a focused political coalition." But who would possibly support messing with a system that had worked so well for so many people for so long?

> What we must do is construct a coalition that will gain directly from its implementation. That coalition should not only consist of those who will reap benefits from the IRA-based private system Ferrara has proposed but also the banks, insurance companies, and other institutions that will gain from providing such plans to the public.

Ah, the banks. That's where the money is. That's who wants this. They'd be *perfect* for the coalition.

Did this aspect of Butler and Germanis's plan bear fruit? To answer that question, I'd like to share with you the story of the person in this world who is most opposed to Social Security privatization. Franni Franken is not an analyst at a liberal think tank, nor a member of the AARP. Well, actually, she is. But that's not the reason she goes ballistic anytime she hears the word "private" in the same paragraph as the words "Social Security." Franni takes the same attitude toward Social Security that she took to our kids when they were toddlers. *Don't touch. If you touch them, I will destroy you.*

See, when Franni Bryson was seventeen months old, her father, Donald, a World War II vet, died in a car accident on his way home from his job at the paper mill. That left her twenty-nine-year-old mother to take care of Franni and her four siblings—Kathy, seven; Carla, five; Neil, three;

and Bootsie, three months old. Franni's mom had a high school education and, as soon as Bootsie started school, got a job working odd hours in the produce department at a nearby supermarket. Her paycheck, a very small veterans' widows' benefit, and the survivor benefits from Social Security weren't always enough to keep the heat on during the Maine winters, or the telephone or the lights for that matter, but they did put food on the table. (Though a terrific cook, my mother-in-law sometimes had to serve fried dough to feed her family.) Neil went into the Coast Guard, and all the girls went to college. If it hadn't been for Social Security, I never would have met Franni in Boston my freshman year, deflowered her, and gotten her to renounce the Pope.

But I digress.

Bush's privatization plan had Franni on edge for months, and she read every article about it that she could find. When she read in *The Wall Street Journal* that, if Bush's plan passed, "only two or three firms" would wind up managing "the tens of billions of dollars that will pour into private accounts each year," and that one of those firms was the State Street Corporation, it rang a bell.

Sure enough, Franni dug up the August 1999 issue of the *Investment Dealer Digest*, an industry journal, which chronicled State Street's role as part of the coalition of "banks, insurance companies, and other institutions that will gain from providing such plans to the public."

> Besides making direct political contributions, various financial services firms and banks have financed think tanks, research projects and public-policy forums that promote privatization. State Street, which manages $485 billion in assets, including index funds, has been the most prominent.

Financing think tanks and research projects? Franni wondered if they had anything to do with the Cato Institute, which published the Leninist essay in the first place. The answer came in the next paragraph:

State Street has been a major financial backer to the Cato Institute, the libertarian think tank that has endorsed full-scale privatization of Social Security, with Cato officials even calling for a sale of federally owned parks to pay for the costs if necessary.

If the libertarian Leninists were wrong about the old people, at least they were right about the banks. And State Street wasn't the only business interest in their "coalition." By the spring of 2005, Karl Rove had assembled an armada of well-financed right-wing operatives to push the privatization agenda.

One star player was the United Seniors Association, a GOP astroturf[4] front group, whose board has, at times, included such luminaries as "Casino Jack" Abramoff. The group, which also goes by the name "USA Next," hired the guys who did the ads for the Swift Boat Vets to help them attack the AARP, which had called Social Security privatization "a threat to the retirement security of millions of Americans and their families." Charles Jarvis, a former Reagan official and USA Next's president, called the AARP "the boulder in the middle of the highway to personal savings accounts." And Jarvis knew how to deal with boulders. "We will be the dynamite that removes them."

Out of the gate, the dynamite took the form of an on-line ad exposing the AARP's "real agenda": opposing our troops and supporting gay marriage. This may have surprised some AARP members, millions of whom are veterans.

In all, pro-privatization forces aimed to raise as much as $100 million

---

[4]An astroturf group is a corporate-funded organization that tries to present itself as a grassroots group. Take the Alliance for Worker Retirement Security. Sounds like a worker group, doesn't it? But it isn't. It was created by the National Association of Manufacturers to push for private accounts. Its members now include the right-wing U.S. Chamber of Commerce, the very-right-wing Business Roundtable, and the nutcase-right-wing USA Next. Chuck Blahous, the guy who used to run it, left to become Bush's special assistant on Social Security.

USA Next rips the lid off the secret agenda of America's retired people.

for a scorched-earth air war to convince Americans that their safety net would be more effective if it were divided into tens of millions of little pieces. That way, every American could have his own private piece of netting.

All in all, the best explanation for Bush's total commitment to private accounts came, oddly enough, from someone other than Bush himself.

For a decade, Michael Tanner of the Cato Institute has been an omnipresent champion of private accounts, pushing them on virtually every TV network other than the Spice Channel. When *Los Angeles Times* columnist Michael Hiltzik interviewed him in February of 2005, Tanner was thrilled by the White House's commitment to the fight:

> I'm stunned at the level at which they're treating this. They're pulling out all the stops. It's going to be virtually like a presidential campaign.

Tanner was enough of a team player to change the name of the Cato Institute's "Project on Social Security Privatization" to the more politically palatable "Project on Social Security Choice" in 2002. Why let accurate terminology get in the way? But perhaps because of his euphoria about the impending victory, Tanner let his guard down about what this was really all about:

> In the end, this isn't a debate about the system's solvency in 2018
> or 2042. It's about whether you think the government should be
> in control of your retirement or people should take ownership
> and responsibility. That's why the debate is so intense—why
> would anyone get so excited about transition costs? This is
> about whether we redefine a relationship between individuals
> and government that we've had since 1935. We say that what was
> done was wrong then, and it's wrong now. Our position is that
> people need to be responsible for their own lives.[5]

Bingo. Thank you, Michael. You know, I *thought* that's what it was, but it was nice to hear it put so directly. It makes me feel less paranoid.

Oh, and by the way, Michael, I'm sorry the privatization campaign turned out so badly. I hate to break this to you—although I'm sure that, deep inside, you already know this—but your life's work is a bust.

It's easy in retrospect to think of the implosion of the privatization scheme as an inevitability. But back when the scope and intensity of Bush's Social Security push was just coming into view, Democrats felt that a defining battle for the soul of the country was being joined. The outcome was in question, and after the election, there was every reason to think Bush and Rove would find a way to hoodwink the public yet again.

But two things happened. Number one, our team pulled together. Number two, the more the American people learned about what Bush was sellin', the less they were buyin'.

Democrats may have been in the minority in both houses, but they knew that on an issue as explosive as this one, Republicans needed cover. Privatization was dead in the water unless it could be seen as bipartisan. If they could just get some conservative Democrats to sign on, they might be able to pull this one off. But they didn't get some. They got *one*. Out of the 245 Democrats in Congress, Bush managed to persuade only Allen Boyd, Democrat of Tallahassee, who joined Republican Congressman Jim

---

[5] This comes from Hiltzik's excellent book, *The Plot Against Social Security.*

Kolbe (R-AZ) in introducing HR 440, aptly named "The Bipartisan Retirement Security Act."

The day after the State of the Union Address in which the President called on America to "join together to strengthen and save Social Security," White House Press Secretary Scott McClellan worked his usual magic:

> **REPORTER:** Does the President feel as if he's able to persuade Democrats last night with his speech?
>
> **MCCLELLAN:** Some Democrats I don't think necessarily needed persuading about the need to strengthen Social Security. You have people like Congressman Boyd, who I've talked about recently, who has already signed on to legislation to address Social Security's—the insolvency facing Social Security.
>
> **REPORTER:** He's the only one in all of Congress, right? The only Democrat?
>
> **MCCLELLAN:** I don't know that I would describe it that way.

The press secretary also fielded some questions about the President's upcoming town hall–style "Social Security Conversations" in Fargo and Great Falls, Montana, which he promised would be "open and candid." When pressed about whether the ticketed events would truly be open and candid, McClellan attempted a similar gambit:

> **REPORTER:** Is every single person, both in the audience and on the panel, are they all supporters of the President's plan?
>
> **MCCLELLAN:** I don't know.

Scott McClellan, ladies and gentlemen.

At this point, the President's approval rating on Social Security was at

43 percent. He clearly had some folks to win over. And, by gosh, he was going to do it out there on the road. After Fargo and Great Falls, it was off to Omaha, where Bush would unleash the full force of both his bully pulpit and his legendary personal charm on behalf of his privatization agenda.

In his conversations with prescreened "regular people," the President displayed his famously dazzling ability to instantly connect with people from all walks of life:

> BUSH: Mary is with us. Mary Mornin. How are you, Mary?
>
> MORNIN: I'm fine.
>
> BUSH: Good. Okay, Mary, tell us about yourself.
>
> MORNIN: Okay, I'm a divorced, single mother with three grown, adult children. I have one child, Robbie, who is mentally challenged, and I have two daughters.
>
> BUSH: Fantastic.

It's not necessarily how I would have described Mary's situation. But that's why he's president and I'm just a comedian, author, and radio host. Without skipping a beat, Bush leavened the moment with some disingenuous pap:

> BUSH: First of all, you've got the hardest job in America, being a single mom.
>
> MORNIN: Thank you. (Applause.)

Moving on, Bush got back on script. And Mary was right there with him.

> BUSH: You and I are baby boomers.
>
> MORNIN: Yes, and I am concerned about—that the system stays the same for me.

BUSH: Right.

MORNIN: But I do want to see change and reform for my children because I realize that we will be in trouble down the road.

BUSH: It's an interesting point, and I hear this a lot—

Yeah. He heard that point a lot—in rehearsal.

BUSH: Will the system be the same for me? And the answer is, absolutely. One of the things we have to continue to clarify to people who have retired or near retirement.

Yes. It was part of the "over and over again" strategy. Buy off the over-55s. Now done with the heavy lifting, the President and Ms. Mornin participated in some lighthearted banter that brought gales of laughter from the carefully preselected crowd.

BUSH: —you fall in the near retirement.

MORNIN: Yes, unfortunately, yes. (Laughter.)

BUSH: Well, I don't know. I'm not going to tell your age, but you're one year younger than me, and I'm just getting started. (Laughter.)

MORNIN: Okay, okay.

BUSH: I feel great, don't you?

MORNIN: Yes, I do.

Only a grump like Ebenezer Scrooge or Bob Novak could fail to be charmed by such authentic, down-home ribbing. But then it was back to work. The President circled back to the crucial point:

BUSH: Thank you for asking that. You don't have to worry.

MORNIN: That's good, because I work three jobs and I feel like I contribute.

BUSH: You work three jobs?

MORNIN: Three jobs, yes.

I don't have a source on this, but I'm guessing that Mary was off script. Wildly groping for a way to keep things cheery, the President put the best spin on the predicament facing a single mom who had to work three jobs to support her mentally challenged adult child.

BUSH: Uniquely American, isn't it? I mean, that is fantastic that you're doing that. (Applause.) Get any sleep? (Laughter.)

MORNIN: Not much. Not much.

BUSH: Well, hopefully, this will help you get your sleep to know that when we talk about Social Security, nothing changes.

There. He stuck it. Nothing could throw him off message for long, not even the harsh realities of the working poor in the economy he presided over.

But somehow, even after a string of such impressive performances, the poll numbers didn't seem to be heading in the President's direction. In the three weeks following the State of the Union address, Bush's approval rating on his handling of Social Security plunged from the tepid 43 percent to a dismal 35 percent. Meanwhile, pro–Social Security forces were gaining steam. Democrats in Congress were holding firm, under the watchful supervision of the blog police, led by Commissioner Joshua Micah Marshall of TalkingPointsMemo.com, who mercilessly pummeled any Democrat who threatened to stray off the reservation. Also, Harry Reid and

Nancy Pelosi were cracking the whip with ruthless synchronicity. The AARP, MoveOn.org, the AFL-CIO—every major progressive group was mobilizing its members, running ads, rocking the vote, doing whatever it could.

Then there was the X-factor. A new power center in the progressive movement was making its presence felt in cars, offices, and construction sites across the land. Air America Radio, led by its award-winning flagship program, *The Al Franken Show*, was broadcasting the unalloyed truth about Bush's campaign of deception, and it was doing so with unmatched wit, including daily segments in which host Al Franken would say "Oy" with a comically exaggerated Jewish accent.

There was only one thing for the President to do. More road trips. On March 2, the Bush administration launched an unprecedented sixty-stop cross-country tour. It was a bold move, especially during a time of war, when one might think the commander in chief would want to stay close to his military advisers. Bush barnstormed the nation, traveling everywhere from Noblesville, Indiana, to Kalispell, Montana; from Muskegon, Michigan, to Smyrna, Georgia; from Las Cruces, New Mexico, to Yuba City, California. Wherever two hundred shills could be gathered, he pitched his deeply dishonest and horribly misguided scheme. He was unrelenting.

But Bush was punching a pillow. As hard as he worked, the sweatier he got, the less progress he made. The polling didn't improve. If anything, it slumped even further. George W. Bush was covered in feathers—and, though he tried to choke them back, bitter tears of disappointment.

Things were no better for nervous Republican congressmen who were traveling back to their districts for town hall meetings. If anything, they had it even worse, because unlike Bush, they didn't have the luxury of prescreening their audiences. Everywhere they went, Republican congressmen were confronted by their worst nightmare: a furious and well-informed citizenry.

Which isn't to say the Republican National Committee didn't declare victory. In a March 24 news release headlined "What They're Saying:

Social Security Town Halls—More Americans Support Call to Strengthen Social Security," the RNC offered "a glimpse of what is being said around the country," featuring brief quotes from local news stories. To the untrained and/or unskeptical eye, the quotes provided compelling evidence that the gloomy polls masked a groundswell of public support. But our friends at the Center for American Progress, whose eyes are both trained and skeptical, saw a smelly rat. The quotes in the RNC release had been plucked from news articles and stripped of their actual meaning. It was a time-honored RNC technique, one that you might call a "nuisance."

From Missouri, according to the RNC:

> Clif Smith, A Retiree From Joplin: "I Believe [Social Security] Needs Improved [Sic]." (Jeff Wells, "SS: Privatize Or Leave Alone?" *Joplin Globe*, 3/24/05)

The full quote from the *Joplin Globe*:

> "I believe it needs improved," said Clif Smith, a retiree from Joplin, at the AARP gathering. "But nothing of the nature of what is being talked about in Washington."
>
> Smith said he opposes private accounts because he thinks they would drain money from the trust fund, but he said the fund itself should own stock.

From Wyoming, RNC-style:

> "[Kimberly] Holloway Sees Advantages In Personal Accounts In That It Would Encourage More Savings And Financial Responsibility . . ." (Tom Morton, "What's A Mother To Do?" *Casper* [WY] *Star Tribune*, 3/24/05)

The full quote from the *Star Tribune*:

Holloway sees advantages in personal accounts in that it would encourage more savings and financial responsibility, she said.

But she's wary that this proposal feeds into the Bush administration's trend to encourage self-centered thinking away from considering the welfare of the general society, she said.

"We all should care because you don't know what (misfortune) will happen," Holloway said. "Don't fiddle with the social safety net."

And now my favorite, from North Dakota. Here's the RNC version:

Scott Savelkol, Recent Graduate From Dickinson State University: "Doing Nothing Is Not An Option." (Dave Kolpack, "Social Security Overhaul Discussed At Hearing In Fargo," The Associated Press, 3/23/05)

Okay, here's the real quote:

Scott Savelkol, who recently graduated from Dickinson State University, said he also opposes to private accounts [sic]. He would prefer lawmakers lift a $90,000 cap on wages taxed for Social Security.

"Doing nothing is not an option," Savelkol said.

Scott Savelkol was mostly right. Lifting the cap is a perfectly sensible idea. And private accounts, a terrible option. But as long as Bush was insisting that any Social Security bill would include private accounts, doing nothing was the only reasonable response. Because private accounts are actually worse than doing nothing.

But how can that possibly be? Bush, like all privatizers in government and the media, tells us over and over again that private accounts will give a higher rate of return than the Social Security system. Here's the President from that town meeting near Rochester:

> With your money in your payroll taxes—after all it's your money—is earning about a 1.8 percent rate of return over time in the Social Security system. You can do better than that. You can do better than that with T-bills, which have very little risk to them.

Wait a minute. The Trust Fund *is* T-bills! Treasury bonds. Remember? The worthless IOUs? They're treasury bonds! Bush saw them himself in Parkersburg, West Virginia.

How could an individual do better by investing in treasury bonds than Social Security does by investing in treasury bonds? The answer is a pretty fundamental one. It's called the legacy debt.

Here's how Social Security works. Workers pay payroll taxes. Some of that money turns into benefit checks for retirees (and survivors and people on disability) and what's left over goes into the Trust Fund, which is invested in T-bills.

You might say, "That's so unfair! Why am I paying for my parents' retirement?" Ah! But your parents paid for *their* parents' retirement. And your children will pay for *your* retirement.

"I see," you say. "It's kind of a grand intergenerational covenant. A 'social contract,' if you will. Wise."

But then your stupid, right-wing brother-in-law pipes up. "Why *is* that? Wouldn't it just be easier for every generation to take care of its own damn retirement?"

You're flummoxed and turn to me. But I'm ready for your idiot brother-in-law.

"Well, that would be nice, sort of. But it's too late now. Your parents already paid for their parents' retirement. If you don't pay for your parents, they'll starve. Or more likely, move in with you."

"I wouldn't want that," your moron Dittohead brother-in-law admits.

It's time to press my advantage. "The legacy debt is the money that each generation owes to the generation before. For example, my parents' generation went through the Depression and won World War II. For that reason, Tom Brokaw dubbed them the Greatest Generation."

"I've heard of them," says the moron.

The tension is slowly draining from the room. I sense that your brother-in-law and I are bonding. Coffee is offered, and accepted. I spend the next hour sitting at your kitchen table, explaining to your brother-in-law, who turns out to not be such a bad guy after all, that it makes no sense to compare the "rate of return" of Social Security to returns on any kind of investment. Because with Social Security you have to cover the legacy debt. If tomorrow you switched to an entirely private system, sure, you'd own some stocks, but your retired parents or grandparents would still be checking their mailboxes for those precious checks that keep them out of your spare bedroom. The Greatest Generation beat the Nazis. If we broke the social contract and stopped paying into Social Security, imagine what they'd do to us. Let's face it. We're kind of soft.

During the spring of 2005, conversations like this one took place across the country. It didn't dawn on the Bush administration that such conversations were hurting them instead of helping. On March 24, three weeks into the sixty-city tour, Treasury Secretary John Snow (whom the White House had desperately tried to get rid of, but kept when they realized they couldn't find anyone with any credibility who would be willing to toe their line)[6] pointed to these conversations as evidence of tremendous progress:

> **REPORTER:** You say there's a climate of ideas. Are they reaping some results beyond the personal retirement accounts?
>
> **SNOW:** Oh, I think absolutely, without any doubt, this is reaping rich rewards. All over America today, at lunch counters and

---

[6]In the *Washington Post's* November 29, 2004, write-up on Bush's plan to "tap some prominent replacements" for his economic team, Mike Allen reported that "one senior administration official said Treasury Secretary John W. Snow can stay as long as he wants, provided it is not very long."

dinner tables, breakfast tables, the evening news, the morning news, Social Security's being discussed.

In truth, Snow was underselling the case. Social Security was also being
discussed in breakfast nooks. At brunch. By vending machines. At water
coolers. With street vendors. At lap dance tables, sushi bars, and in dentist
chairs. (Not by the patients, obviously. More by cute dental hygienists.)

But in all these conversations, Americans were gaining newfound
appreciation for FDR's vision of retirement security for all. In a society
where every person faces greater and greater economic risk, Social Security represents our best ideals—the deeply held conviction that we're all in
this together.

Sometimes when I'm feeling unmoored, I reach for the collected letters of Dwight Eisenhower—a Republican of a different era, and a different stripe. Here's what Ike wrote about Social Security in a November 8,
1954, letter to his brother Edgar:

> Should any political party attempt to abolish Social Security,
> unemployment insurance, and eliminate labor laws and farm
> programs, you would not hear of that party again in our politi-
> cal history. There is a tiny splinter group, of course, that believes
> you can do these things. Among them are H. L. Hunt (you pos-
> sibly know his background),[7] a few other Texas oil millionaires,
> and an occasional politician or businessman from other areas.
>   Their number is negligible and they are stupid.

I think it's too easy an out to say that George W. Bush is stupid. But it
certainly was stupid of him to think that his election had anything to do
with a mandate for Social Security privatization. As he found out the hard

[7]In 1948, *Fortune* magazine called H. L. Hunt "the richest man in America." He was a
major funder of the far-right John Birch Society, which, among other things, supported
the abolition of Social Security and called Dwight Eisenhower a Communist.

way, George Bush was the *last* person Americans wanted tinkering with Social Security.

Bush didn't win the election because he was a Social Security president. He didn't win the election because he was a Restore Terri Schiavo's Feeding Tube president. He won because he convinced 51 percent of American voters that he, and only he, had what it took to be a war president.

12 Plan of Attack— Attack the Planning

In 1979, a young Pentagon staffer undertook the first thorough look at America's strategic interests in the Persian Gulf region. The fruit of his labors was a classified report entitled "Capabilities for Limited Contingencies in the Persian Gulf." The author, who inhabited the obscure position of deputy assistant secretary of defense for regional programs, made the case that the Gulf was important to the United States for very specific reasons:

> We and our major industrialized allies have a vital and growing stake in the Persian Gulf region because of our need for Persian Gulf oil and because events in the Persian Gulf affect the Arab-Israeli conflict.

The author was especially clear on that first reason, and went on to give it special emphasis:

The importance of Persian Gulf oil cannot easily be exaggerated.

Years later, the author of that study would make news once again by saying "fuck you" to me at a White House Correspondents Association dinner. But back in 1979, Paul Wolfowitz was much too small a fish to be invited to Washington's most glamorous black-tie gala.[1]

Wolfowitz's report raised some eyebrows. Most people who made it their business to worry about such things were worried that our oil supply might be cut off by a Soviet invasion of the Persian Gulf. Wolfowitz, however, placed his focus on a different concern: the possibility that "Iraq may in the future use her military forces against such states as Kuwait or Saudi Arabia."

It seemed far-fetched. Who would have the gall to order such an invasion? At the time, Iraq's president was the colorless Hassan al-Bakr. But a month and a day after Wolfowitz submitted his report, a dashing young Saddam Hussein engineered the resignation of al-Bakr, who was also his cousin, and consolidated his power over the country he called home.

Ever since the British created Iraq after World War I, the country had been riven by ethnic tensions between the majority Shia Muslim Arabs, the minority Sunni Muslim Arabs, and the Muslim, but non-Arab, Kurds, located mainly in the north. Saddam's Sunni regime crushed dissent with an iron fist, a fist that, on occasion, emitted poison gas.

A year after the release of Wolfowitz's report, Iraq was at war with neighboring Iran, whose ruler, Ayatollah Khomeini, a Shiite, was viewed by Saddam as a total Assaholah. This view was also held widely in the United States, where it formed the basis for much of America's Middle East policy and a popular line of novelty T-shirts. Shortly after Saddam's 1983 gassing of Iranian troops, President Reagan sent his Middle East envoy Donald Rumsfeld to hold friendly talks with Saddam about how to

[1] For a full account of my battle of wits with Paul Wolfowitz, see the chapter "Bush Can't Lose with the Clinton Military" in my #1 bestseller, *Lies, and the Lying Liars Who Tell Them.*

"wipe" the Assaholah. As Rumsfeld reported back to Reagan, the meeting was a "positive milestone in development of U.S.-Iraqi relations."

Rumsfeld was right. In the years afterward, the Reagan and H. W. Bush administrations authorized the sale to Iraq of precursors to chemical and biological weapons, including anthrax and bubonic plague, as well as conventional weapons such as Chilean cluster bombs. (At the same time, of course, Reagan was selling thousands of rockets to Iran. That sounds bad, until you consider that he *needed* to sell those arms to Iran in order to illegally fund the Contras in Nicaragua. So don't be so quick to judge.)

The 1988 gassing of thousands of the aforementioned Kurds hardly dimmed the enthusiasm of the two Republican administrations. In fact, U.S. military intelligence actually expanded its contributions to the Butcher of Baghdad after the gas attack. But all of that came to an abrupt end when Wolfowitz's prophecy came to fruition. On August 2, 1990, Iraq invaded Kuwait. That put Saddam Hussein in control of 20 percent of the world's crude oil reserves. The love affair between the Republican right and the Baathist ultraright was as over as Brad and Jen.[2]

President Bush, father of President Bush and Governor Bush and son of Senator Bush, assembled a mighty coalition to push back the aggressor and reclaim Kuwait's oil for America and its allies. In almost all regards, the war was a huge success. As the remnants of Saddam's Republican Guard retreated, George H. W. Bush decided to keep his word to his allies in the coalition not to march to Baghdad.

Bush explained his reasoning in a 1999 speech to veterans of the first Gulf War:

> Whose life would be on my hands as the commander in chief because I, unilaterally, went beyond the international law, went beyond the stated mission, and said we're going to show our macho? "We're going into Baghdad. We're going to be an occu-

[2] At the time of this writing, Brad Pitt and Jennifer Aniston are on the outs. It is my hope that they will one day get back together, because, according to an article I read, she's heartbroken.

pying power—America in an Arab land—with no allies at our side." It would have been disastrous.

Paul Wolfowitz understood his point. As Wolfowitz wrote in an essay published in 1997:

> A new regime would have become the United States' responsibility. Conceivably, this could have led the United States into a more or less permanent occupation of a country that could not govern itself, but where the rule of a foreign occupier would be increasingly resented.

Bush did keep the pressure on Saddam by encouraging the Shias in the south and the Kurds in the north to rise up against the Sunni dictator. But when they did, Bush left them high and dry. And dead. You see, Saddam was still useful to the United States in order to keep Iran in check. As Colin Powell wrote in his autobiography, "Our practical intention was to leave Baghdad enough power to survive as a threat to an Iran that remained bitterly hostile to the United States." So the Bush administration allowed the Iraqi regime to mow down hundreds of thousands of Shias and Kurds from helicopter gunships before establishing "no-fly zones" and imposing rigorous sanctions.[3]

The sanctions allowed U.N. inspectors to poke around and discover a surprisingly advanced nuclear weapons program. Saddam, it seems, was an even bigger Assaholah than the Ayatollah.

But at long last, he had been brought to heel. He was no longer a threat to anybody other than his own people. As much as Saddam could brutalize, rape, and lethally neglect Iraqis, he couldn't hurt anybody else. He was like a rabid pit bull on a choke chain that extended only to the border of his squalid, blood-drenched little yard.

---

[3] The dead were buried in mass graves that would later provide retroactive justification for our own invasion in 2003.

George W. Bush came to office determined to screw the pooch. I think I know what that means. Point is, he was psyched about overthrowing Saddam. Where did President Bush, who had no opinion at all about most foreign policy issues, acquire his enthusiasm for regime change? Same way he acquired everything. From his friends. Friends inherited from his father.

One of them was Paul Wolfowitz. While he had recognized the folly of taking Baghdad at the end of the first Gulf War, Wolfowitz had also regretted how the United States had abandoned the Shias and Kurds in their hour of getting slaughtered. As Saddam remained in power during the Clinton presidency, Wolfowitz grew increasingly miffed, and began calling for regime change.

But what about the issue he raised before—that if Saddam were kicked out, someone would have to replace him? Luckily, Wolfowitz and the neo-cons had found the perfect guy, a guy who could run the country and eliminate the need for a costly, prolonged, and maybe even bloody U.S. occupation. Ahmed Chalabi, the smooth-talking, power-hungry, CIA-backed, multi-multi-millionaire mathematician, who had left Iraq when he was just twelve years old, was, according to Chalabi, wildly popular in his native country. America could merely hand him the reins and never again worry about its interests in the Gulf. Ahmed Chalabi was the missing piece in the Iraq puzzle.

In 1997, Wolfowitz and a coterie of neo-cons formed the Project for a New American Century, funded by money from Richard Mellon Scaife and his nutty, ultra-right-wing friends, the Olins and the Bradleys. Perhaps you'll recognize some of PNAC's current and former members: Donald Rumsfeld, Dick Cheney, Richard Perle, Richard Armitage, John Bolton, Lewis "Scooter" Libby, and its intellectual furnace, Dan Quayle. All would become key players in the George W. Bush administration, with the mysterious exception of Quayle.

In 1998, after Saddam kicked the U.N. weapons inspectors out of Iraq,

PNAC sent a letter to then-President William Clinton, urging that "removing Saddam Hussein and his regime from power . . . needs to become the aim of American foreign policy." Clinton complied, but not in the way they wanted. He declared "regime change" to be the new policy of his administration, but he didn't invade. Instead, he launched a series of targeted bombing strikes, which, as Bush's handpicked weapons inspectors would later confirm in the Duelfer Report, knocked out all that remained of Saddam's atrophied WMD capacity. The threat to America was obliterated once and for all, even though Saddam was still in place. The neo-cons were enraged. It was so Clinton.

But two years later, with a new president occupying the Oval Office, a president who had traveled overseas only three times in his life, the neo-cons could do more than just write letters. They could plan and execute the invasion of Iraq themselves.

They got to work right away. In Ron Suskind's *The Price of Loyalty: George W. Bush, the White House, and the Education of Paul O'Neill*, which chronicled the former treasury secretary's encounter with the impenetrable ideological clique at the center of the Bush administration, O'Neill was startled to discover that "Mideast Policy," the designated topic of the first National Security Council meeting, referred not to the Arab-Israeli conflict, but to a possible preemptive attack on Iraq. The January 30, 2001, meeting ended with the President asking Rumsfeld to "examine our military options" and see "how it might look" to put U.S. ground forces into north and south Iraq.

Within a month, the NSC principals—including Rice, Rumsfeld, and Cheney—were examining maps of Iraqi oil fields and lists of foreign oil companies that might be interested in divvying them up. Of course, before the divvying could take place, a certain Saddam Hussein would have to be removed from the picture. As Suskind wrote, channeling O'Neill:

> Already by February, the talk was mostly about logistics. Not the *why*, but the *how* and *how quickly*.

In retrospect, you have to admire these guys for thinking, *before 9/11*, that they'd be able to drag their countrymen into a preemptive war against Iraq. I can't for the life of me imagine how they thought that would have worked.

But when the buildings fell on September 11, the neo-cons saw their opportunity. Even though intelligence linking Osama bin Laden to the attacks started flowing immediately, Rumsfeld told his aides that very day to start looking at ways to attack Saddam.

In the chaotic hours following the strike, our resolute president resolutely allowed himself to be ferried around in Air Force One, hopscotching the country in order to evade any Iraqi terrorists that might (a) exist and (b) be trying to kill him.

But by September 12, Bush was back in the saddle. At a White House meeting of top officials, counterterrorism chief Richard Clarke was surprised at the lack of singular focus on the perpetrators of the previous day's mass murder. Don Rumsfeld was concerned about the lack of good bombing targets in Afghanistan, and suggested bombing Iraq, which he said had better targets. Clarke thought Rumsfeld was joking. As Clarke wrote in his book *Against All Enemies*:

> Having been attacked by al Qaeda, for us now to go bombing Iraq in response would be like our invading Mexico after the Japanese attacked us at Pearl Harbor.

But Rumsfeld was deadly serious.

President Bush disagreed with Rumsfeld, but for a very different reason than Clarke. He thought we needed to do more than bomb Iraq. We needed to change the government.

Later that day, the President took Clarke and some of his aides aside. "Go back over everything, everything," Bush told them. "See if Saddam did this. See if he's linked in any way."

Clarke was incredulous:

"But, Mr. President, al Qaeda did this."

"I know, I know. But—see if Saddam was involved. Just look. I want to know any shred—"

"Absolutely, we will look—again." I was trying to be more respectful, more responsive. "But you know, we have looked several times for state sponsorship of al Qaeda and not found any real linkages to Iraq. Iran plays a little, as does Pakistan, and Saudi Arabia, Yemen."

"Look into Iraq, Saddam," the President said testily and left us.

We can't know whether Bush made the decision to invade Iraq that very moment, whether he had made the decision years before, or whether he was still months away from deciding to pull the trigger. If we believe President Bush, and why would we, he wouldn't make up his mind until just before the invasion. As he told the nation on March 8, 2003, "We are doing everything we can to avoid war in Iraq." But even though the administration didn't feel the American people were entitled to know whether they were going to war, the Bush team did let the British government in on the secret.

On July 23, 2002, Prime Minister Tony Blair met with his top diplomatic, military, and intelligence advisers at 10 Downing Street, the secret headquarters of the British government. The minutes of the meeting, which were leaked to the British press in May 2005, offer a valuable window into the state of play at the time. One paragraph describes the report of "C," head of British intelligence. James Bond fans will know "C" as "M." Not to be confused with "Q," the gadget guy, who in real life is known as "P." To the best of our knowledge, "P" was not present.

Here's how the minutes describe what C, whose real name is Sir Richard Dearlove,[4] told the group:

---

[4] Unlike Robert Novak, I'm not blowing anyone's cover. I found this on Wikipedia.

C reported on his recent talks in Washington. There was a perceptible shift in attitude. Military action was now seen as inevitable. Bush wanted to remove Saddam, through military action, justified by the conjunction of terrorism and WMD. But the intelligence and facts were being fixed around the policy.

The fixing of the facts was proceeding apace. All over official Washington, intelligence was being cherry-picked, stovepiped, and twisted by the administration, or when necessary, manufactured out of whole cloth by the humming workshop of Ahmed Chalabi's Iraqi National Congress. But as C reported, there was one aspect of the war preparation that was getting hind tit:

There was little discussion in Washington of the aftermath after military action.

The July 23 minutes were only the first of what would prove to be a Klondike of "Downing Street Memos," secret documents that exposed the United Kingdom's growing agitation about unsettling events unfolding in its former colony. C wasn't the only Brit who expressed concern about the Bush administration's blithe attitude toward postwar planning.

In a March 14 memo, Blair's foreign policy adviser David Manning ("Z") reported to the prime minister on recent meetings with Condi Rice and the National Security Council. "From what she said, Bush has yet to find the answers to the big questions," Manning wrote. One of these questions was, "What happens on the morning after?"

Manning had no confidence that the answer would be found. "I think there is a real risk that the administration underestimates the difficulties. They may agree that failure isn't an option, but this doesn't mean that they will avoid it."

By July, things had hardly improved. According to a memo preparing Blair for the July 23 meeting with C, Z, R, and a group of key advisers collectively known as "the Vowels," "the U.S. Government's military planning is proceeding apace," but "little thought has been given to . . . the aftermath and how to shape it."

In fact, unbeknownst to the British government, a great deal of thought *had* been given to the aftermath of an invasion. The trouble was that the people doing the thinking weren't President Bush, Donald Rumsfeld, and Dick Cheney, who were too busy fixing the intelligence and facts around the policy to read the briefing papers on postwar plans.

The myth that there was no planning for a postwar Iraq was accepted by nearly everyone in the year following the invasion. But it was conclusively debunked by James Fallows in his *Atlantic Monthly* cover article "Blind Into Baghdad," which I believe to be the best article ever published.

As Fallows showed, no less than five separate major studies of how to handle the inevitable postwar challenges were conducted in the lead-up to the March 2003 invasion. Of the five, five were ignored by the administration. Though there is no way to know for certain, had a sixth study been conducted, it seems almost certain that it, too, would have been ignored.

These studies were conducted by organizations that one might expect to know a thing or two about war planning, such as the Army War College, the CIA, and the U.S. Department of State. Certain themes emerged, all of them consistent with common sense. The importance of "an initial and broad-based commitment to law and order," for example. Prevent looting. Secure the nation's borders to block foreign fighters from coming in. Get key services like electricity and clean water up as quickly as possible. Guard weapons caches. Handle the demobilization of the Iraqi Army with great care. That was a big one. As the State Department's Future of Iraq Project noted in a model of understatement, "The decommissioning of hundreds of thousands of trained military personnel . . . could create social problems."

Sure, that was a lot to do. But it was doable if we sent "something on the order of several hundred thousand soldiers," as Army Chief of Staff General Eric Shinseki recommended in testimony to Congress.

If you're curious why Iraq is in the crapper, it's because every one of these eminently reasonable recommendations fell not on deaf ears, but on ears into which fingers had been deliberately inserted.

Why did the Bush administration insert its fingers into its ears? And was the humming absolutely necessary? It was. For two reasons. First, Chalabi. He had assured the Bushies that the postwar would be the easy part. He and his associates had explained that we would be greeted with sweets and flowers, leaving out the crucial modifier, "exploding." After that, Chalabi would take over—and, presto chango, Iraq would be a U.S.-friendly Jeffersonian democracy, an Australia with oil. There would be no need to plow through page after page of boring electrical grids and sewerage maps. Ahmed Chalabi, who hadn't been in Baghdad since 1956, would take care of all of that.

The second reason why the Bush administration ignored the postwar planning tells you everything you need to know about why they shouldn't be running a small-town hardware store, much less the world's only remaining superpower. Here it is:

George W. Bush and his inner circle do not believe in objective reality.

They do believe in objective moral truth, which they and a few enlightened others, like Bob Jones III and James Dobson, have ready access to. But when it comes to *facts*, they're relativists.

To justify the war, they decided upon a set of terrifying "facts": that Saddam was poised to slip Osama a suitcase containing a nuclear bomb coated in anthrax. A second set of terrifying facts, which inconveniently were true, they rejected. Because those facts didn't fit. Since those facts suggested that the war and its aftermath would be difficult, they didn't want to hear about them.

To those of us who believe in objective reality, planning for every possible scenario is something you should do even if you're in favor of a war. In fact, it's something that you do *especially* if you're for a war. But for them, anyone who seemed to be contradicting their message of a cakewalk, followed by sweets and flowers, followed by the free and democratic election of the handpicked Ahmed Chalabi—anyone questioning that story wasn't merely the bearer of bad news. He was an enemy. Facts, like nations, were either for us or against us.

A senior Bush adviser summarized the Bush team's way of thinking to journalist Ron Suskind in the summer of 2002:

> The aide said that guys like me were "in what we call the reality-based community," which he defined as people who "believe that solutions emerge from your judicious study of discernible reality." I nodded and murmured something about enlightenment principles and empiricism. He cut me off. "That's not the way the world really works anymore," he continued. "We're an empire now, and when we act, we create our own reality. And while you're studying that reality—judiciously, as you will—we'll act again, creating other new realities, which you can study too, and that's how things will sort out. We're history's actors . . . and you, all of you, will be left to just study what we do."

Doesn't that sound like the kind of speech a Bond villain would make just before falling into his own shark tank? Bad screenwriters get paid good money to come up with monologues like that. But this is real. The Bush inner circle sees the world as having spectators and participants. Almost everybody—you, me, Scott McClellan—is a mere spectator, trapped in the reality-based universe. The participants, "history's actors," aren't constrained by the rules of evidence and consequence that govern us mere mortals. And there aren't many participants. As an administration official who'd been involved in the planning for the Iraq war told James Fallows:

> There was absolutely no debate in the normal sense. There are only six or eight of them who make the decisions, and they only talk to each other. And if you disagree with them in public, they'll come after you, the way they did with Shinseki.

Once your divorce from reality is final, you can choose whatever fantasy world it is you want to inhabit. Bush seems to have chosen the world of B-movie heroics. In Bob Woodward's *Plan of Attack*, which could easily be the title of the movie George Bush thinks he's starring in, we see Bush fully inhabiting his role with Stanislavskian élan:

> "Are you with me on this?" the President asked [Colin Powell]. "I think I have to do this. I want you with me."
>
> "I'll do the best I can," Powell answered. "Yes, sir, I will support you. I'm with you, Mr. President."
>
> "Time to put your war uniform on," the President said to the former general.

Powell, of course, was the only one in the inner circle who actually owned a war uniform. Which perhaps explained why his attitude to the entire enterprise was lukewarm.

It would not be that long before the President would put on a war uniform of his own (a flight suit with a noticeably bulbous codpiece), and strut manfully across the deck of the USS *Abraham Lincoln*. It would be the first time Bush had worn a flight suit since the years, months, or perhaps only days he spent in the Alabama Air National Guard.

George W. Bush's B movie wasn't the only thing showing at the imaginary multiplex where he seemed to spend so much of his time. There was also Donald Rumsfeld's movie, *Plan of Attack II: The Army You Got*. Here, the secretary of defense (Donald Rumsfeld) informs the Saudi ambassador, Prince Bandar (Prince Bandar) about the planned invasion of Iraq:

> Rumsfeld looked Bandar in the eye. "You can count on this," Rumsfeld said, pointing to the map. "You can take that to the bank."

The subsequent rise in the price of oil would give Bandar many reasons to visit the bank.

"Saddam, this time, will be out period?" Bandar asked skeptically. "What will happen to him?"

In Dick Cheney's movie, *Plan of Attack III: Sticking to the Plan*, it was the vice president who had all the good lines. "Prince Bandar," Cheney intoned, "once we start, Saddam is toast."

As opposed to *the* toast, as in "the toast of the terrorist community." That role is currently being played by Osama bin Laden, who fell out of favor at the White House when he proved difficult to capture.

A movie entitled *The Judicious Study of Discernible Reality* would not have sold a lot of tickets in Bush's fantasy multiplex. "Take that to the bank!" "Saddam is toast!" "Put on your war uniform!" That's leadership. That's decisiveness. In *Plan of Attack*, you didn't hear lines like "Putting on your war uniform would help to convince Saddam that we're serious about backing up the U.N. weapons inspectors, thereby possibly averting a horrible war."

There's also no scene where Bush meets with his advisers and says, "Give me twelve reasons to do this and twelve reasons not to." No meeting where he asks one team of intelligence analysts to make the case that Saddam did have weapons of mass destruction, and another team to make the case that he didn't.[5] No assessment of the worst-case scenario. No consideration of "opportunity costs"—all the things we could have done with the resources that would be poured into the sand in Iraq.

Bush didn't even consult the only U.S. president who had fought a war against Saddam Hussein. It wasn't that Bush didn't have his own father's phone number. "I can't remember a moment where I said to myself, 'Maybe he can help me make the decision,' " he told Woodward. "He was the wrong father to appeal to in terms of strength. There is a higher father that I appealed to."

Prayer is a perfectly legitimate supplement to a decision-making

---

[5] If I had been president, I would have then asked the two teams of analysts to switch sides and argue the opposite positions. That's how we did it in high school debate.

process, but not a substitute. And when Bush talked to God, he wasn't even asking *Him* whether or not to go in. All he seemed to want from the Almighty was the fortitude to continue looking resolute.

Freed from the constraints of reality, everything for the Bush team was just politics. The only requirement of victory is convincing 50 percent plus one of the voters, or five Supreme Court justices, to pick your story line over the other guy's. That was the strategy in 2004, when Bush convinced a bare majority of Americans that the only way to protect their children from nuclear annihilation was to reject the flip-flopper for the unyielding man of God. Bush and his advisers approached the war with the same mind-set. The German military theorist Carl von Clausewitz famously said that "war is politics conducted by other means." For Bush, war was politics conducted by the same means. Politics.

Relying on fantasy was a bad way to win an election. But clinging to a fantasy when you're leading a country to war is inexcusable.

But that's how they did it. In the months leading up to the war, the Bush administration tried to sell its version of reality to a skeptical America. Earlier in this book, I described the administration's lies regarding Iraq's ties to al Qaeda and its perilously advanced WMD arsenal. That was all to convince the public that not going to war would be dangerous. The other half of their case was that attacking Iraq would be easy, cheap, quick, and fun. Fun, in a gee-whiz, shock-and-awe kind of way.

Easy? Invading and occupying an Arab country of 25 million people? The most militarized country in the region? And a country where the majority Shia still hated us for double-crossing them in 1991, and where the Sunni had nothing to gain from a democracy in which they'd be at the mercy of the ethnic groups they'd been oppressing for decades?

A cinch.

"My belief is we will, in fact, be greeted as liberators," Dick Cheney said on *Meet the Press* on March 16, 2003. Wide-eyed Tim Russert, uncharacteristically, followed up with a skeptical question:

> RUSSERT: If your analysis is not correct, and we're not treated as liberators, but as conquerors, and the Iraqis begin to resist, particularly in Baghdad, do you think the American people are prepared for a long, costly, and bloody battle with significant American casualties?

> CHENEY: Well, I don't think it's likely to unfold that way, Tim, because I really do believe that we will be greeted as liberators.

He'd already said that. But that was part of the strategy. If you want someone to remember something, you have to say it over and over again. That's the way to get an idea to sink in: Say it over and over again. If you're serious about getting your point across, say it over and over again. That's the only way to get people to remember your point. Say it over and over again. Then they'll remember it.

Cheney again put this theory into practice only seconds later:

> CHENEY: The read we get on the people of Iraq is there is no question but what they want to get rid of Saddam Hussein and they will welcome as liberators the United States when we come to do that.

Exactly how many liberators were the Iraqis going to be greeting? That was the question, not just for Iraqi florists and candy shops, but for the Pentagon. Would seventy-five thousand liberators be enough to do the job, as Donald Rumsfeld believed? Or would it take the hundreds of thousands of liberators that Army Chief of Staff General Eric Shinseki had calculated were necessary?

Testifying before Congress, Shinseki had been asked how many troops would be needed for a postwar occupation. Shinseki replied:

> **SHINSEKI:** Something on the order of several hundred thousand soldiers are probably, you know, a figure that would be required. We're talking about post-hostilities control over a piece of geography that's fairly significant, with the kinds of ethnic tensions that could lead to other problems. And so it takes a significant ground-force presence to maintain a safe and secure environment, to ensure that people are fed, that water is distributed, all the normal responsibilities that go along with administering a situation like this.

Clearly, Shinseki hadn't gotten the memo that Chalabi's Iraq wouldn't need to be secured by U.S. troops. Or if he had gotten the memo, he'd sure done a bad job of internalizing it. Shinseki, a thirty-eight-year military officer and proud member of the reality-based community, had reached his estimate using a study by the Army War College and his own experiences in the Balkans. His dangerous and unwelcome attempt to inject reality into the Iraq debate had to be met, unlike Iraq itself, with overwhelming force—as well as an exit strategy. The latter was easy. Shinseki "resigned" a few months later. (There is no record of whether or not the door struck him on the ass on the way out.) As for the overwhelming force, the Pentagon's top civilian officials led the charge against the military brass.

"What is, I think, reasonably certain," Donald Rumsfeld told reporters two days later, "is the idea that it would take several hundred thousand U.S. forces is far from the mark."

Paul Wolfowitz, testifying to Congress the same day, concurred that Shinseki's assessment was off the mark.

> We can say with reasonable confidence that the notion of hundreds of thousands of American troops is way off the mark.

Wolfowitz knew the power of the "over and over again" approach. In the same testimony:

> Some of the higher-end predictions that we have been hearing recently, such as the notion that it will take several hundred thousand U.S. troops to provide stability in post-Saddam Iraq, are wildly off the mark.

As it turned out, Shinseki was wildly *on* the mark. It was Wolfowitz who was wildly off the mark. Not only on troop strength, but also on the financial cost of the war.

According to Wolfowitz, it was gonna be cheap. In fact, the war would pay for itself. Wolfowitz explained in that day's testimony that Iraq had "$15 billion to $20 billion a year in oil exports," that there were "I believe, over $10 billion" in an escrow account run by the U.N., and that even Saddam's personal bank account had "I don't know how many billions." It was just a matter of getting hold of Saddam's ATM card and turning him over to Lynndie England to get the PIN out of him.

"There's a lot of money there," Wolfowitz marveled, "and to assume that we're going to pay for it is just wrong."

As Wolfowitz summed it up to a House committee a few weeks later, "we're dealing with a country that can really finance its own reconstruction, and relatively soon."

The party line was firm. Here's Andrew Natsios, the Bush administration's chief for international development at the State Department, appearing on *Nightline*. To be fair, Natsios didn't paint the war as quite the financial opportunity that Wolfowitz had described. Still, the price tag for the reconstruction of Iraq was both attractively low and extremely precise: exactly $1.7 billion.

> **KOPPEL:** I want to be sure that I understood you correctly. You're saying the, the top cost for the U.S. taxpayer will be $1.7 billion. No more than that?

NATSIOS: For the reconstruction.

Ted Koppel tried again.

KOPPEL: As far as reconstruction goes, the American taxpayer will not be hit for more than $1.7 billion no matter how long the process takes?

NATSIOS: That is our plan and that is our intention.

An incredulous Koppel tried a different angle.

KOPPEL: If it's cost-plus, in other words, if they come back to you in another six months or in another year and say, gee, you know, we gave you the best estimate we could but here's what it ended up costing and it ended up costing double what we said it was gonna cost—

NATSIOS: Oh, no, no, we have, that's the amount of money we have to spend. We're gonna do less if it costs more than that, because we have an appropriation, we're gonna go within the limits of the appropriation.

KOPPEL: But what you are saying is, maybe, maybe fewer tasks will be accomplished. The amount of money, however, is gonna be the same?

NATSIOS: That's correct. 1.7 billion is the limit on reconstruction for Iraq.

Like all encounters with the press, this interchange was posted on a government website, but was taken off when it was proven to be embarrassing and crazy. Natsios still has his position at State. However, he has not yet been awarded the Presidential Medal of Freedom.

Natsios understood his job. Not so Lawrence Lindsey, director of Bush's National Economic Council, who had pulled a Shinseki[6] while talking to *The Wall Street Journal* the previous fall. After Lindsey committed the unpardonable sin of telling the *Journal* that the war could cost up to $200 billion, in retrospect an optimistic underestimate, he was fired. "Larry just didn't get it," an anonymous administration official (wild guess: Karl Rove) told the *Washington Post.*

Natsios, Wolfowitz, and the anonymous administration official were wildly off the mark. As of this writing, the war has cost $183 billion. As of the writing I'm planning to do next week, the war will have cost $184.5 billion. See how this works?

Of course, if we cut and run by the time this book hits the shelves, maybe the whole disaster will slide in under the $200 billion mark. On the other hand, if the nonpartisan Center for Strategic and Budgetary Assessments is correct, the cost of the Iraq War could exceed $700 billion. That's more than the cost, in current dollars, of either the Korean War ($430 billion) or the Vietnam War ($600 billion), and without the prospect of the clear and decisive victories we achieved in those conflicts.

How much you think the war is going to cost depends on how long you think we're going to be there. On February 7, 2003, Donald Rumsfeld said, "It could last six days, six weeks. I doubt six months." Of course, he was talking about how long it would take to topple Saddam, not how long an occupation might last. If someone asked Rumsfeld that now, you might imagine he'd say "six years, six decades. I doubt six centuries." You might imagine that, but you'd be wrong. This June, he said on Fox that the insurgency might last "five, six, eight, ten, twelve years." But before the war, no one in the administration wanted to acknowledge the possibility of a messy aftermath. That would be Chalabi's problem. We'd be invading Iran by then.

---

[6]This was in September 2002, long before Shinseki pulled *his* Shinseki.

So at the same time America was presented with a nightmarish vision of what could happen if we didn't go in (millions infected with smallpox before being mercifully vaporized by nuclear bombs), it was also presented with a dreamlike picture of what would happen if we did invade: instant victory, rivers of oil, chocolate-covered flowers. Not to mention the peace of mind that comes from eliminating the people who attacked us on 9/11. This was going to be such a good war that it would make World War II look like World War I.[7]

In the inner sanctum of Bush's war cabinet, not everyone was buying into this having-your-cakewalk-and-eating-it-too scenario. Although Colin Powell had put on his war uniform, he had not taken off his thinking cap. The Old Soldier didn't think things were going to be as quick, cheap, and easy as the rest of the gang. Powell seemed reluctant to entrust Iraq's postwar fate to the shady Chalabi. The Iraqi exile leader was regarded with distrust by both the State Department and the CIA after feeding them inaccurate intelligence and wildly exaggerating his own popularity. Furthermore, Chalabi had been convicted in absentia of thirty-one counts of embezzlement, theft, misuse of depositors' funds, and currency speculation after he fled Jordan in the wake of the collapse of the bank he had founded there. In Powell's view, the mere fact that he would be better than Saddam Hussein was hardly a sufficient qualification to recommend Chalabi as the next leader of Iraq.

Until the time that a democratic, self-sufficient Iraq was able to handle its own affairs, Powell felt that the person most likely to wind up holding the bag in Iraq was his boss, George Bush. It was the Pottery Barn Rule. "You break it, you own it," Powell argued. Once the United States invaded Iraq—"broke it"—it would fall to the United States to govern ("own") that country and its 25 million people, give or take however many we

---

[7]Most of you are too young to remember World War I, but that's where poison gas got its bad name.

killed in the invasion. To the rest of the inner circle, invoking the Pottery Barn Rule was a namby-pamby, passive-aggressive way to argue against the war itself. For Powell, it was meant as a reminder that with victory would come great responsibility.[8]

But Bush didn't get it. Or, more likely, didn't want to get it. Even when they were presented in the simplistic form of the Pottery Barn Rule, Bush couldn't or wouldn't grasp the full dimensions of the responsibilities he was about to undertake.

Bush's failure to look reality full in the face extended to even the most basic facts about the country he had chosen to invade. There is one anecdote in particular that I keep coming back to. David Phillips, a former State Department official, tells the story in his book, *Losing Iraq: Inside the Postwar Reconstruction Fiasco*. Phillips was in charge of the Democratic Principles Working Group of the Future of Iraq Project, where he convened a variety of Iraqi exiles to envision how Iraq would be governed after the fall of Saddam. The most prominent exile in the group was Brandeis professor Kanan Makiya, one of Ahmed Chalabi's chief deputies. Makiya was the man who had famously told Bush that Americans would be greeted in Iraq with sweets and flowers. In late January 2003, less than eight weeks before the war began, Phillips wrote:

> Kanan was invited to watch the Super Bowl at the White House;
> he told me later that he had to explain to the President of the
> United States the differences between Arab Shi'a, Arab Sunnis,
> and Kurds.

---

[8]What Colin Powell didn't know was that there is no such rule at Pottery Barn. If you break something at Pottery Barn, you might feel bad. But you don't have to pay for it. I learned this the easy way. By calling Pottery Barn and talking to their director of public relations, Leigh Oshirak. She told me in no uncertain terms that if you accidentally break one of their pieces of pottery, or whatever it is they sell in their barns (I've never been; that's Franni's department), corporate parent Williams-Sonoma, Inc., is happy to mark it out of stock and pick up the full cost of the item.

I talked to David Phillips over breakfast and asked what Makiya had meant by this. Did he mean that Bush didn't understand the fine points of their cultural and religious differences? No.

> PHILLIPS: What Makiya told me was that he didn't know there *was* a difference. That among Iraqis there were Arab Shia, Arab Sunni, and Kurds. [9]

> ME: He didn't know that there existed those three groups?

> PHILLIPS: That's right. This is pretty basic. You're going to go to war in a country, you should know who lives there.

Remember, Bush is a man who ran for president in 2000 on a pledge to "usher in an era of responsibility." In his acceptance speech at the Republican Convention that year, he was specific. "To lead this nation to a responsibility era," he said, "that President himself must be responsible."

Once Powell had told Bush that he would be responsible for Iraq and its people, not to mention our troops as well, you would think that Bush would have done everything in his power to make sure he was doing the right thing.

In a *Frontline* report on the 2004 presidential election, Richard Clarke contrasted the way in which the last two presidents processed information. Of Bush, Clarke said:

> He doesn't reach out, typically, for a lot of experts. He has a very narrow, regulated, highly regimented set of channels to get advice. One of the first things we were told was "Don't write a lot of briefing papers. And don't make the briefing papers

---

[9] When I e-mailed Makiya about this, he denied the story. David Phillips stands by his account.

very long." Because this President is not a reader. He likes oral briefings, and he likes them from the national security adviser, the White House chief of staff, and the vice president. He's not into big meetings. And he's not into big briefing books.

With Clinton, it was different:

The contrast with Clinton was that Clinton would hold a meeting with you. And he read your briefing materials. But also, having read your briefing materials, he would have gone out and found other materials somehow. He would have directly called people up. Not people in the government, necessarily. Experts, outside the government. Or he would have found magazine articles, or—or books on the subject. So that, when you were briefing him, frequently you had the feeling that he knew more about the subject than you did. And he wasn't showing off. He had just done his homework.

We know George W. Bush is not an intellectually curious person. But he's president. And when he was about to send American men and women to war, it was his responsibility to suck it up and do the reading. It was all there for him. All he had to do was care enough to look at it.

Anthony Zinni, a four-star general who as commander in chief of the U.S. Central Command held the same job as Norman Schwarzkopf and Tommy Franks, summed up the consequences of Bush's style of leadership:

In the lead-up to the Iraq war and its later conduct, I saw at a minimum, true dereliction, negligence and irresponsibility; at worst, lying, incompetence and corruption.

Every day our soldiers and Marines are paying for choices made not just during the war, but before it. And President Bush still refuses to hold anyone accountable for prewar failures—least of all, himself.

At 5:30 A.M. Baghdad time on March 20, 2003, the first Tomahawk missile slammed into a bunker where Saddam Hussein wasn't. Bush's war on terrorism had entered its most irrational phase yet.

13 | Mission Redacted

Off the Coast of San Diego—May 1, 2003

"Remember, Mr. President; don't touch anything when we're landing, sir."

Commander John "Skip" Lussier was concerned. The President had tried manning the controls for a moment after takeoff and had almost rolled the S-3B Viking.

"I'm a trained pilot, Commander," Bush said churlishly. "And I outrank you."

"I know, sir. But seriously, Mr. President, a carrier landing is very precise. Really. Just keep your hands to yourself. Please."

"Can I at least lower the gear?"

"No!"

Lussier immediately regretted snapping at his commander in chief.

"No, sir," the pilot corrected himself.

The President fidgeted in his seat for a moment, and then tried a different tack. "You know, I was an ace fighter pilot when you were in diapers."

"We both know that isn't true, sir. Now, please, if you could just keep quiet for these last few minutes. I'm trying to call for a clearance."

The President sat back, adjusted his codpiece for what seemed like the ninety-ninth time, and began humming "Hail to the Chief."

"Please, sir," Lussier said through clenched teeth. "Please don't hum 'Hail to the Chief.'"

Sweat rolled down the pilot's brow as he approached the rolling carrier deck. Commander Lussier mustered every ounce of his training as both a sailor and a pilot to tune out his aggravating passenger and focus on the task at hand. But Bush couldn't help himself and flipped a circuit breaker, setting off an ear-piercing alarm in the cramped cockpit. Distracted, Lussier came in a little too high and too fast, his tailhook snagging the fourth and final wire. The rugged thirty-nine-year-old pilot knew he'd get a razzing in the ready room, in addition to the razzing he was currently getting from the President, who knew just enough about flying to be a critic.

Bush's codpiece led the way onto the carrier deck, followed a few inches later by the President himself. As the young men and women in uniform gathered around him, cheering and slapping him on the back, he gave a thumbs-up in the general direction of one of the thirteen cameras Karl Rove had strategically placed around the USS *Abraham Lincoln* with an eye toward dynamite footage for a campaign commercial. It was the kind of movie moment the President relished. He hadn't felt so much like Tom Cruise since he had danced around the White House in his underwear, lip-synching to Bob Seger, much to the embarrassment of his daughters and their friends.

The President took his place at the podium photogenically positioned in front of the enormous "Mission Accomplished" banner that Rove had ordered up and that Halliburton subsidiary Kellogg, Brown and Root had manufactured at a cost of $738,000 after being awarded a no-bid contract. Major combat operations in Iraq, he told the world, were over.

Roll credits.

Eight thousand miles away, a very different kind of movie was unfolding. Instead of a Hollywood blockbuster, the movie taking place in Iraq at that moment was more like a gritty documentary that may win an award or two, but that no one really wants to see.

Hospitals, government ministries, and arms depots were being looted; yet another attack on American soldiers in Fallujah foreshadowed what would become a vicious and virulent insurgency; and Iraqis struggled to survive without basic services, which had been destroyed in the early days of the fighting and which to this day remain far short of their prewar standard. Weeks into the war, American viceroy Jay Garner didn't even have access to a working telephone to use to report to Washington on how badly things were going.

Iraq was descending into chaos. Exactly as the unheeded postwar planners had prophesied. But you don't need to be an expert to know that looting is a bad idea. It spits in the face of the rule of law. It rips the very fabric of civil society. It turns ordinary people into criminals. And on a more practical level, looting means that things that you need won't be there when you need them. In the first days after the fall of Saddam's regime, seventeen of the government's twenty-three ministries were not just looted, but gutted—stripped of wiring, insulation, and plumbing.

No one in their right mind thinks that there's any justification for looting. Except, that is, for the man who was in charge of preventing it, United States Secretary of Defense Donald Rumsfeld. On April 11, 2003, as the international looting Olympics were getting under way in Baghdad, Rumsfeld was asked whether there had been a plan to restore law and order after the war. His answer:

> **RUMSFELD:** Stuff happens! . . . And it's untidy. And freedom's untidy. And free people are free to make mistakes and commit crimes and do bad things.

I didn't know that. I didn't know that I was free to walk over to Broadway, throw a brick through the window of Circuit City, and make off with a fifty-five-inch Fujitsu flat-screen plasma television. I mean, I want one of those babies. And I live in a free society.

But, of course, I am not free to loot. Looting has nothing to do with freedom, any more than any other crime does. Rumsfeld was sending a clear message to the Iraqis: You're not as good as us. We don't care about you.

It wasn't just words that sent that message. The 3rd Infantry Division, which had heroically led the drive to Baghdad, didn't have enough troops to prevent the ransacking of almost every official building and major business in Baghdad. But they were able to surround the oil ministry with fifty tanks, reinforcing the suspicion that America was in Iraq not for Iraqis but for their oil. There could be an innocent explanation for this. Maybe we had to protect Iraq's oil ministry, because only the oil could provide the money to rebuild what was being destroyed—for example, the other ministries. But, boy, did it look bad.

It's not like the looting wasn't anticipated. Every expert had warned that looting would pose a crucial challenge in the aftermath of the war and had suggested specific measures to prevent it.

One of those experts, Robert Perito, had given a presentation to the influential Defense Policy Board about this very danger:

> It was very likely, we thought, that there was going to be widespread civil disturbance. It was also going to be necessary for the U.S. to be prepared going in to deal with that. So my presentation was largely about the kinds of forces that we would need in order to deal with that kind of violence. The recommendations were to create a constabulary and a police force and rule-of-law teams that would be able to go in and deal with civil disturbance.

But Rumsfeld had made ignoring experts like Perito a top priority. And that's why nobody told the 3rd Infantry what to do when the chaos began. As the 3rd Infantry's after-action report says, there was "no plan from higher headquarters," and "no guidance for restoring order in Baghdad." Had they been told from the beginning that preventing looting would be part of their mission, things almost certainly would have been different. Listen to Lieutenant General James T. Conway, who commanded the 1st Marine Expeditionary Force:

> **CONWAY:** When the troops entered Baghdad and there was a level of looting, I think I understood, so long as Iraqis were taking office furniture out of the government buildings in a regime headquarters location, those types of things. We watched it for two or three days, I think, pretty much with that attitude.
>
> **FRONTLINE:** And you think you could have stopped it?
>
> **CONWAY:** I think so. I think—if we had been told to stop the looting and secure key elements of the city, we could have brought a force to do that.

Army Secretary Thomas White summed it up:

> We *immediately* found ourselves shorthanded in the aftermath. We watched people dismantle and run off with the country basically.

Of course, it's one thing to allow looters to plunder Iraq's cultural heritage along with computers, bathroom fixtures, and insulation from the Irrigation Ministry. It's quite another to allow looters to make off with hundreds of tons of high-grade explosives from sites that had been previously identified as probable WMD caches.

In 2003, Christmas came early for Iraq's burgeoning bombmaker class. The weapons dump at al Qaqaa, some thirty miles south of Baghdad, held 377 tons of extremely powerful explosives. Enough high explosives to make an Improvised Explosive Device for every Iraqi man, woman, and child, with enough left over to detonate the six nuclear bombs that North Korea has developed while we were concentrating on Iraq.

Here's how the U.S. troops who witnessed the looting described it to the *Los Angeles Times*:

> "We were running from one side of the compound to the other side, trying to kick people out," said one senior noncommissioned officer who was at the site in late April 2003. "On our last day there, there were at least 100 vehicles waiting at the site for us to leave" so that they could come in and loot munitions.
>
> "It was complete chaos. It was looting like L.A. during the Rodney King riots," another officer said.
>
> The soldiers said about a dozen U.S. troops guarding the sprawling facility could not prevent the theft of the explosives because they were outnumbered by looters.

The only consolation was that while al Qaqaa did contain massive quantities of materials suitable for nuclear detonators, Iraq didn't have a nuclear weapon to detonate. Nor, it would turn out, did it have a program to develop such a weapon. But presumably Donald Rumsfeld hadn't known that. And that's just one of the reasons why it was so infuriating that he didn't give the military the resources it needed to secure the site. As one weapons expert said of al Qaqaa:

> This is not just any old warehouse in Iraq that happened to have explosives in it; this was a leading location for developing nuclear weapons before the first Gulf War. The fact that it had been left unsecured is very, very discouraging. It would be like invading the U.S. in order to get rid of WMD and not securing Los Alamos.

The Bush administration took special pains to cover up this particular failure. When *The New York Times* broke the story on October 25, 2004, the Pentagon tried to push the line that the explosives had been removed before American troops had arrived. The right-wing press jumped on board immediately, and by October 27 Sean Hannity was saying that "the story has been totally and completely and utterly debunked."

Hannity never apologized after a Minnesota news crew dug up some video they had shot in Iraq on April 18, 2003, of box after box clearly marked "explosives" and "al Qaqaa." After seeing the tape, Bush's weapons inspector David Kaye said it was "game, set, match" that the explosives had still been there when American forces came through.

As a former federal prosecutor, Rudy Giuliani knew who was guilty of negligence in the case of al Qaqaa:

> No matter how you try to blame it on the President, the actual responsibility for it really would be for the troops that were there. Did they search carefully enough? Didn't they search carefully enough?

Call me crazy, but I don't blame the troops. Here's former secretary of the Army Thomas White:

> I think from an Army perspective, the concern was the troop levels after the war. Our concern—Shinseki's concern, my concern—was if you were to look at the postwar tasks that had to be accomplished, the fact that this was a country as large as the state of California with a population of 25 million people, we were very concerned that there wouldn't be sufficient boots on the ground after the operation to provide for security and get on with the stabilization activities.

A large majority of the 1,833 U.S. troops who have died in Iraq as of this writing—not to mention the 13,000+ wounded—were hit by

IEDs and suicide bombers. It's hard to believe that none of these bombs were made with explosives looted from al Qaqaa. In President Bush's war movie, nobody wasted time on details like calculating the number of soldiers needed to secure ammunition dumps. No, I don't blame the troops. I blame their commander in chief, who was serving the military even less as president than he had as an Alabama National Guard pilot in 1972.

Considering how well not reading had worked for him, it is probably not surprising that Bush fostered a culture of illiteracy, demanding that his advisers also not read certain key documents. It was sort of like a book club in reverse: "This month, we're all going to be not reading the final report of the State Department's Future of Iraq Project."

Lieutenant General Jay Garner was a reluctant member of the Bush nonreading group. Appointed by Rumsfeld to run postwar Iraq, Garner thought the conclusions of the seventeen-agency Future of Iraq Project might be something he should take a look at, if, for no other reason, than to get their point of view. But for a voracious nonreader like George Bush, even this modest notion proved threatening.

One month after Garner arrived in Baghdad, he received some unwelcome news. He was out—a scapegoat for the lawless chaos that the Bush administration had been unable to keep off the front pages and the nightly news. Someone had to take the fall besides that statue of Saddam Hussein.

What had gone wrong?

> **GARNER:** I think that it was a mistake that we didn't use that. I agree with that. It was my intent to use that, but we didn't.
>
> **FRONTLINE:** Why didn't we use the Future of Iraq [Project]?
>
> **GARNER:** I don't know. I don't know the answer to that. I was just told, and now it's just a decision they made that we're not going to do that.

FRONTLINE: Who told you that?

GARNER: I got that from the Secretary, and I don't think that was his decision.

FRONTLINE: Secretary Rumsfeld?

GARNER: Mm hmm.

Garner had actually tried to hire Tom Warrick, head of the Future of Iraq Project, as part of his staff for postwar reconstruction. At a lunch with *The New Yorker*'s George Packer, at which we were waited on by Jay Garner himself, Packer told me that it was Dick Cheney who had personally blackballed Warrick. Why? Because he came from the opposing team. No, not the terrorists. Not the Democrats. He came from the reality-based community over at the State Department.

As Packer told me:

> The Future of Iraq Project wasn't the key to all solutions in Iraq. It was just a very useful compendium of information, a fantastic resource for anyone who wants to tackle all the range of problems in the postwar that would have been of great use to any postwar administration.
>
> Rumsfeld and Cheney didn't believe the State Department's version of the electrical grid in Iraq was worth looking at. Because it's the State Department version. We have our own version of the electrical grid in Iraq, which is that it's actually in very good shape and it's not going to need a whole lot of repair.

When Garner was recalled to Washington, Packer reports, he was brought to the White House for a meeting with Bush. During the forty-five-minute encounter, you might have expected the President to ask questions like "G-man, how's it going in Baghtown?" Or "General Jay, what's rockin' in Iraq?" Or "Given everything that's happened, how can we win the trust of the Iraqi people and put the reconstruction effort back on track?"

But instead of dealing with substance, the meeting consisted largely of idle and perfunctory chitchat peppered with occasional joshing.

"You want to do Iran for the next one?" the President joked.

"No, sir. Me and the boys are holding out for Cuba."

Ha ha ha. HA HA HA HA HA.

But what about the other Future of Iraq Project? The project to turn the future of Iraq over to the shifty Ahmed Chalabi? If Chalabi could carry the ball, who gave a shit about the Irrigation Ministry? That was *his* problem.

On April 6, two weeks after the start of the war, Ahmed Chalabi made his triumphant return to the country of his birth and early childhood, flown by the U.S. military into Nasiriyah with seven hundred members of his own militia.

Expectation: A broad-based spontaneous popular uprising would crystallize around the charismatic Chalabi, simplifying even further the job of the coalition forces, and sweeping him into power as the pro-Western head of a new democratic government.

Reality: A curious throng, long starved for entertainment, gathered to stare at the first non-Baath politician most had ever seen. While they listened politely, there were few recruits for the two-hundred-and-thirty-mile march to Baghdad.

Unimpressed, American generals deposited Chalabi and his men at a derelict military base in the desert, which he failed to use as a staging ground for his popular rebellion based on the philosophy of Chalabiism.

Jay Garner's replacement in Baghdad was L. Paul Bremer, career foreign service officer, protégé of Henry Kissinger, former ambassador-at-large for counterterrorism, graduate of Harvard and Yale, and speaker of eight languages including Arabic, Norwegian, and English. If anyone could realize the neo-cons' vision for Iraq, Bremer could. The fact that he couldn't proves what a bad idea the enterprise was.

In point of fact, Bremer did an absolutely terrible job during his one-year tenure in Baghdad, for which he was awarded the Presidential Medal of Freedom, not to be confused with the Presidential Medal of Competence, which has only been awarded twice—both times to Donald Rumsfeld.[1]

Unlike Garner, Bremer didn't have to be ordered to ignore the guidance of the postwar planners. Right after unpacking his toothbrush, Bremer began a sweeping de-Baathification of the Iraqi government, throwing the baby out with the Baath water.[2] On May 16, his first decision was to fire 120,000 Iraqi officials—teachers, engineers, civil administrators, and public health officers, most of whom were nominal Baath Party members in the same way my wife and I are supporting members of the Museum of Natural History, even though we haven't been there since our children were very small. Apparently Bremer's impressive résumé didn't prepare him for the task of distinguishing essential civil servants from the cadre of hard-core Saddam loyalists who had to be held to account for the atrocities they had committed, such as torturing prisoners.

Giving 120,000 pink slips to people with vitally needed skills would accelerate the collapse of whatever institutional infrastructure remained. Bremer's next move, firing 400,000 more government employees, would complete it. In this case, it wasn't just that they would have been helpful in the reconstruction and peacekeeping efforts. It was also that they had guns. On May 23, the multilingual Bremer fired the entire Iraqi military and canceled their pensions, neglecting to first disarm them. With military employment now out of the question, these angry, Kalashnikov-owning young men were obliged to find other ways to keep themselves busy. You know what they say about the Devil and idle hands.

---

[1] There it is, the other joke.
[2] Bonus joke.

It was a dramatic departure from the commonsense approach of the departed Jay Garner:

> **GARNER:** Our plan then is we were going to use most of the army, the Iraqi army, for reconstruction. We were going to hire them and make them, for lack of a better word, reconstruction battalions and use them to help rebuild the country.
>
> **FRONTLINE:** Did that seem like a good plan to you at the time?
>
> **GARNER:** Seemed like a great plan, yeah, because they had the skill set to do everything I thought we needed to do. I mean, they know how to fix roads. They know how to fix bridges. They know how to move rubble around. They are all trained, to a certain degree. They knew how to take orders. They have a command-and-control system over them. They have their own transportation, you can move them around, that type of thing. So that was a—that was a good concept.

Without the army to fix bridges, etc., these tasks naturally fell to Halliburton, Dick Cheney's old outfit, which had secretly received a $7 billion no-bid contract coordinated by the vice president's office. Halliburton's financial future was secure and, along with it, the financial future of the Cheney family, which was receiving $12,000 a month from the company and owned 400,000 options on its stock—one for each former Iraqi soldier now roaming the streets of Baghdad, Fallujah, and Najaf.

But without the Iraqi army and civil service to help, the job at hand was too big for even Halliburton. Companies like Bechtel, DynCorp, and the newly formed Custer Battles LLC stepped into the breach.

To oversee the work of these contractors, Bremer didn't want to rely on the dinosaurs who had successfully managed the transition in the Balkans in the nineties. He wanted fresh blood; energetic new faces, who wouldn't be boxed in by the conventional wisdom. It wasn't that Clinton's approach hadn't worked. It was that Clinton was involved. And Paul Bremer knew exactly where to find people who hadn't worked for Clinton.

Among the new hires were Casey Wasson, twenty-three, a recent college grad who needed a job; Anita Greco, twenty-five, a former teacher, who also needed a job; John Hanley, twenty-four, a website editor (i.e., also needed a job). And then there was Scott Erwin, twenty-one, a former intern for Dick Cheney and Tom DeLay, who didn't need a job because he was still in college. Erwin marveled to the University of Richmond newsletter that "in one week I went from chatting on the quad, eating in the Heilman Dining Center and attending ODK [Omicron Delta Kappa] meetings to being briefed in the Pentagon, flying in a C-130 military plane from Kuwait City to Baghdad and living in one of Saddam's many palaces."

Erwin soon landed a gig as the top Coalition Provisional Authority (CPA) official managing the finances of Iraq's civilian security forces— fire units, customs, border patrols, and police. What a great job! Almost as much fun as his previous favorite job, which he told the *Richmond Times-Dispatch* was "my time as an ice cream truck driver."

Erwin was one of the six youngsters given control of Iraq's $13 billion budget. "The Brat Pack," as they inevitably came to be known, were understandably startled to find themselves with awesome new jobs in Baghdad, especially since they hadn't applied for them. Each had received an unsolicited e-mail from the Pentagon inviting them to join in the liberation effort. After comparing notes, the twenty-somethings realized the one thing they all had in common. They had all sent their résumés to the notoriously unreliable Heritage Foundation.

The Brat Packers, the contractors, and Bremer were all operating under the aegis of the CPA, which, depending upon who you talk to, was created by a secret presidential directive or by a resolution of the United Nations Security Council. An extensive investigation by the nonpartisan Congressional Research Service was unable to determine whether the CPA was a "federal agency" or an "amorphous international organization." This ambiguity provided excellent legal cover for the tremendous amount of irregular activity, such as stealing, that took place during Bremer's tenure, activities that continued even after the CPA was officially dissolved.

CPA Inspector General Stuart Bowen concluded that no less than $8.8 billion went unaccounted for on Bremer's watch. Where did this money go? Perhaps it's out there now working to improve the lives of ordinary Iraqis. Perhaps. But somehow I doubt it.

Entire books could be written about the unchecked corruption that occurred after the fall of Saddam. None of them by me. I do, however, have some favorite examples that I'd like to share with you.

As part of an audit of Halliburton subsidiary Kellogg, Brown and Root, Bowen tried a little experiment. KBR's Baghdad office had been entrusted with 20,531 pieces of U.S. government property valued at $61.1 million. Bowen selected 164 of those items at random and asked KBR to produce them. Out of the 164 items, 52 were either missing or could not be accounted for, including two electric generators, six laptops, and an eight-by-twenty-foot trailer. And eighteen trucks.

Overall, Pentagon auditors found that Halliburton couldn't account for $1.8 billion of work they had done in Iraq and Kuwait.

But that's not my favorite story. My favorite story involves a company called Custer Battles.

Now, if your name were Jim Custer and you decided to start a new company with your friend Joe Battles and you wanted to be sure that when people thought of your company they thought of it as a winner, you probably wouldn't call it Custer Battles. You'd call it something like Consolidated International Solutions. However, when former CIA officer, unsuccessful Republican congressional candidate, and Fox News commentator Michael Battles teamed up with his pal Scott Custer, a former Army Ranger and defense contractor, the pair showed an admirable disdain for modern business's obsession with perception management. No, they didn't name their company Fuck You. They just ran it that way. They actually called their security firm Custer Battles. This time they were determined that by hook or by crook, especially crook, Custer would win the battle.

In the spring of '03 Custer Battles received a $16 million contract to provide security inspection for civilian flights at Baghdad International Airport. The fact that there were no civilian flights into BIAP at the time and haven't been since is what makes this one my favorite. But Custer and Battles didn't sit around the Iraqi Airways Sultans Club just filing their nails. According to a lawsuit filed by former employees, they stayed busy repainting forklifts, specifically forklifts abandoned by Iraqi Airways, which they then leased back to the United States. Next, Custer Battles got a contract guarding the Security Exchange where Iraqis were required to exchange their old currency with Saddam's picture on it for new currency with Paul Bremer's picture. It was every contractor's favorite kind of contract: "cost-plus," where no matter how much you spend (cost), the U.S. government gives you 25 percent more (plus). Not satisfied with that markup, according to the former employees, Custer Battles created a series of sham companies registered in the Cayman Islands and elsewhere that forged invoices claiming to be leasing equipment back to Custer Battles.

All told, Custer Battles stands accused of stealing somewhere in the neighborhood of $50 to $60 million. That's nowhere near the $1.8 billion that Halliburton was able to make disappear, but still, pretty good for a start-up.

Ironically, as all this money was being showered on contractors, very little of the money appropriated for reconstruction was actually being spent. By late June 2004, only $366 million of the $18.4 billion appropriated for reconstruction had actually been spent to address the urgent and growing needs of Iraqis. The two most fundamental services, electricity and clean water, were absolute disasters. Hepatitis shot up 70 percent in Iraq in 2003 because of untreated water. A particularly virulent form killed pregnant women in Baghdad's vast slum of Sadr City. Before the war, residents of Baghdad had about twenty hours of electricity a day. By

June 2004, that was down to less than ten hours a day, in DVD-viewing-experience-ruining two-hour chunks.

The longer we waited to spend the money, the more the price of rebuilding Iraq went up. By the fall of 2004, only 27 cents of every dollar spent on reconstruction actually reached projects to help Iraqis. The rest went to contractors, administrative costs, mismanagement and corruption, and, most of all, security. The less progress was made on rebuilding Iraq, the more alienated Iraqis became, the less they trusted America, and the more the insurgency was able to attract recruits. That September, the Pentagon announced that $3.46 billion was going to be rerouted from reconstruction to security.

A responsible administration would have been apoplectic about all of this. It certainly would have responded to the new facts on the ground by changing course, flip-flopping, if you will. But here again, the administration's incapacity to admit a single mistake assured that mistake after mistake after mistake would go uncorrected.

Even the seemingly noncontroversial issue of cracking down on corruption ran afoul of the Bush administration's policy of rewarding cronies. As of today, unlike the people of Iraq, Custer and Battles are thriving, though no longer as Custer Battles LLC, which was finally banned from bidding on further government contracts. Instead, the executives formed new companies that are housed in the firm's old offices and run by the company's old executives. When two whistleblowers sued Custer Battles for defrauding the United States, Bush's Justice Department refused to take part. Justice lawyers took the dubious position that the entity that was ripped off, the Coalition Provisional Authority, was an international agency rather than a part of the U.S. government—and therefore outside of their jurisdiction.

As you might imagine, Halliburton has enjoyed an even more airtight immunity from government busybodies. On October 8, 2004, the Defense Contract and Audit Agency discovered that Halliburton's KBR had overcharged the U.S. government $108 million for importing fuel from

Kuwait to Iraq. When a U.N. monitoring board asked for the DCAA's report, the Pentagon allowed KBR to black out almost all negative references to the company before handing it over. Sometime later, hero congressman Henry Waxman (D-CA) uncovered an un-redacted copy of the audit, and discovered that sentences like "KBR did not demonstrate the prices for Kuwaiti fuel and transportation were fair and reasonable" had been covered with thick black ink, ink for which the Defense Department was charged an amount of money that was itself blacked out.

But the dimensions of the corruption cover-up were far greater than the Defense Contract and Audit Agency. Perhaps the most shocking story of all about Halliburton is one that involves not just money, high government officials, and guns, but sex—and one of today's top box-office stars.

Iraq had become what one former CPA senior adviser called a "free-fraud zone." In its "Global Corruption Report 2005," the nonprofit group Transparency International warned that "If urgent steps are not taken, Iraq . . . will become the biggest corruption scandal in history."

Steps, urgent or not, were not taken. No one was surprised that Dick Cheney was reluctant to investigate Halliburton. But that's why Congress was invented. The nice thing about having multiple branches of government is that they can balance each other, or, when necessary, even check one another. This system of balances and checks is the cornerstone of our democracy. Unfortunately, this Republican Congress sees itself as a rubber stamp.

The body that should have been investigating the corruption in Iraq is the Senate Committee on Homeland Security and Governmental Affairs, chaired by Maine Republican Susan Collins, who likes to flaunt her supposed independence. Since 2003, that committee has conducted eight hearings on the postal service, two on Defense Department employees' improper use of airline tickets, and two on diploma mills. They have conducted none on corruption in Iraq.

But maybe you're thinking to yourself, "This is something they should start looking at in subcommittee to see if it rises to the level of a problem, like diploma mills, that merits the attention of the full committee." Valid point. In fact, there's a Permanent Subcommittee on Investigations. That seems like the *perfect* place to investigate Scott Custer and KBR. But I'm afraid, dear reader, you're once again being hopelessly naive. The subcommittee's chairman, Minnesota Republican Norman Coleman, is one of the administration's leading butt boys. He hasn't held a single hearing on postwar corruption.

If Norm Coleman is serious about realizing his ambition to become vice president in the third Bush administration, he'd do well to follow the example of Harry Truman. In early 1941, Truman took a ten-thousand-mile tour around the United States to look into rumors of defense contractor mismanagement. When he returned, he convinced a Senate and a president from his own party that waste and corruption would impair the nation's mobilization for war. On March 1, 1941, the Truman Committee was born, launching a three-year marathon investigation into "waste, inefficiency, mismanagement, and profiteering," saving millions of dollars and the lives of American soldiers.

Truman considered war profiteering "treason." It still is. And the senators who stand by and allow it to happen must be called to account. Their refusal to act is killing our men and women in uniform.

Jim Leach is a Republican congressman from Iowa. I've known him for some time because of his good work as chairman of the House Banking Committee, where he has fought powerful interests in support of the Community Reinvestment Act, which forces banks to lend money to people who historically have been denied access to capital: minorities, women, and the poor. For three years, Leach has been calling for a modern-day Truman Committee to investigate war profiteering in Iraq. I had Leach on my radio show, and although the mild-mannered Iowan avoided the term "butt boy" when describing his Republican colleagues, I could tell he was as mad as I was about the way this Congress is putting party above patriotism.

On the Senate side, Chuck Grassley, also a Republican from Iowa, wants the Bush administration to join the suit against Custer Battles, because, based on the precedent it could set, "billions of taxpayer dollars are at stake."

This war cannot be about partisan politics. But for George W. Bush and Karl Rove and Dick Cheney, nothing but partisan politics exists. Man's genetic relationship to apes is a partisan political issue. The effect of atmospheric carbon on the Earth's absorption of heat from the sun is, to them, a partisan political issue. The likelihood of Terri Schiavo joining the Rockettes is a partisan political issue. And on this, the most solemn duty of a commander in chief, war, they still can't reach past politics and touch reality. They will not die in battle. Their children will not die in battle. Short of a Congress with a backbone, there is nothing that will shake them from the fantasy that they're winning this war. And that the only battle that requires their attention is the battle of perception. As we lose the hearts and minds of Iraqis day after day, the White House's obsession remains the hearts and minds and future votes of Americans.

Last we left him, Ahmed Chalabi was cooling his heels in a not-so-cool abandoned military base in the desert southeast of Baghdad. It was a far cry from the gated estate in Tehran that the American government had bought for him, and from which he had watched his deeply laid plans for a U.S. invasion of Iraq bear fruit. Or, for that matter, the hillside mansion outside of Amman, Jordan, where his children had ridden horses with that country's royal family while he stayed busy embezzling $230 million through the Petra Bank that he founded there. Or the country squire's estate in Middleburg, Virginia, purchased with some of those embezzled funds and to which he fled after being indicted in Jordan. Most galling, it was a far cry, and at the same time just a little too far, from the million-plus square meters of downtown Baghdad that had belonged to Ahmed Chalabi's family before the 1958 Baathist Revolution, and which he believed it was his birthright to reclaim.

What happened next is a testament to the extended family values that have enabled Chalabi to insert tentacles into a variety of corrupt and/or powerful institutions that should have known better. Institutions like the Swiss investment firm Socofi, the CIA, the Pentagon, and, in this case, *The New York Times*. Upon learning by satellite phone that her uncle was languishing in the desert, the manager of the *Times* office in Kuwait, Sarah Kahlil, Chalabi's niece, tapped funds from Chalabi's exile group, the Iraqi National Congress, and personally liberated her uncle and his men with a fleet of SUVs.

Chalabi was back.

Having failed to gain power as the leader of a popular uprising, he adapted with the kind of flexibility that the Bush administration could have learned from, deciding instead to win power as a warlord. After a certain amount of looting and pillaging on his way into Baghdad, Chalabi called in one final chit from his patrons at the Pentagon and was awarded a coveted seat on the twenty-five-member Iraqi Governing Council. Moving decisively to consolidate power, he appointed friends and family members as heads of the oil, finance, and trade ministries, as well as the Central Bank.

Chalabi's lifelong interest in financial matters extended to Iraq's newly privatized private sector. One crony received millions of dollars to secure the country's oil infrastructure, and another was given an enormous cell-phone contract. Though Chalabi was far and away the winner of a March

2004 poll asking whom Iraqis trusted least (beating out second-place finisher Saddam Hussein by more than three to one), everything seemed to be falling into place for Ahmed Chalabi.

But somehow, amid all the lying, all the cronyism, all the scheming, all the looting, somehow he had fallen out of favor with the Bush administration, which was slowly coming to the same conclusion as the Iraqi people. When U.N. envoy Lakhdar Brahimi was asked by the White House to put together a new interim government, Chalabi's name was not on his list. Though Paul Bremer and the U.S. government overruled Brahimi on many of his choices, they declined to reinstate Chalabi.

The United States had declared war on Ahmed Chalabi.

Chalabi declared war right back—this time, without the support of the Pentagon.

14 Werewolves of Washington

Having been accomplished once, the mission was accomplished a second time, on June 28, 2004. At an understated ceremony held two days early deep inside the heavily fortified Green Zone, L. Paul Bremer handed over a leather-bound document transferring sovereignty from the mysteriously constituted Coalition Provisional Authority to Iyad Allawi, America's handpicked interim prime minister.

Within two hours, Paul Bremer had flown out of Iraq and was onto his next assignment, a nationwide after-dinner speaking tour that went off without a hitch. Until, that is, conference organizers at the Council of Insurance Agents and Brokers released some excerpts from his remarks at their annual summit. Bremer, now liberated from Iraq, felt free to speak his mind about the looting. "We paid a big price for not stopping it, because it established an atmosphere of lawlessness," he told the agents and brokers. "We never had enough troops on the ground." The implications for the insurance industry were clear. Do not write any insurance policies for anything in Iraq. But the media saw wider implications. Perhaps things weren't going so well in Iraq after all. When a reporter dug up a previous Bremer speech at DePauw University, the plot thickened still further. Bremer had told his audience at DePauw:

> The single most important change—the one thing that would have improved the situation—would have been having more troops in Iraq in the beginning and throughout. Although I raised this issue a number of times with our government, I should have been more insistent.

The implications for the students at DePauw were clear. Do not enlist in the U.S. Army after graduating from DePauw. Not only was the situation on the ground out of control, but the Bush administration was refusing to adapt, fearing that increasing troops levels would be tantamount to admitting a mistake.

Despite the occasional stumble, Bremer's speaking tour was a well-deserved victory lap. Bremer had left his mark. Iraq was well on its way to becoming whatever it was going to become.

There is a monument to L. Paul Bremer in Iraq. And it's as perfect a symbol as the Statue of Liberty or Mount Rushmore, and an even better one than the Washington Monument, which I never "got." It's called a Bremer wall. And there's not just one Bremer wall, but many, many Bremer walls.

A Bremer wall is a twelve-foot-high, five-ton reinforced concrete barrier that proved to be an innovative solution to the biggest problem in postwar Iraq: explosions.

The Bremer walls represented Bremer's legacy in many ways. Instead of providing security for *all* Iraqis, Bremer walls provided security for people lucky enough to live inside the Bremer walls—people like Paul Bremer. They reinforced the Iraqis' perception that our mission was not to protect them, but to protect ourselves *from* them. This is what reconstruction in Iraq has become. Building barriers instead of rebuilding Iraq's infrastructure.

Let me give you a concrete example. The concrete. Before the war, Iraq had nineteen operating cement factories and was a major cement exporter. Because of looting and electrical outages, the plants are now operating at only one sixteenth of their prewar capacity. None of these factories has been awarded a single contract to supply the reconstruction. Instead, the cement for the Bremer walls must be imported from Turkey, driven in via an increasingly hazardous route by increasingly reluctant Turkish truck drivers. As a result, the cost of each Bremer wall is approximately $1000. Iraqis, who are currently enjoying an unemployment rate of anywhere from 27 percent (the official U.S. government figure) to a more likely estimate of more than 50 percent, say they could make them for $100.

The Bremer walls are a daily reminder to Iraqis of everything that has gone wrong since the Americans arrived. And they're not a reminder that can be easily tuned out. Just ask Khalid Daoud, a worker in Iraq's Culture Ministry, who described his personal encounter with a Bremer wall to *The New York Times*. It was every homeowner's worst nightmare.

> A few months ago, [Daoud] said, the American military arrived with a crane and tore up the trees in his garden, smashed the low wall surrounding it, swung the slabs into place and topped them with concertina wire.

The beauty part of Bremer walls is that the more we build, the more we need.

Bush partisans like to point out that after World War II, it took years to form democratic governments in Germany and Japan. What they won't tell you is that the total number of post-conflict American combat casualties in Germany, Japan, Haiti, Bosnia, and Kosovo is zero, a number invented by Arab mathematicians like Ahmed Chalabi.

Speaking of inventing things, Donald Rumsfeld and Condi Rice claim that there was a postwar insurgency in Germany that bears many parallels to the Iraqi insurgency today. Trying to put one over on, of all people, the Veterans of Foreign Wars, Condi and Rummy, in separate speeches on the same day, both drew the comparison:

> RICE: SS officers—called "werewolves"—engaged in sabotage and attacked both coalition forces and those locals cooperating with them—much like today's Baathist and fedayeen remnants.

> RUMSFELD: One group of those dead-enders was known as "werewolves." They and other Nazi regime remnants targeted Allied soldiers, and they targeted Germans who cooperated with the Allied forces. Mayors were assassinated, including the American-appointed mayor of Aachen, the first major German city to be liberated. Children as young as ten were used as snipers, radio broadcasts and leaflets warned Germans not to collaborate with the Allies. They plotted sabotage of factories, power plants, rail lines. They blew up police stations and government buildings, and they destroyed stocks of art and antiques that were stored by the Berlin Museum. Does this sound familiar?

No. And it probably didn't ring a bell to the Veterans of Foreign Wars, either. Why? It didn't happen! According to Golo Mann, author of *The History of Germany Since 1789*:

> The [Germans'] readiness to work with the victors, to carry out their orders, to accept their advice and their help was genuine; of the resistance which the Allies had expected in the way of "werewolf" units and nocturnal guerrilla activities, there was no sign.

International security scholar Daniel Benjamin, writing in *Slate*, noted:

> When an officer in Hesse was asked to investigate rumors that troops were being attacked and castrated, he reported back that there had not been a single attack against an American soldier in four months of occupation.

What about the mayor of Aachen, whom Rumsfeld had mentioned so dramatically? Well, he *was* assassinated. On the orders of Himmler. How, you ask, could Himmler be in a position to give orders? I'll tell you how. The war wasn't over yet! The mayor of Aachen was assassinated on March 25, 1945, six weeks before the Nazi surrender at Reims.

Why would Rice and Rumsfeld spin such a far-fetched yarn? Habit.

One of the few habits that the administration was finally forced to break was insisting that the war had been justified by Saddam's growing stockpile of Weapons of Mass Destruction. At first, they made a small adjustment, saying that Iraq's grave threat to America had actually come from Weapons of Mass Destruction–Related Program Activities. When it turned out there were none of those either, they had to change the subject entirely.

Errrr . . . Freedom. That was it. That's worth fighting for! We're all for that. Right? In his second inaugural address, President George W. Bush completed the bait and switch. Goodbye, imminent threat and the ties to al Qaeda. Hello, world freedom.

> All who live in tyranny and hopelessness can know: The United States will not ignore your oppression, or excuse your oppressors. When you stand for your liberty, we will stand with you.

There were some exceptions to what seemed to be a line in the sand. Among those who live in tyranny and hopelessness with whom we have been somewhat reluctant to stand are those who live in countries that have been kind enough to grant basing rights to our military.

On my first USO tour to Iraq and Afghanistan, our group flew to southern Uzbekistan to entertain the troops at an airbase that served as a staging ground for combat operations in Afghanistan. There, I fell into conversation with two scruffy PSYOPS guys (Psychological Operations— you know, unconventional warfare, demoralizing the enemy, winning the hearts and minds). It was my experience at every base I visited that the PSYOPS guys were the chattiest. So I asked one of them, "What do you think of the Uzbek regime?"

"They're great!" he said enthusiastically. "They're incredibly cooperative. They'll do whatever we ask."

"Really?" I said. "Because I heard that they were the most repressive of all the former Soviet Republics."

He understood instantly. "Oh, yeah—they're *horrible!* They *boil* people."

I happened to tell this story on my radio show, but got it slightly wrong. I recalled that the PSYOPS guy had said the Uzbek regime boils people in *oil.* That sounded fishy to my cohost, Katherine Lanpher, who is always eager to take me down a peg. She Googled "Uzbekistan," "boil," and "oil," and found nothing about torture in that country. She did, however, find what sounded like a delicious recipe for one of my favorite dishes, rice pilaf.

Other than injustice, nothing makes me madder than when I make a factual error on my show and I am unable to immediately blame it on someone else. But I was reluctant to cede my point, which, by the way, is that our ally Uzbekistan is not even a model dictatorship, let alone a model democracy. Perhaps I had gotten it wrong. Perhaps they boil their prisoners in some sort of bouillon. I asked Katherine to remove "oil" from the search.

"Oh," said Katherine, "here it is. Yup. They boil people."

In 2002, the Bush administration gave Uzbekistan $500 million for the use of the airbase I visited. In the interest of fairness, I should point out that not all of that went for torture. Only $79 million was given to the police and intelligence service, which, according to the State Department, uses "torture as a routine investigation technique." An intelligence official estimated that from early 2002 to late 2003, the Bush administration "rendered" dozens of terrorist suspects to Uzbekistan. President Bush has even received the country's psycho president Islam Karimov in the White House, where they signed a declaration agreeing to "strengthen the material and technical base of [their] law enforcement agencies." In other words, bigger, better man-boiling pots.

Torture has been something of a sore point in the War on Terror.

When the photos of the abuse at Abu Ghraib first surfaced on Saturday, May 1, 2004, most people around the world were appalled. Not Rush Limbaugh. Over the course of the next week, Limbaugh would come down squarely on the pro-torture side. On Monday, May 3:

> LIMBAUGH: I thought, as I've said, it looked like anything you
> could see at a Madonna or Britney Spears concert.

I've never been to either, and if this is true, I'm staying away. The idea of listening to Madonna or Britney sing while dogs attack naked men—well, it's just not my idea of a fun evening out.

The next day, Rush drew a different parallel:

> LIMBAUGH: This is no different than what happens at the
> Skull and Bones initiation and we're going to ruin people's
> lives over it, and we're going to hamper our military effort,
> and then we're going to really hammer 'em because they had

a good time. You know, these people are being fired at every day—I'm talking about the people having a good time. You ever hear of emotional release? You ever hear of "need to blow some steam off"?

By then we had learned from the Taguba Report, an internal military investigation, that one of the ways that Abu Ghraib guards had blown off steam was by sodomizing detainees with a glow stick.

On Wednesday, Rush offered to take a more formal role in the developing scandal:

> **LIMBAUGH:** If they need an apologist, I'm going to be their apologist.

By Thursday, Rush had clearly given the issue a lot more thought:

> **LIMBAUGH:** All right, so we're at war with these people. And they're in a prison where they're being softened up for interrogation. And we hear that the most humiliating thing you can do is make one Arab male disrobe in front of another. Sounds to me like it's pretty thoughtful. Sounds to me in the context of war this is pretty good intimidation—and especially if you put a woman in front of them and then spread those pictures around the Arab world. And we're sitting here, "Oh my God, they're gonna hate us! Oh no! What are they gonna think of us?" I think maybe the other perspective needs to be at least considered. Maybe they're gonna think we are serious. Maybe they're gonna think we mean it this time. Maybe they're gonna think we're not gonna kowtow to them. Maybe the people who ordered this are pretty smart. Maybe the people who executed this pulled off a brilliant maneuver. Nobody got hurt. Nobody got physically injured.

> But boy there was a lot of humiliation of people who are try-
> ing to kill us—in ways they hold dear. Sounds pretty effective
> to me if you look at us in the right context.

Nobody got hurt. Nobody got physically injured. Here, Rush was not just being obscene, he was being, as he so often is, factually incorrect. Two of the photos released from Abu Ghraib were of dead prisoners, one packed in ice and the other badly battered.

Brilliant maneuver. Pretty smart. Pretty thoughtful. Pretty *effective*. Remember, 22 percent of Americans gets their news from talk radio. And this is what they were hearing.

Also, Rush Limbaugh is broadcast in Iraq. On the American Forces Network operated by the Pentagon.

Why was the Abu Ghraib abuse such a bad idea, other than the fact that it was morally wrong? Let's take a look at a cultural sensitivity pamphlet made by the U.S. military and given to our troops in Iraq:

> Do not shame or humiliate a man in public. Shaming a man will
> cause him and his family to be anti-Coalition.

Pretty effective.

According to the International Red Cross, our own military intelli-gence had estimated that "between 70 percent and 90 percent of the per-sons deprived of their liberty in Iraq had been arrested by mistake." There's no justification for torture, but purely from a practical perspec-tive, torturing innocent people is even worse than torturing enemies. And let me explain why. You see, innocent people could be your friends. Until you torture them. After that, they're very likely to resent you. And not just them, but their families and pals.

That's one of the reasons that while the Abu Ghraib photos were a shock to Americans, they weren't so shocking to Iraqis. Word had already gotten around.

But Rush was right on one point. A tremendous amount of thought had gone into the torture at Abu Ghraib, and indeed the whole torture system that our civilian leadership had crafted since 9/11. Lawyers, including Bush's top attorney Alberto Gonzales, Cheney's counsel David Addington, and Rumsfeld's general counsel William Haynes, had pored over anti-torture treaties and U.S. law to find loopholes that would allow interrogators to torture detainees with near impunity. These weren't rogue lawyers trying to circumvent their bosses' wishes. Many of the worst practices used at Abu Ghraib had been beta tested at Guantanamo, where a team of operational behavioral psychologists and goons had worked on innovative techniques to break the prisoners.

These practices, so at odds with American tradition going back to the Revolutionary War, ignited a firestorm within the military, law enforcement, and intelligence communities. According to witnesses, whenever Colin Powell tried to question detainee abuse with his colleagues in Bush's war cabinet, he was subjected to "frat-boy bully remarks about what these tough guys would do if THEY ever got their hands on prisoners."

When an FBI report about prisoner abuse at Gitmo was leaked to the press, Rush was ready with another zinger:

> **LIMBAUGH [Quoting an AP article]:** "One detainee wrapped in an Israeli flag, some were shackled hand and foot in fetal position for eighteen to twenty-four hours, forcing them to soil themselves." (Gasping in mock horror.) I thought they did that anyway over there. This is news to me that this is news.

Major General Geoffrey Miller so impressed his superiors with his work commanding the detention facility at Gitmo that he was brought over to Abu Ghraib to work his special kind of torture magic.

Donald Rumsfeld took a very hands-on approach to the torture. He personally approved the lifting of restrictions on abusive interrogation methods, like clothing removal, hooding, and the use of dogs to terrify prisoners. His approach to the torture cover-up was equally hands-on. In a March 2005 press conference, Rumsfeld and Joint Chiefs of Staff Vice Chairman General Peter Pace took a page from my favorite old vaudeville team, Deny and Obfuscate.[1]

> **REPORTER:** I wonder if you would just respond to the suggestion that there is a systemic problem rather than the kinds of individual abuses we've heard of before?
>
> **RUMSFELD:** I don't believe there's been a single one of the investigations that have been conducted, which has got to be six, seven, eight or nine . . .
>
> **PACE:** Ten major reviews and three hundred individual investigations of one kind or another.
>
> **RUMSFELD:** And have you seen one that characterized it as systematic or systemic?
>
> **PACE:** No, sir.
>
> **RUMSFELD:** I haven't either.

Both of them must have been skimming the reports, particularly General Taguba's finding of "systemic and illegal abuse of detainees" and General Fay's report of "systemic problems and issues."

When the photos from Abu Ghraib surfaced, Senator Lindsey Graham (R-SC), who served as a JAG officer in the Air Force for six years on active duty and continues to serve as a reservist, was incensed. He didn't buy the "a few bad apples" line that many of his fellow Republicans were parroting. "Not only should we focus on the privates, and the sergeants,

---

[1] In 1987, Herb Deny and Bernie Obfuscate died within a week of each other after torturing audiences for more than sixty years at Grossinger's Hotel and Resort in the Catskills. This page is dedicated to them.

and the specialists who did criminal activity," Graham said in a hearing, "but we also should have a higher accountability."

Since that time, many more details have emerged. We know now, for example, that 108 detainees have died in our custody during the almost four years we've been in Iraq and Afghanistan. One hundred and fourteen American POWs died in North Vietnamese captivity during the eleven years of the Vietnam War.

George H. W. Bush's personal physician, Dr. Burton J. Lee III, who served in the Army Medical Corps, wrote in a *Washington Post* op-ed:

> Torture demonstrates weakness, not strength. It does not show understanding, power or magnanimity. It is not leadership. It is a reaction of government officials overwhelmed by fear who succumb to conduct unworthy of them and of the citizens of the United States.

As Lindsey Graham feared, no one above the rank of captain is scheduled to be court-martialed for crimes at Abu Ghraib or anywhere in Rumsfeld's global network of detention centers, many of them secret. And the worst part is that the White House refuses to put an end to this once and for all. The day I wrote this, the White House blocked a Senate vote on a measure sponsored by John McCain (himself a victim of torture as a POW in Vietnam) and a bipartisan group of senators that would create a uniform code prohibiting inhumane interrogations.

Which brings me to another funny story.

I am, as far as I know, the only comedian who has performed at Abu Ghraib. It was during my last visit to Iraq with the USO. The leader of our tour was Sergeant Major of the Army Ken Preston. As the highest-ranking noncommissioned officer in the Army, he's a living god to ordinary soldiers. When Ken Preston was introduced, our host, the commander of the base, actually said—without a trace of irony—"Let's give a very warm Abu Ghraib welcome to Sergeant Major of the Army Preston!"

The crowd of MPs did just that.

We had gone to Abu Ghraib because, in the Christmas of 2004, the soldiers there needed a morale lift. Although the Lynndie Englands and the Charles Graners were long gone, these guys were operating under a stigma. In a way, the men and women I performed for at Abu Ghraib were victims of torture as well. And so are all our troops in Iraq.

Testifying before Congress on April 29, 2004, Paul Wolfowitz was asked how many Americans had been killed in Iraq. Wolfowitz replied:

> It's approximately 500, of which—I can get the exact numbers—approximately 350 are combat deaths.

The actual number at the time was 722, of which 521 were killed in combat. He was off by a third, and, not surprisingly, on the low end. How could Paul Wolfowitz, the number two man in the Pentagon, the man more responsible than anyone for the invasion of Iraq, make such a bad guess? And why did he have to guess at all?

As people who listen to my show know, I have thought and thought about that moment. And the only explanation I can come up with is that he does not care.

The next Saturday, I happened to run into Wolfowitz at the White House Correspondents Dinner. "You want to hear the joke I've been using about your not knowing how many of our troops had died in Iraq?" I asked. The small group that had gathered around us made it impossible for him to say no.

"Okay. Here it is. 'Paul Wolfowitz was off by a third when he was asked how many Americans have died in Iraq. The good news, however, is that he won the office pool.' " As the others laughed, Wolfowitz gave a wan smile, as if to acknowledge that it was bad form for the deputy secretary of defense to be so unfamiliar with the casualty count in an ongoing war.

One guy who you'd think would *definitely* know how many troops have died in Iraq would be Donald Rumsfeld. After all, the family of every soldier killed in action receives a personally signed letter from the secretary of defense. It's the least he could do. Or so I thought. Actually, it turns out that the least he could do was send form letters to the next of kin signed with an Autopen.

When former Colonel David Hackworth wrote a column on November 22, 2004, reporting that two colonels had told him that Rumsfeld had "relinquished this sacred duty to a signature device," Pentagon spokesman Jim Turner denied the charge, saying that "Rumsfeld signs the letters himself."

Stars and Stripes reporter Leo Shane hammered away at the story until he got a straight answer. Sort of. "In the interest of ensuring timely contact with grieving family members," Pentagon spokesman Lawrence Di Rita said of Rumsfeld, "he has not individually signed each letter." Perfect. Not only did he not sign the letters. He lied about it.

What kept Rumsfeld so busy that he couldn't sign the killed-in-action letters by hand? As it so happens, my researchers obtained a document that might shed some light.

OFFICE OF THE SECRETARY OF DEFENSE OF THE UNITED STATES OF AMERICA

DONALD RUMSFELD

Dear Chip,

Congratulations on Molly's acceptance to Princeton. Did my recommendation help? Sure. Would Molly have gotten in on her own merit? Probably. Are these things totally fair? Of course not. Does Molly deserve her acceptance? Absolutely. See you at the reunion.

Best regards,
Don

By the spring of 2004, Ahmed Chalabi had been bloodied in his first skirmishes with his former ally, the Bush administration. In early May, the Defense Intelligence Agency ended its monthly $340,000 stipend to Chalabi's Iraqi National Congress. A few weeks later, U.S. soldiers and Iraqi police raided his home and offices, seizing computers, dozens of rifles, and a large number of documents, as well as detaining three guards.

An Iraqi judge issued an arrest warrant, charging Chalabi with counterfeiting and money laundering. Even worse, he was accused by top U.S. intelligence officials of feeding sensitive intelligence to the Iranian government, including security information that could "get people killed."

Paul Wolfowitz, Chalabi's former patron, admitted at the time, "There are aspects of his recent behavior that are puzzling to me."

Operating on the principle that the enemy of my enemy is my friend, Chalabi found an unlikely ally in the erratic Shiite cleric Moktada al-Sadr, who had led several bloody uprisings against U.S. troops in the holy cities of Karbala and Najaf. Al-Sadr, who was wanted in connection with the murder of a pro-American cleric, had a Chalabi-like knack for landing on his feet. In one of his many uprisings against U.S. and Iraqi authorities, al-Sadr supporters holed up in Najaf's most holy sites, including the most sacred Shia shrine in the entire country, the Iman Ali mosque, killing twelve American soldiers.[2] On the condition that the Coalition promise not to arrest him, al-Sadr negotiated his way out of the siege in Najaf, pledging to give up violence and go into politics.

A friend of Chalabi's described the marriage of convenience thus: "Ahmed has brains but no guns. The Sadris have the guns but not the brains."

In Iraq's January 2005 elections, with the backing of al-Sadr, Chalabi did well enough to claim a powerful position as a deputy prime minister. From there, he resumed his long-standing project of enriching and empowering the family of Ahmed Chalabi. One nephew was given the

---

[2] Rush Limbaugh suggested America respond by raising the stakes even further: "Looks like we're soon going to be making a parking lot out of Najaf, mosque or no mosque, and it's about time."

finance ministry. Another is in charge of the prosecution of Saddam Hussein. For himself, he kept the oil ministry, which is considered the "it" ministry by Iraqis in the know.

Chalabi's current projects include lobbying for the release from prison of hundreds of violent followers of al-Sadr, and attempting to fire the judge who issued the warrant for al-Sadr's arrest. Yes, things are looking up for Ahmed Chalabi. Proof that in Iraq you can't keep a good man down. Or, for that matter, a very bad one.

If Paul Wolfowitz didn't care enough about U.S. troops to know how many had died in his war, you can just imagine how little he cared about the number of dead Iraqis.

No one knows how many civilians have died in Operation Iraqi Freedom. The fuzziness of the estimates (from 25,000 to over 100,000) gives you some idea of the priority that the administration has given to the protection of Iraqi lives. If you want to win hearts and minds, the first thing you should do is protect people's chests and heads.

In this area, as in so many others, the Pentagon's political leadership has let down our soldiers. Some civilian casualties are inevitable. But without a system for keeping track of them, much less compensating their families or, better yet, systematically trying to minimize casualties, it fell to individual soldiers to try to do what they could. There has been imaginative and effective work done by soldiers and Marines acting on their own initiative. So often in Iraq, success on the ground has been the work of a single soldier or group of soldiers, not executing a grand plan—there are none of those—but deciding independently to rebuild a school, mediate a feud, or distribute food and medicine.

Civilian casualties, as much as anything else, fuel the insurgency. The administration's approach has been to ignore them. It's another example of the administration pretending a problem doesn't exist, rather than solving it. In the fall of 2004, when a Johns Hopkins study estimated that

100,000 Iraqi civilians had been killed, the White House spokesman offered up this bland rehash of administration boilerplate:

> **REPORTER:** The administration has said in the past that it doesn't do body counts, but do you consider one hundred thousand to be in the ballpark of the number of Iraqis killed as a result of the war?
>
> **MCCLELLAN:** I don't know of any specific estimates on the civilians. I know that the United States military goes out of its way to minimize the loss of Iraqi civilian life. And what we're working to achieve in Iraq is an important cause that will make America more secure.
>
> **REPORTER:** Just to follow up: Does the President have an estimate before him on the number of Iraqis killed?
>
> **MCCLELLAN:** I'm not aware of any precise estimate or estimate of that nature.

It's disgusting to be indifferent to human suffering, but to do such a lousy job of pretending that you care is just stupid. When the American military did solve Iraq's chronic parking problem once and for all, not by turning Najaf into a parking lot, as Rush Limbaugh had suggested, but by blasting Fallujah into a sea of softball-size rubble, care was taken to compensate the city's soaring homeless population. Displaced families were given "one bottle of water and one emergency food pack per person, and a set of yellow flowered sheets."

Seven months into the war, Donald Rumsfeld wrote a memo asking whether we were creating more terrorists than we were eliminating. "We lack the metrics to know," he lamented at the time. Nine months later, he gave a speech indicating that he had made no progress in creating such metrics:

What we don't know is what's coming in in the intake. How many more of these folks are being trained and developed and organized and deployed and sent out. The civilized world doesn't know the answer to that question.

While we don't have an actual head count of terrorists, there are certain indicators. And all these indicators suggest that to the extent that the war in Iraq was ever about fighting terrorism, it has been a spectacular failure. An obvious metric, or as I prefer to call it, "measure," of the success of the War on Terror is the number of terrorist attacks worldwide. At least that's what the State Department boasted when it initially released its annual "Patterns of Global Terrorism" report in 2004. The report showed that the incidence of terrorist attacks was down to its lowest level in more than thirty years—a 45 percent decrease since 2001. "You will find in these pages clear evidence that we are prevailing in the fight," Deputy Secretary of State Richard Armitage proudly announced.

It wasn't long before the State Department realized they had made a number of small mistakes, including leaving out the terrorist attacks that had taken place during an unusually busy terrorist attack season from November 12 through December 31. An embarrassed Colin Powell did some damage control, telling the easily deceived Tim Russert, "I'm not a happy camper on this. We were wrong. We're going to get to the bottom of it." Once the books had gone through the State Department's de-cookerator, they told a very different story. The number of "significant" terrorist attacks had shot up from the previous year, reaching, not the lowest, but the *highest* level ever recorded.

The next year, the State Department was determined not to repeat its mistake. Breaking with twenty years of precedent, the administration's congressionally mandated report on terrorism did not include statistics on terrorist attacks—the very activity that defines terrorism. Which isn't to say they didn't *collect* the statistics. It's just that when they learned that the number of "significant" attacks had tripled from the previous year's record high, they realized that the number was useless as a metric to prove that terrorist attacks had gone down.

In May 2004, around the same time Ahmed Chalabi's home and office were being raided, Paul Wolfowitz asked William Schneider, Jr., chairman of the Pentagon's Defense Science Board and an old buddy from the Project for a New American Century, to conduct a study on how America could improve its strategic communication in the global war on terror. Wolfowitz wanted to know how America could convince the world's Muslims that America was not their enemy. It was a move I had been calling for since President Bush referred to the War on Terror as a "Crusade" and Lieutenant General William G. Boykin, the deputy undersecretary of defense for—get this—intelligence, said, in full dress uniform, at a *church*, that the War on Terror was a fight between "a Christian nation" and "Satan."

Schneider's report was slightly more critical of the Bush administration's approach to fighting terror than, say, I am. It noted that "opinion surveys" of Muslims worldwide "reveal widespread animosity toward the United States and its policies."

> A year and a half after going to war in Iraq, Arab/Muslim anger has intensified. Data from Zogby International in July 2004, for example, show that the U.S. is viewed unfavorably by overwhelming majorities in Egypt (98 percent), Saudi Arabia (94 percent), Morocco (88 percent), and Jordan (78 percent).

Hmm. Something good is going on in Jordan. Maybe it was that Queen Noor book.

Back to the Defense Science Board report. After being delivered to Wolfowitz in September of 2004, the incredibly important document was somehow held for weeks, only to be released after the election. And not just after the election, but on the Wednesday before Thanksgiving, when news takes a well-deserved holiday. Because so few Americans ever heard about it, I think the report is worth quoting at some length. Remember, this isn't an open letter from Tim Robbins and Susan Sarandon. This is a formal report from an advisory board to Donald Rumsfeld and Paul Wolfowitz's Pentagon.

> The larger goals of U.S. strategy depend on separating the vast majority of nonviolent Muslims from the radical-militant Islamist-Jihadists. But American efforts have not only failed in this respect: they may also have achieved the opposite of what they intended.
>
> • Muslims do not "hate our freedom," but rather, they hate our policies. The overwhelming majority voice their objections to what they see as one-sided support in favor of Israel and against Palestinian rights, and the longstanding, even increasing support for what Muslims collectively see as tyrannies, most notably Egypt, Saudi Arabia, Jordan, Pakistan, and the Gulf states. Thus when American public diplomacy talks about bringing democracy to Islamic societies, this is seen as no more than self-serving hypocrisy.
>
> • Furthermore, in the eyes of Muslims, American occupation of Afghanistan and Iraq has not led to democracy there, but only more chaos and suffering. U.S. actions appear in contrast to be motivated by ulterior motives, and deliberately controlled in order to best serve American national interests at the expense of truly Muslim self-determination.
>
> • Therefore, the dramatic narrative since 9/11 has essentially borne out the entire radical Islamist bill of particulars. American actions and the flow of events have elevated the authority of the Jihadi insurgents and tended to ratify their legitimacy among Muslims.
>
> • Finally, Muslims see Americans as strangely narcissistic—namely, that the war is all about us. As the Muslims see it,

everything about the war is—for Americans—really no more than an extension of American domestic politics and its great game. This perception is of course necessarily heightened by election-year atmospherics, but nonetheless sustains their impression that when Americans talk to Muslims they are really just talking to themselves.

So, to summarize the conclusions of the Defense Science Board:

- Worse, not better
- Hypocrisy
- Noor
- 9/11
- Ulterior motives
- Chaos
- Narcissistic

That last one, narcissistic, I find particularly intriguing. I think about narcissism a lot. One of the things people like most about my books is how I relate politics and global events to anecdotes about myself, especially my USO tours and the repeated confrontations in which I get the better of Deputy Secretary of Defense Paul Wolfowitz. But enough about me. Let's talk about my conclusions.

Muslims aren't crazy to think that, as things have gotten worse and worse, the conduct of the global war on terror has devolved into an exercise in self-serving political ass-covering in the United States.

On May 30, 2005, Dick Cheney told Larry King that the Iraq insurgency was in its "last throes." That was less than a month before Rumsfeld said on *Fox News Sunday* that the insurgency would last "five, six, eight, ten, twelve years." Which is it, guys? Inquiring families of soldiers would like to know.

Let's face it. You can't count on them to give you straight information. You can't count on them to tell us straight why we're going to war. You can't count on them to tell us what's happening over there.

You can't count on them to do their homework. To keep track of our money. You can't count on them to punish war profiteers. You can't count on them to protect our troops.

You can't rely on them for much of anything. Armor. Veterans' benefits. You can't count on them for the true story of how Jessica Lynch was captured, or how Pat Tillman died. Even for how the "Mission Accomplished" sign went up on the USS *Abraham Lincoln.* They actually lied about that.

You can't count on them to count terrorist attacks. You can't count on them to count civilian victims. You can't count on them to listen to military commanders and send in enough troops, or to not lie about the commanders asking them to send more troops, or to listen to Colin Powell and not torture people, or to not lie about whether the torture policies started at the top.

You can't trust them to *care.* About Iraqis. About Americans.

You can't trust them to do the work of actually signing killed-in-action letters. You can't trust them not to lie about not signing killed-in-action letters.

You can't count on them to acknowledge any mistakes whatsoever. You can't trust them not to lie when confronted with those mistakes.

You can't trust them not to believe their own propaganda.

You can't trust them. Period.

I don't know what to do in Iraq. I don't trust them to stay, and I don't trust them to leave. They send the right-wing media out there to say that any of us who have been critical of the war at all just want to cut and run. I don't. I want us to succeed in Iraq, but I don't know if it's possible. I've wrestled with this, talking to people on all sides of the issue. Some people think that our presence there creates more chaos, and that we should leave. Other people think leaving will cause a civil war, but others say we already have one. Most believe that whenever we leave, there will be more chaos—but that that will be true whether we leave now or five years from now, so we should start phasing out now.

Other people think it's possible to negotiate with the Sunni insurgents, and work with other countries to seal the borders and stop foreign jihadists from entering. Some people think that the only way to defeat an insurgency is to send in hundreds of thousands more troops—and others think that that would have helped three years ago, but that it's too late now.

But as much as I and others have agonized over this, it doesn't matter. The Bush administration does not care what you or I think should happen in Iraq. Six to eight people make the decisions, and they don't listen to anybody else. And the Republican Congress has let them get away with it. They have refused to hold anyone to account. Every day, they have a chance to do their job—and they don't do it.

If you want to know what I think we should do in Iraq, it's that we should think about what we have to do in America. We have to throw these guys out.

Step one is 2006.

The work starts now.

Epilogue

The Resurrection of Hope

15 A Letter to My Grandchildren

October 2, 2015

Dear Barack, Hillary, and Joe III,

Your grandmother and I were married forty years ago today. Little did we dream back then that we would have three grandchildren as beautiful as you.

Barack, I'll never forget the moment I first saw you in the maternity ward at the hospital, and your mother asked me to suggest a name. In retrospect, I guess it was kind of an obvious choice, but at the time I had no idea that Barack would soon become America's second most popular baby name, after Aidan. Hillary, when you came along two years later, you had your mother's eyes and your father's hemophilia. Thanks to advances in stem cell science, we were able to take care of the hemophilia. The eyes we left alone.

Joe III, you're the baby of the family. Although you can't read this yet, I think that one day, you'll find what I'm about to write as interesting as you currently find my ring of shiny, jangling keys.

This letter is my legacy to you, my beloved grandchildren, along with the million dollars each of you will receive thanks to your grandmother's prudent investments in T-bills, which are backed by the full faith and credit of the United States government. Thanks to the fiscal prudence of Democrats after Bush left office, that makes them the most secure investment we can possibly leave you.

Here's what I want you to know.

Just as I used to sit on my father's knee and ask him about him about the Great Depression and World War II, I know that you are probably curious about what I did during the Dark Time from the late fall of 2000 to January 2009. I stood up and fought, along with millions of Americans, and we took our country back. This letter is your record of how and why we did it, so that if the specter of corrupt and unaccountable conservatism should ever cast its long shadow on this fair land again, you'll know exactly what to do.

These days, the 2004 election is mostly remembered as the beginning of the end of the Republican hammerlock on America. But back then, it seemed, at best, like the end of the beginning. Air America was just a radio network, as opposed to the international media behemoth it is today. Back then, you couldn't turn on a television without hearing about the death of the Democratic Party and the collapse of liberalism. The radical Republican elite controlled the White House, both houses of Congress, and to a greater and greater extent, the courts, along with a well-oiled media machine and a network of well-funded think tanks, such as the extremely untrustworthy Heritage Foundation. The right had divided us along many lines: age, class, religion, race, sexuality, and color of state. And when it came to Iraq, anyone who dared point out any of Bush's mistakes, even the blindingly obvious ones, was labeled unpatriotic. The conventional wisdom held that the 2004 election was just the first blow, and that America was doomed to generations of GOP misrule.

But as we know now, there was fire in the ashes of that defeat.

Although you didn't hear it on television, anyone who read the coffee grinds could see that the Democrats were getting their act together. In fact, I myself made a strong case at that point, that we were poised for a resurgence, and wrote a bestselling book on the subject.

One group of Kerry voters in particular gave us hope: your parents' generation. I'm talking about young people. (I know it may seem hard to believe, but your folks were young at one time. They were pretty wild, too! Not really. But your grandparents were!!!) While voters over thirty went for Bush by a seven-point margin, the under-30s went overwhelmingly for Kerry: 54–45 percent. Youth turnout had shot up from 42.3 percent in 2000 to 51.6 percent—reaching 64 percent in battleground states. (I know that you'll be able to understand these percentages, because of the dedicated teachers in your public school who now receive such excellent salaries.)

There were other hopeful signs. Democrats gained more than sixty seats in state legislatures, winning majorities in so-called "red states" like Colorado and Montana. And Democrats, even though they weren't as rich as Republicans, gave almost as much money to their candidates. That was a big change. Al Gore had only gotten contributions from 155,000 people. John Kerry received contributions from well over a million. Yes, back then, people gave money to politicians. That was before the second McCain-Feingold bill, the Feingold-McCain Bill, finally got it right.

One key to the Democrats' success was that we had begun to build a new progressive movement. And to support the movement, we were building an infrastructure.

Your granddad had just started on the radio back then. No, radio wasn't a new medium. But progressive radio was. This may sound crazy, but back in 2004, liberal radio was a new idea. It was *conservatives* who dominated radio. In every city in America, radio stations were devoted to nothing but right-wing talk, every hour of every day. What did they talk about? It's a good question. They had to make stuff up and call us names, something I know you kids are much too grown-up to do. Except for baby Joe III. You can't talk. Yet!

I didn't have to go into radio. There was a whole bunch of other stuff I could have done. After all, I had quite a career in television, and writing movies and books. And there was the Al Franken All-Girl Orchestra. I would have loved to have gone back out on tour with them. Someday, I'll tell you about the Al Franken All-Girl Orchestra. Someday. But you're not quite old enough. Please don't ask your Grandma about it either.

But the All-Girl Orchestra was perhaps the most minor part of the emerging progressive infrastructure. Along with Air America, there was David Brock's progressive media watchdog group, Media Matters for America, which drove conservatives crazy by paying attention to what they said. Very, very, very, very carefully. It turned out that a lot of what they said wasn't true. And when your Uncle David called them on it, they squealed like pigs.

And there were the new liberal think tanks, like the Center for American Progress, which, true to its name, almost immediately became a genuine center for American progress. One of the differences between the liberal think tanks and conservative think tanks is that liberal think tanks were much less frequently funded by huge corporations that stood to benefit financially from the foregone conclusions of their research. That gave our think tanks the advantage of *accuracy*, which became invaluable when the reality-based community came back into power.

This new infrastructure helped us prevent the 2004 election from being an unmitigated disaster. But it became even more important afterward. Following the election, Bush and the Republican Congress proceeded to completely blow it by flashing, if only for a moment, their true colors. When they alienated the public by ignoring the nation's priorities and screwing up on Schiavo, Social Security, and Iraq, Air America was right there, poised to use statistics provided by our think tanks and audio clips pulled by unpaid interns at Media Matters to heap scorn and ridicule upon the hapless Republicans. That was our mission, and we did it well.

By the 2006 election, the Republican dam was beginning to crack.

That year, voters expressed their disgust with a Republican Congress that had completely betrayed the promises they had made in order to win power in 1994. Back then, Republicans had vowed in their Contract with America to "end the cycle of scandal and disgrace" and to "restore accountability to Congress." When Americans were reminded of those quotes and of the fact that 226 of the 231 Republicans in the House had received campaign cash from Tom "Forced Abortions" DeLay (as he had come to be known), they scoffed.

The unfathomable corruption and moral bankruptcy of Tom DeLay and his dearest friend, a man named Jack Abramoff, were just the beginning. The public was also enraged by the way Congress circled the wagons around the White House even as its betrayals of the public trust were becoming clear. For the second time in thirty-two years, a cancer had begun to grow on the presidency. This time, the tumor was Karl Rove–shaped, and though the President could have caught it in its early stages, when it was first revealed that Rove had outed an undercover CIA agent, he failed to do so. And Congress, instead of performing emergency surgery on national television by holding hearings on BlowCIAAgent's-CoverGate, held more and more hearings on the postal service and diploma mills. Congress even failed to address those two issues, which, as you kids will one day learn, remain extremely minor problems to this day.

Most of all, people were angry about Iraq. The politically motivated premature withdrawal was a disaster. The militarily necessary reinvasion was even worse.

It was a miracle that the Republicans managed to cling to fifty seats in the Senate in 2006. Vice President Cheney had to cast tie-breaking vote after tie-breaking vote, cursing all the while. (When you're all a little older, I'll tell you what Cheney said, and why C-SPAN had to become a pay channel.) But it was no surprise that we Democrats regained control of the People's House, the House of Representatives.

Republicans had spent the previous six years saying that Democrats were just a party of obstructionism, and that if we ever gained power, we'd just pass resolutions attacking Republican proposals without offering any new ideas of our own. But, defying expectations, the Democratic House wasted no time in passing bills big and small, each containing at least one idea, and some, such as the Omnibus Idea Bill, containing hundreds. A few of the smarter Republicans in the Senate, now terrified of the burgeoning progressive movement, soon started voting with their Democratic colleagues, which drove Cheney to almost constant explosions of obscenity and sent a string of excellent bills to the President's desk.

Bush was finally forced to use his veto. After first vetoing the Waxman-Castle Universal Prenatal Care Act, the President soon became so busy vetoing worthwhile legislation that he was forced to borrow Donald Rumsfeld's Autopen. But because Bush neglected to reprogram the Autopen, the first ten bills were "vetoed" by Donald Rumsfeld and, thus, became law.

Bush tried to take credit for the precipitous drop in infant mortality, the expansion of rural broadband Internet access, and the increase in the minimum wage. But because of the liberal infrastructure's new ability to rapidly expose the President's flip-floppery, the credit went instead to Democrats in Congress and, to a lesser extent, to the secretary of defense.

Unfortunately for Donald Rumsfeld, all the undeserved popularity in the world couldn't protect him from the subpoena power of Henry Waxman's Committee on Government Reform. As investigation after investigation uncovered ever deeper layers of corruption, fourteen fifteenths of the President's cabinet was forced to resign, leaving Secretary of Transportation Norman Mineta pretty much in charge.

The stage was set for the 2008 presidential elections.

Our party was fortunate to be blessed with a field of outstanding candidates. But thanks to your Granddad's early and vocal support, we selected the perfect nominee without a long and bruising primary campaign. Some criticized me for getting behind the President so early, but my gutsy move put me on the cover of *Newsweek* with the headline: "The Kingmaker?" Your Uncle Howard Fineman and I still fight about that question mark, but he points out that it certainly didn't hurt me in my victorious 2008 Senate race.

The President won in a landslide, defeating Republican nominee Bill Frist, whom Karl Rove had been advising from prison. (Not because of Plame. He punched a cop.) And not only did we gain an additional forty seats in the House, but we took the Senate. It was the happiest day of my life, except for the day I married Grandma, the days your parents were born, the days each of you were born, and the day I'm about to tell you about.

Can you guess which day that is? That's right, Barack. The quickie impeachment of George W. Bush.

Yes, kids, it was an actual historical event before it became a popular Saturday morning cartoon show. As you no doubt have learned from the cartoon, each new Congress is sworn in a few weeks before the presidential inauguration. The old president, in this case, George W. Bush, becomes a lame duck.

The quickie impeachment was your grandfather's idea. Everyone in our caucus said, "Why bother? He'll be out of power on January 20 whether we impeach him or not. Why do it?"

My answer, "Because we can," led to my second *Newsweek* cover.

Besides, I wanted to usher in an era of personal responsibility. And what better way of kicking it off?

But it wasn't until I proposed my Grand Bargain that the caucus and, it would turn out, virtually the entire House and Senate fell in love with the idea. Here's how it worked. In exchange for impeaching and voting to convict George W. Bush of the many high crimes and misdemeanors that the House investigations had uncovered, Democrats would agree to share power with their Republican colleagues, giving them a few committee chairmanships in an unprecedented Unity Congress. Unlike the GOP, we were magnanimous in victory, and gave some authority to those Republicans who weren't crazy or big jerks.

On January 18, 2009, President Bush was impeached, convicted, and began drinking again, all in the space of a single afternoon. America's reputation around the world was restored.

Dick Cheney, who, up until that day, had suffered a mere four heart attacks in his entire lifetime, managed to double that total in his forty-eight hours as president.

At long last, the country was united. Your namesake's famous words, Barack, turned out to be half-right. There were no red states and blue states that day. Only blue states.

The fun was over. It was time to restore honor and dignity to the Oval Office, to usher in a new era of personal responsibility, and to leave no child behind—but this time, for real.

We Democrats had come to power in a nation and a world beset by problems. At home: unaffordable health care, job and retirement insecurity, crumbling schools, and a crippling addiction to foreign oil. Abroad, a disastrous war. Plus poverty, terrorism, tyranny, global warming, and epidemic disease. Also, a comet was hurtling toward the Earth.

But we were fortunate to have a president with a sweeping vision, and the wisdom and courage to make that vision a reality. On Tuesday, January 20, 2009, our new head of state delivered an inaugural address that moved America to tears of joy and hope. In stirring words that will never be forgotten, the President explained that from now on, instead of serving special interests, politics would serve the public interest. And in return, Americans would be challenged to meet a new standard of patriotism. I don't remember exactly how it went, but it was unbelievably eloquent and moving. You can look it up.

The gist, basically, was that we were now in a global society full of great opportunities but also great risks. And that the job of America's government was to shield people from those risks so they could seize those opportunities. Imagine that sentiment put in a very eloquent way. The President has a particular gift for that.

It was more than just rhetoric. In the first one hundred days, the President and the President's allies in Congress, including your Granddad, enacted one hundred pieces of legislation, all of them flowing from the one simple uniting idea that we are all in this together.

They were the hundred days that changed America.

Day 1. Universal health care. Would you believe that our universal health care system, the "fourth rail" of American politics, didn't exist until 2009?

When your Granddad started his radio show back in '04, I thought the biggest problem in America was dishonesty in public discourse. I had spent a great deal of time and effort combating it. But as I learned, day by day, about all the problems facing our country, I started detecting a common thread. Whether it was the crisis in veterans' benefits, the causes of bankruptcy, the pressure on corporate pensions, or the health of our nation, there was one root cause. It wasn't Ann Coulter, as bad as she was. It was the fact that America, unlike every other developed nation in the world, didn't guarantee that every one of its citizens would have access to health care.

At that time, America spent a far higher fraction of its income on health care than any other industrialized country, but got far less in return. In terms of health status and patient satisfaction, the U.S. was at the very bottom. And Americans were the fattest people on earth.

Why hadn't we fixed the problem? It wasn't that Americans didn't *want* universal health care. For decades, opinion polls had showed that large majorities of Americans supported it. But since the 1940s, every time universal health care had been proposed, the special interests—the drug companies, the insurance companies, the for-profit hospitals owned by the Frist family—had killed it.

Now the game had changed. Government was finally aligned with the special-est interest of all: the people. And the people got what they wanted and needed.

This sent a message to the special interests: You're not so damn special anymore. Get over yourselves.

The national health system saved America a mind-boggling amount of money and lives by adopting new information technology. The transition to a more high-tech system was overseen by Newt Gingrich, who was in turn overseen by a team of ethicists. The number of hospital deaths caused by medical error dropped from 98,000 a year to only 12,000. (Your Grand-dad believes that at least 5,000 of those are murders by rogue male nurses, but has not yet been able to prove it in any of his Senate investigations.)

That was Day 1. A Wednesday.

Day 2. Thursday. Your Granddad and Representative Sherwood Boehlert (R-NY) proposed a new Apollo Project to end America's dependence on fossil fuels. Kids, every once in a while you still see a car that runs purely on gasoline. Can you imagine if *every* car worked that way? Well, at one time, they did. But that was before the President and Congress decided to fund the biggest research project since John Kennedy announced we'd put a man on the moon.

Can you guess which special interests were against this one? That's right. The fossil fuel people. They *loved* America's dependence on fossil fuels. Two of them had even been elected president (the Bushes), and a third was president for two days after the second Bush was impeached. But Democrats knew that America would reap many benefits by finding new, renewable sources of energy. It wasn't just that burning fossil fuels was heating up the planet. Taking on a national project like this would lead to a surge of innovation and new technology, which in turn would create high-paying jobs—and not just for computer whizzes in India, but for Indian computer whizzes right here in America. Barack, your friend Vijay's father invented the world's first dolphin-safe tidal dam. The day is coming soon when we won't have to organize our foreign policy around protecting our access to oil in the Persian Gulf. Maybe then we'll finally be able to withdraw once and for all from Iraq.

Already, the technologies developed by people like Vijay's dad are helping the world's poor countries become less poor, and to do so without poisoning the planet the way we had. Speaking of which, thanks to the new Apollo Project, our air and water are the cleanest they've been since the Clinton administration!

An interesting side note here. The President signed the Franken-Boehlert Act in Portland, Oregon. Why? Because in 1993, Portland had decided to adopt its very own global climate change policy. By 2005, the city had reduced its carbon emissions to below 1990 levels, behaving as though the Kyoto Protocol had never been torpedoed by President Bush. Had Portland's economy been wrecked? After all, Bush said, "Kyoto would have wrecked our economy." Nope. Portland boomed, becoming a center for energy efficiency technology and the burgeoning bike path industry. Because of its clean air, Portland was a great place to visit, until its residents became a little too pleased with themselves.

The President flew commercial back to D.C. and was selected for a random search, surrendering a nail clipper.

Day 3. Friday. Homeland Security reform. The end of the wasteful, useless random searches. The random-search industry was furious.

Day 4. Saturday. Tax fairness. Democrats believe that all Americans have been given an incredible gift, living in America. And with that gift comes certain responsibilities. That applies especially to those who have been fortunate enough to find themselves at the top of our income pyramid. No American gets rich on his or her own. Every one of us rich people stands on the shoulders of people who stood on the shoulders of people who stood on the shoulders of people who stood on the necks of Native Americans. Some rich people, such as a man named Jack Abramoff, cut out the middle man and stood directly on the necks.

The President reminded our Republican friends in Congress how they had opposed Clinton's tax increase on the top 1 percent. How they had predicted it would lead to a recession, but how instead it had been followed by eight fat years. Humbled, a few of them joined the Democrats to repeal the Bush tax cuts for people at the top, and restored the estate tax for estates over $5 million. Outraged, rich people staged a Million Millionaire March, but only a thousand millionaires showed up (although they claimed it was twelve hundred).

Just as importantly, we required that America's corporate citizens accept the responsibilities of citizenship. If they do business here, they would have to pay their taxes here. It was only fair. No more fake headquarters in the Bahamas. If some tax-dodging corporation really wanted its headquarters to be a PO box, they could rent post office boxes here in

America. "American post office boxes," the President told *The Tonight Show*'s Conan O'Brien, "are the finest post office boxes in the world."

The crowd loved it. And so did the American people.

Day 5. Sunday. The President rested. You might not realize that the President's political beliefs are rooted in a profound religious faith. That's because our nation's leader doesn't make a big show of it.

Day 6. Monday. What better day to fix American public education than on a Monday? With a touch of gentle irony, Ted Kennedy and I introduced the "Let's Stop Leaving Children Behind Act," which guaranteed small classes taught by well-paid teachers with plenty of up-to-date books, state-of-the-art computers, and "safety scissors" that lived up to their name. And thanks to federally funded bonuses, teachers fought to get a chance to teach in the nation's poorest school districts. The results were immediate. By Tuesday, kids were reading better, enjoying school more, and staying in school longer.

Day 7. Tuesday brought a flurry of activity. In rapid succession, the President signed—by hand!—the "End the Stupid Drug War Act," the "Secure Loose Nukes Like We Should Have Ten Years Ago Act," the "You'd Think Stem Cell Research Would Be a No-Brainer Act," and the "End Malaria Act," which really did end malaria, saving the lives of 2 million children a year.

On Days 8 through 99, we passed initiatives both great and small. We ended the Star Wars program and redirected the funds to provide body armor for our troops. We reformed the election system, in one fell swoop mandating paper trails on electronic voting machines, making Election Day a national holiday, and allowing people to vote by Instant Messenger, which pushed youth turnout to even higher highs. We also tackled global trade, protecting worker rights at home and around the world; international terrorism; and poverty. It was a heady time.

Then, on Day 100 of the first one hundred days, the President announced that, thanks to improved funding for scientific research, NASA had determined conclusively that the comet was going to miss the Earth and crash harmlessly into the moon.

The remainder of the President's first term was devoted to addressing unforeseen problems arising from the legislation passed in the initial exuberance. The President was able to fine-tune, overhaul, and in some cases abandon (Instant Messenger voting) legislation without fear of being called a flip-flopper. People were tired of that.

Today, as the President approaches the end of an equally accomplished second term and prepares to move on to the Supreme Court, America is inarguably a better place. Those of us who stood up during the Dark Time can look back proudly, not just because we won a victory for our party, but because we did something with it.

When Republicans had control of the whole government, they had the chance to pass their own solutions to American problems. But what they did showed what they really cared about. Themselves and their cronies.

I'm glad my party cares about something bigger than that.

Liberals believe that government, at its best, is the way we come together to tackle problems we can't solve on our own. I'm a liberal, and as it turns out, most Americans are liberals, too. A lot of them had forgotten they were, until President Bush tried to mess with Social Security.

My brother (your Great-Uncle Owen) and I grew up in suburban Minneapolis. We always had three squares a day, and a roof over our heads. A man named Bill O'Reilly, who was a popular conservative television commentator, grew up in a house a lot like ours, in Westbury, Long Island, and once told a newspaper that "you don't come from any lower than I came from on an economic scale."

When I was growing up, I thought I was the luckiest kid in the world. And I was. Bill O'Reilly was, too. But he just didn't seem to know it. That's the difference between liberals and conservatives. They think it's dog-eat-dog out there, that people's position in life is the result of their personal success in the marketplace, and that if you're rich or you're poor, it's only because you deserve it.

I just thought we lived in a great country.

Both my parents worked hard and had to overcome adversity in their lives. Like almost everyone does. My Mom developed rheumatoid arthritis at an early age and was in constant pain most of her life. She was married on crutches. Still, she told us, "It's a great life if you don't weaken." And she didn't. After my brother and I were old enough, she became a real estate agent. At dinner, she made sure we had meat and always, always, a fresh vegetable. At the table, she'd tell us about her business and things like "redlining." Banks wouldn't lend money to black people who wanted to buy houses in certain neighborhoods. She told us that was wrong. And that's why your Granddad works so hard with Congressman Leach to make sure that banks continue lending money to the poor, to minorities, and to women, not just to buy homes, but to start businesses.

My Dad, your great-grandfather, was born in New York. *His* father died of tuberculosis when Dad was sixteen. That's why Dad, who was a very smart man, didn't graduate high school. Instead, he went right to work. A lot of smart people who don't get a formal education end up being great businessmen and make enormous fortunes. Not your great-grandfather. Frankly, he wasn't the most ambitious man in the world, but he sure was devoted to his family. He'd come home at about five and spend time with my brother and me. It wasn't necessarily "quality time," but "quantity time." A lot of it spent watching TV. Dad loved comedians, and I guess that might be why I became one.

That's right. Before I got so involved in politics, I was a comedian. Then I wrote my first political book, *Rush Limbaugh Is a Big Fat Idiot.* (Rush and I would become fast friends after his fourth rehab took, and he made personal amends to me and thousands of other people and started working a twelve-step program of rigorous honesty.) A few years later, I wrote *Lies, and the Lying Liars.* The reaction I got to both books was different than anything I had done before. Don't get me wrong. There's still nothing better than making people laugh. But my books made me realize that maybe I could have an effect on the things I cared about.

That's why I went into radio. And that's why I eventually decided to run for the Senate, although I didn't make the final decision until 2007.

My brother and I weren't just lucky because we had parents who sacrificed for us. We were lucky because we lived in America, where millions of parents have sacrificed for millions of kids. And I want you guys, my grandkids, to know that you're inheriting the same incredible gift.

There's still a long way to go and a lot of work to be done. Before long, you'll be old enough to pick up where we left off. You don't have to go into politics or liberal radio to do it. Barack and Hillary, you could become teachers, like your mom. Or Joe III, you could design fuel-efficient cars like your dad. Or Joe could become a teacher, and Barack and Hillary could design cars. It's a free country.

The best gift I got from my parents was my values. Mom used to give us lectures at the dinner table about ethics. My Dad, your great-grandfather, Joe the First, mostly taught by example. What I learned from them was basically what Thomas Jefferson said: Be just and good.

Be just and good, kids, and you just might make your great-grandfather Joe smile down from Heaven. Though I doubt it. Because he's on your Great-Uncle Owen's mantelpiece in an urn.

With all my love,
Grandpa Al

NOTES AND SOURCES

For links to electronic versions of many of these sources, as well as further reading personally compiled by me, Al Franken, visit me on-line at www.AlFranken.com.

Book One: The Triumph of Evil

Chapter 1: Election Day

Vice President Cheney used the inaccurate terms "broad nationwide agenda," "mandate," and "clear agenda" in his speech introducing President Bush at the Ronald Reagan Building in Washington on November 3, 2004.

Here are the false "mandate" claims, listed in order of appearance:
- Bill Bennett: "The Great Relearning," *National Review* website, November 3, 2004
- Tucker Carlson: CNN's *Crossfire*, November 3, 2004
- Peggy Noonan: Fox's *The Sean Hannity Show*, November 3, 2004
- Bill Kristol: "Misunderestimated," *Weekly Standard*, issue of November 15, 2004
- *The Wall Street Journal*'s editors: "The Bush Mandate," November 4, 2004
- Tony Karon for *TIME*: "Victorious Bush Reaches Out," posted on Time.com November 3, 2004

- David Sanger for *The New York Times*: "Relaxed, Certainly, but Keeping One Eye on the Clock," November 5, 2004
- Doyle McManus and Janet Hook for the *Los Angeles Times*: "Majority Win Could Make Second Term More Partisan," November 4, 2004
- Wolf Blitzer: CNN's "Breaking News" coverage, November 3, 2004
- Renee Montagne for NPR: *Morning Edition*, November 3, 2004

President Bush announced the discovery of his stock of political capital in a press conference in Washington on November 4, 2004.

Chapter 2: How Bush Won: Fear

For more on the "Wolves" ad and its debunk, including a video of the commercial and copies of legislation proposed by John Kerry and Porter Goss, visit *www.factcheck.org/article291.html*.

The President's October 30, 2004, speech in Orlando, like all public presidential remarks, is transcribed at the White House's website, *www.whitehouse.gov*.

Vice President Cheney warned Americans about "making the wrong choice" at a "town hall meeting" in Des Moines on September 7, 2004.

Tom Ridge's comment on the terror alert system is in a May 10, 2005, *USA Today* article titled "Ridge Reveals Clashes on Alerts." He pooh-poohed the notion that the department was politicized in an August 2, 2004, press conference. The Associated Press then revealed, in a February 18, 2005, article titled "Ridge Met with GOP Pollsters," that Ridge had, in fact, met with GOP pollsters Frank Luntz and Bill McInturff.

The TMT study I discussed is properly cited as follows:

Landau, Mark J., et al. 2004. "Deliver Us From Evil: The Effects of Mortality Salience and Reminders of 9/11 on Support for President George W. Bush." *Personality and Social Psychology Bulletin* 30 (9): 1136–1150.

The "terribly designed" exit poll can be found at *www.cnn.com/ELECTION/2004/pages/results/states/US/P/00/epolls.0.html*.

The *Economist* article on the non-barking of the moral values dog was titled "The Triumph of the Religious Right," and ran on November 13, 2004.

Chapter 3: Bush's Little Black Dress

The complete anthology of President Bush's approval ratings can be found at *www.pollingreport.com/BushJob.htm*.

The August 6, 2001, Presidential Daily Brief has been declassified and is now available on-line at *news.findlaw.com/hdocs/docs/terrorism/80601pdb.html*.

The report of the 9/11 Commission is available at your local bookseller. You can also read it on-line at no cost by visiting *www.9-11commission.gov/report/index.htm*.

George Tenet's reaction to the 9/11 attacks was described in "The Wrong Man at Langley," in the October 28, 2002, issue of the *National Review*. It was later confirmed to me personally by 9/11 Commissioner Jamie Gorelick.

Al Gore's speech on October 18, 2004, was delivered at Georgetown University. The text is available on-line at *www.moveonpac.org/gore5*.

Yes, I know, you think it's **My** *Pet Goat*, not **The** *Pet Goat*. But it's *The Pet Goat*. It was published in an anthology called *Reading Mastery—Level 2 Storybook 1*, written by Siegfried Engelmann and Elaine Bruner.

The "Phoenix memo" is available on-line at *www.thememoryhole.org/911/phoenix-memo*.

The Associated Press reported on the warning from the Minneapolis FBI agent in a September 23, 2002, article titled "FBI Agent Cited Trade Center Attack Ahead of Sept. 11."

Details of Condi Rice's planned speech on 9/11 can be found in an April 1, 2004, *Washington Post* article titled "Top Focus Before 9/11 Wasn't on Terrorism; Rice Speech Cited Missile Defense."

President Bush blamed the loss of a million jobs on 9/11 in Wilkes-Barre, Pennsylvania on October 6, 2004. The Bureau of Labor Statistics statistics debunking that claim can be found on-line at *stats.bls.gov/mls/mlsimpac.htm*.

President George H. W. Bush spoke about Iraq at the "8th Annual Reunion of Our Victory in the Desert," an event for Gulf War vets, on February 28, 1999.

The State Department website no longer features a transcript of Colin Powell's February 24, 2001, remarks in Cairo. Fortunately, TheMemoryHole.org has a mirror of the site available at *www.thememoryhole.org/war/powell-cairo.htm*.

Condi Rice discussed Saddam's military impotence on CNN's *Late Edition* on July 29, 2001.

President Bush warned the nation about Iraq's connection to al Qaeda in Cincinnati on October 7, 2002. He also discussed this phony assertion on September 25, 2002, in a photo op in the Oval Office.

The results of the *New York Times*/CBS News poll regarding the nation's belief that Saddam Hussein had been involved in 9/11 are available on-line at *www.nytimes.com/packages/html/politics/20030311_poll/20030311poll_results.html.*

The *Christian Science Monitor* reported on the lack of a perceived al Qaeda–Saddam connection in a March 14, 2003, article titled "The Impact of Bush Linking 9/11 and Iraq."

Vice President Cheney appeared on *Meet the Press* on December 9, 2001 (Atta-Prague) and September 14, 2003 (major blow).

The text of President Bush's letter announcing the war is available on-line at *www.whitehouse.gov/news/releases/2003/03/20030321-5.html.*

A GPO search of presidential documents for the year 2003 yielded four examples of the President speaking the words "bin Laden":
- June 24 [with President Musharraf of Pakistan]: "If Usama bin Laden is alive—and the President can comment on that if he cares to—but the people reporting to him, the chief operators, people like Khalid Sheik Mohammed, are no longer a threat to the United States or Pakistan for that matter."
- July 3: "Well, I would have to say obviously there needs to be an education program, because Usama bin Laden is nothing but a killer who has hijacked a great religion."
- September 11: "And it just reminds us of the duty we have got to do. And I say "we," my administration and all who serve our country, our duty is to protect our fellow citizens from people like bin Laden."
- October 19: "I think that the bin Laden tape should say to everybody the war on terror goes on, that there's still a danger for free nations and that free nations need to work together more than ever to share intelligence, cut off money, and bring these potential killers or killers to justice."

By way of comparison, he publicly mentioned his dog Barney five times.

The BBC-leaked intelligence memo was reported:
- In the *Press Trust* (India) on February 5, 2003
- In the *Gold Coast Bulletin* (Australia) on February 6, 2003
- In *The Scotsman* (Scotland) on February 6, 2003

- By the Chinese Xinhua Newswire on February 5, 2003
- In the *Village Voice*'s February 18, 2003, issue
- In the February 14, 2003, edition of the *LA Weekly*
- By the Associated Press in a wire story that was picked up by Salt Lake City's *Deseret News* on February 5, 2003
- In the *Washington Post* on February 8, 2003 ("Blair Acknowledges Flaws in Iraq Dossier")
- And in a cogent op-ed column entitled "Iraq-Terrorist Link Is Flimsy" that appeared in the *Cleveland Plain Dealer* on February 9, 2003

A transcript of Colin Powell's remarks to the United Nations is available on-line at *www.cnn.com/2003/US/02/05/sprj.irq.powell.transcript.09*. Powell confessed to the inaccuracies in those remarks on *Meet the Press* on May 16, 2004.

The President's "Mission Accomplished" speech was delivered on May 1, 2003.

The "Case Closed" argument about the Iraq–al Qaeda connection was made by Stephen F. Hayes in the November 24, 2003 issue of *The Weekly Standard*, but by that date, it had already been debunked by Michael Isikoff and Mark Hosenball on *Newsweek*'s website on November 19, 2003.

Cheney appeared on CNBC's *Capital Report* on June 19, 2004.

President Bush "pirouetted" in a June 17, 2004, press availability.

The *New York Times* article discussing the President's fumfering ran on April 15, 2004, and was titled "Bush Takes Strategic No-Remorse Stance."

The transcripts of Republican National Convention speeches are available on-line at *rncnyc2004.blogspot.com/2004/09/rnc-official-speeches-list-full-text.html*.

The other TMT study I read, available at *www.apa.org/divisions/div46/images/cohen.pdf*, is properly cited as follows:

Cohen, Florette, et al. 2004. "Fatal Attraction: The effects of mortality salience on evaluations of charismatic, task-oriented, and relationship-oriented leaders." *Psychological Science* (in press).

Chapter 4: How Bush Won: Smear

The *Los Angeles Times* debunked the false claims of the Swift Boat Veterans for Truth in an August 20, 2004, article titled "Kerry Starts Firing Back at Critics of War Record."

The *Washington Post*'s "opus," "Swift Boat Accounts Incomplete: Critics Fail to Disprove Kerry's Version of Vietnam War Episode," was published on August 22, 2004. Mike Medeiros's comments came from this article.

The *New York Times* added some debunking and examined the close ties between the Swifties and the Bushies in an August 20, 2004, article titled "Friendly Fire: The Birth of an Attack on Kerry."

Supporting documentation for Kerry's Navy awards, in .pdf format, is available on-line at *www.factcheck.org/article231.html*. Here are the documents cited in the chapter:

- The citation for John Kerry's Silver Star, signed by U.S. Navy Vice Admiral Elmo Zumwalt
- A supporting citation noting Kerry's "extraordinary daring and personal courage," signed by U.S. Navy Admiral John J. Hyland
- George Elliott's July 21, 2004, affidavit supporting the Swifties' claims
- George Elliott's second affidavit, dated August 6, 2004, in which he retracts the retraction published in the *Boston Globe*

Michael Kranish's profile of John Kerry, in which George Elliott stood behind John Kerry's version of the "loincloth" story, was titled "Heroism, and Growing Concern About War," and was published on June 16, 2003. Kranish's report on Elliott's retraction of the July 21 affidavit, "Veteran Retracts Criticism of Kerry," was published on August 6, 2004.

Jim Rassman was Bill O'Reilly's guest on the August 10, 2004, edition of *The O'Reilly Factor*.

William B. Rood's firsthand account, "What I Saw That Day," was published on August 22, 2004.

Andrew Morse summed up the results of *Nightline*'s investigation in an October 14, 2004, piece on ABCNews.com titled "What Happened in Kerry's Vietnam Battles?"

Joshua Green's article on Karl Rove, "Karl Rove in a Corner," was published in the November 2004 issue of *The Atlantic Monthly*.

Chapter 5: A Brief Recuperative Debunk

Jonathan Chait's article, "The Invention of Flip-Flop," appeared in the October 18, 2004, issue of *The New Republic*.

Here are the sources for the debunking of Sean Hannity's lie-tany on his March 25, 2004, show. They are all collected at *The Al Franken Show*'s website (*shows. airamericaradio.com/alfrankenshow/node/1345*):

Here's a guy who supported gay marriage, now against it.
- Kerry's speech against the Defense of Marriage Act was delivered on September 10, 1996.

Here's a guy that by my count has had six separate different unique positions on the war on Iraq.
- The President's interchange with a reporter took place during a September 19, 2002, news conference in the Oval Office.
- Kerry's speech on the Iraq resolution was delivered on October 9, 2002.
- Kerry appeared on *Face the Nation* on September 14, 2003.
- The *San Francisco Chronicle* debunked the lie thoroughly in a September 23, 2004, article titled "Flip-flopping Charge Unsupported by Facts."

Here's a guy that voted for the $87 billion to fund the war before he voted against it.
- Kerry voted against tabling (i.e., voted for) Senate Amendment 1796 to S. 1689. This amendment would have suspended "a portion of the reductions in the highest income tax rate for individual taxpayers" to pay for the $87 billion. The amendment was tabled by a vote of 57–42.
- The amendment having failed, Kerry then voted against S. 1689, which passed by a vote of 87–12.

Here's a guy that was for the Patriot Act. Now against it.
- Kerry spoke about this at Iowa State University on December 1, 2003.

No Child Left Behind, for it, now against it.
- Kerry voted for HR 1, the No Child Left Behind Act, which passed by a vote of 91–8. His criticism of Bush and his pledge to "fully fund" the act was widely reported, including in the *San Francisco Chronicle* on May 7, 2004.

Here's a guy that supported—was against the death penalty for terrorists who kill Americans. Now he's for it.
- As noted in the text, fair enough.

The only thing he seems consistent on is that, throughout the nineteen years he was in the Senate, he voted to raise taxes consistently 350 times.
- Factcheck.org provides the documentation for my thorough debunking of this lie at *www.factcheck.org/article.aspx?docID=159*. But it's more fun to read Michael Kinsley's March 23, 2004, *Slate* piece on the subject.

Chapter 6: With Friends Like Zell

For more on the unprecedentedly negative Bush advertising campaign, see "From Bush, Unprecedented Negativity," an article in the May 31, 2004, *Washington Post*.

Matt Bai's piece on Kerry was titled "Kerry's Undeclared War" and appeared in *The New York Times* on October 10, 2004.

If you think it should be *My Pet Goat*, as opposed to *The Pet Goat*, then not only are you wrong, you didn't read the notes from Chapter 3.

For more on the post-convention bounces, check out *Newsweek's* web exclusive, "Bush's Big Bounce," published on September 4, 2004. The web address is *www.msnbc.msn.com/id/5915140/site/newsweek*.

The text of Zell Miller's speech at the Republican National Convention can be found on-line at *www.cbsnews.com/stories/2004/09/01/politics/printable640299.shtml*.

A transcript of Miller's far-less-insane speech at the 2001 Jefferson-Jackson Dinner can be found at *www.buzzflash.com/alerts/04/09/ale04045.html*.

Kerry voted for the B-1 Bomber Defense System Upgrade as part of the 2002 Department of Defense Appropriations Act. He voted for a total of more than $16 billion in authorizations for the B-2 bomber in the Defense appropriations bills from 1985 to 2003.

Then–Secretary of Defense Cheney's cancellation of the B-2 program, as well as the story of the 1991 Defense Appropriations Act that Kerry voted against, was chronicled in Fred Kaplan's piece "John Kerry's Defense Defense," published on *Slate* on February 25, 2004.

Cheney testified before the Defense Subcommittee of the Senate Appropriations Committee on June 12, 1990.

Judy Woodruff and Wolf Blitzer challenged Zell Miller on CNN on September 1, 2004.

John McCain appeared on *The Sean Hannity Show* on May 12, 2004. Hannity claimed on May 13, 2004, that Kerry had "voted against every major weapons system."

Zell Miller spoke at the 1992 Democratic Convention on July 13, 1992.

Barack Obama spoke at the 2004 Democratic Convention on July 27, 2004.

Chapter 7: How Bush Won: Queers

The *Detroit Free Press* reported on the gay marriage robo-calls in a November 1, 2004, article titled "Presidential Campaigns, Voters Upset About Misleading Calls."

Thanks to Joshuah L. Bearman and Stephen Elliott for the story of the "pro-gay Kerry supporters" and the photo. Check out their full account at *laweekly.blogs. com/joshuah_bearman/2004/10/how_they_do_par_1.html.*

The episode of *Frontline* discussing the Compassion Capital Fund was called "The Jesus Factor" and aired on April 29, 2004. You can view the transcript on-line at *www.pbs.org/wgbh/pages/frontline/shows/jesus/etc/script.html.*

The January 18, 2005, *Los Angeles Times* article about Jim Towey and the Swing-State Faith-Based Initiatives program was titled "Bush Rewarded by Black Pastors' Faith."

Jim Towey fretted over the fate of the faith-based program under a President Kerry in the June 12, 2004, issue of *World* magazine, in an article titled "A Lasting Legacy?"

Luke Bernstein's e-mail was reported by the Associated Press in a June 2, 2004, article titled "Pennsylvania Political Push for Bush Could Cost Churches Tax Break."

The Associated Press reported the strange case of Chan Chandler in a May 8, 2005, article titled "N.C. Church Kicks Out Members Who Do Not Support Bush."

Cal Thomas's column, "John Kerry's Catholic Problem," was published on the Internet on April 26, 2004.

Presumptive ex-Catholic Sean Hannity weighed in on the Kerry-Communion debate on *The Sean Hannity Show* on April 12, 2004.

A CBS News poll conducted May 20–23, 2004, found that 28 percent of American Catholics felt that abortion should not be permitted.

Bob Novak tangled with Paul Begala about Bob Casey on the June 28, 2004, episode of *Crossfire.*

Michael Crowley wrote about the Bob Casey Myth in his September 23, 1996, *New Republic* article "Casey Closed."

Russell Shorto's excellent piece in *The New York Times Magazine* tracking the anti-gay marriage movement ran on June 19, 2005, under the headline "What's Their Real Problem with Gay Marriage? It's the Gay Part."

The Internet Archive preserved Bob Jones III's letter to President Bush just as it appeared on the Bob Jones University website. You can read it at *web.archive. org/web/20041113005205/http://www.bju.edu/letter.*

Alan Abramowitz's analysis of the religious vote appeared in a post on Ruy Texeira's blog on November 6, 2004. It's still available at *www.emergingdemocratic majorityweblog.com/donkeyrising/archives/000930.php.*

The Ray C. Bliss Institute study is available on-line at *pewforum.org/docs/ index.php?DocID=55.*

Charles Stewart and Stephen Ansolabehere's analysis, "Truth in Numbers," appeared in the February/March 2005 issue of the *Boston Review*. It's available on-line at *www.bostonreview.net/BR30.1/ansolastewart.html.*

Paul Weyrich is quoted in a documentary by the BBC's Adam Curtis, *The Power of Nightmares: The Rise of the Politics of Fear,* which originally aired on October 20, 2004. You can watch the whole documentary on-line at *www.archive.org/ details/ThePowerOfNightmares.* It's mind-blowing.

James Dobson made his claim to a mandate in his January 2005 Focus on the Family newsletter.

The *New York Times* article on November 4, 2004, detailing the victory lap of the religious right was titled "Some Bush Supporters Say They Anticipate a 'Revolution.' "

Chuck Colson's reality check came in his November 8, 2004, syndicated column, "It's Not Payback Time."

Chapter 8: Al Franken Talks About God

No notes.

Book Two: Seeds of Collapse

Chapter 9: "A Great Political Issue"

One thing I didn't mention in the chapter is that the House Committee on Government Reform actually *subpoenaed* Terri Schiavo. On March 18, the day the feeding tube was to be removed, subpoenas were issued for Michael Schiavo (who was to bring with him the "nutrition and hydration equipment in working order"), three physicians who had treated Terri, and Terri herself. The subpoenas were eventually quashed on account of ridiculousness.

Leon Fuerth's *New York Times* op-ed "Looking for the Next Tsunami" was published on January 7, 2005.

President Bush's response to the tsunami was discussed in a December 29, 2004, *Washington Post* article, "Aid Grows Amid Remarks about President's Absence."

Richard Cizik's comments were reported in the March 21, 2005, *New York Times* article titled "Supporters Praise Bush's Swift Return to Washington."

ABC News has the text of the Schiavo memo at *abcnews.go.com/Politics/ Schiavo/story?id=600937&page=2.*

The official poll archive of *The Truth (with jokes)* is *www.pollingreport.com.*

PowerLineBlog.com's asinine case for the phoniness of Brian Darling's memo can be viewed on-line at *powerlineblog.com/archives/009929.php.*

Fred Barnes's column "The ABCs of Media Bias" appeared in the April 4, 2005, issue of *The Weekly Standard.*

Howard Kurtz's column "Doubts Raised On Schiavo Memo" appeared in the *Washington Post* on March 30, 2005.

For more on Mel Martinez's history of bad hires, check out *mediamatters.org/ items/200504080009.*

Tom DeLay's comments before the Family Research Council were reported by *TIME* magazine on March 23, 2003.

The *St. Petersburg Times* article reporting DeLay's suggestion that Terri Schiavo was sentient was titled "Political Heft behind Bill" and ran on March 21, 2003.

Senator Frist's comments about Senator Edwards were reported by CNN on October 12, 2004.

Frist's Senate floor speech in which he diagnosed Terri Schiavo is available on-line at *www.govtrack.us/congress/record.xpd?id=109-s20050317-7&bill=s109-653.*

I made up the FristCam thing.

Rush Limbaugh's explanation of why liberals wanted Terri Schiavo to die was part of his radio show on March 23, 2005.

Bay Buchanan unveiled her feminist theory on CNN's *Inside Politics* on March 25, 2005.

Bill O'Reilly pondered the motivations of the tube-yankers on March 24, 2005.

Michael Schiavo slander collection:
- *Scarborough Country* guest William Hammesfahr appeared to talk about the "huge hoax" Michael Schiavo was pulling on March 21, 2005.
- Tom DeLay railed against Michael Schiavo at a March 18, 2005, press conference.
- Bill Bennett denigrated Schiavo on the March 24, 2005, episode of *The Sean Hannity Show*.

Tom DeLay thundered against Justice Kennedy on Fox News Radio on April 19, 2005.

An excellent time line of the Schiavo legal case can be found on-line at *www.miami.edu/ethics/schiavo/timeline.htm.*

The tragic and ironic story of Charles DeLay is told in the March 27, 2005, *Los Angeles Times* article titled "DeLay's Own Tragic Crossroads."

Chapter 10: The Tom DeLay Saipan Sex Tour and Jack Abramoff Casino Getaway

You can relive the original Battle of Saipan by watching a 1944 newsreel about it at *www.archive.org/details/1944-06-30_Saipan_Is_Ours.*

Brian Ross's first report on Saipan appeared on *20/20* on March 13, 1998. His second report appeared on *20/20* on May 24, 1999.

Marshall Wittmann was quoted in a *New York Times Magazine* article on Jack Abramoff titled "A Lobbyist in Full," published May 1, 2005.

The *Washington Post* article about Tom DeLay's Judeo-Christian worldview was titled "Absolute Truth" and ran on May 13, 2001. This article also referenced the peculiar political philosophy ("beat him over the head with a baseball bat") of Michael Scanlon.

DeLay's adoring toast to Jack Abramoff was reported by James Harding for *Slate* on April 7, 2005.

The Senate Indian Affairs Committee, as I mentioned, has posted some of the e-mail correspondence between Abramoff, Scanlon, and Ralph Reed on its website. It's worth reading through at *indian.senate.gov.*

Timothy Noah wrote about Jack Abramoff's early days, including his "Abraham Jackoff" moniker, in a piece titled "Jack Abramoff's School Days—The Making of a Sleazeball," published in *Slate* on April 27, 2005.

Michael Isikoff's *Newsweek* article about the Tom DeLay–Jack Abramoff relationship was titled "With Friends Like These . . ." and ran on April 18, 2005.

The *New York Times* reported on the plight of the Tigua tribe in a June 13, 2005, article titled "For a Tribe in Texas, an Era of Prosperity Undone by Politics."

The story of David Grosh was detailed in a June 23, 2005, *Washington Post* article titled "One Committee's Three Hours of Inquiry, in Surreal Time."

The *Galveston Daily News* article on DeLay's denial, published May 15, 2005, was titled "DeLay Disputes Charges of Abuse in Saipan."

The *National Journal* article about Peter Hoekstra, "Former House Staffers Say DeLay's Office Derailed Northern Marianas Investigation," ran on May 6, 2005.

Chapter 11: Social Security: Franni vs. Bush

When President Bush was sworn into office in 2001, the federal debt was $5.7 trillion. When I wrote this in the summer of 2005, it was over $7.8 trillion. You can find official statistics on the federal debt on-line at *www.publicdebt.treas.gov/cgi-bin/cgiwrap/~www/opdpen.cgi.*

Information about the poverty rate of seniors comes from a February 2005 report by the Center on Budget and Policy Priorities (CBPP), available on-line at *www.cbpp.org/2-24-05socsec.htm.*

The letter from the American Academy of Actuaries, dated December 19, 2003, is available on-line at *www.actuary.org/pdf/socialsecurity/tech_dec03.pdf.*

Secretary Snow was asked about the eighty-three-year retirement at a press conference on March 23, 2005, at the Treasury Department.

Many of the statistics in this chapter, including the projected dates on which the Trust Fund will zero out, were collected in a report prepared by Dean Baker and

David Rosnick for the Center on Economic and Policy Research. It's on-line at *www.cepr.net/publications/facts_social_security.htm.*

Mark Weisbrot's column, which appeared in several newspapers in October 2004, was titled "Social Security: It's Not Broken, So Don't Fix It."

The February 2, 2005, background briefing in which the "senior administration official" (Laura Bush) admitted to the pointlessness of private accounts was transcribed by the *Washington Post.*

President Bush's fact-finding mission to Parkersburg, West Virginia, took place on April 2, 2005.

Charles Krauthammer's column, "2042: A Fiscal Odyssey," appeared in the *Washington Post* on February 18, 2005.

The Heritage Foundation's pamphlet claiming that the Trust Fund was a sham, "The Social Security Trust Fund Fraud," was written by Daniel Mitchell and published in February 1999.

The President spoke about Social Security during a news conference on April 28, 2005.

The President conversed with Bob McFadden at an event in Washington, D.C., on January 11, 2005.

The Heritage Foundation's "extremely untrustworthy" study, titled "Social Security's Rate of Return," was published in January 1998. Stephen Goss criticized that report in a memorandum available on-line at *www.cbpp.org/10-5-98socsec. htm#IV.%20%20Appendices.* Heritage "replied" to its critics with "Social Security's Rate of Return: A Reply to Our Critics" in December 1998.

The "significantly more trustworthy" Government Accountability Office study on minorities and Social Security can be found on-line at *www.gao.gov/new.items/ d03387.pdf.*

Joshua Micah Marshall has the full text of the Peter Wehner memo on his blog. Check it out at *www.talkingpointsmemo.com/archives/004348.php.*

"Achieving a 'Leninist' Strategy," by Stuart Butler and Peter Germanis, was published in the Fall 1983 *Cato Journal.*

The President gave his Lenin-inspired speech while on his fact-finding mission to Parkersburg, West Virginia, on April 5, 2005. He noted the repetitiveness of his line on May 24, 2005, in Greece, New York.

In this chapter, I was helped greatly by Michael Hiltzik's book *The Plot Against Social Security*.

Scott McClellan's press gaggle took place on February 3, 2005.

The President's conversation with Mary Mornin took place on February 4, 2005.

Chapter 12: Plan of Attack—Attack the Planning

James Mann's excellent book *Rise of the Vulcans* provided much of this chapter's background information on the history of our nation's Iraq policy, including the 1979 study by Paul Wolfowitz.

The text of President George H. W. Bush's 1999 speech can be found on-line at *www.fas.org/news/iraq/1999/03/a19990303bush.htm*.

Paul Wolfowitz's 1997 comment about the potential "permanent occupation" of Iraq by the United States appeared in *The Future of Iraq*, edited by John Calabrese and published in November 1997.

The Project for a New American Century's 1998 letter to President Clinton can be found on-line at *www.newamericancentury.org/iraqclintonletter.htm*.

Paul O'Neill's account of the rush to war, including the divvying-up of Iraq oil fields, comes from Ron Suskind's *The Price of Loyalty*.

Richard Clarke wrote about his experiences in the Bush administration after 9/11 in his book *Against All Enemies*.

President Bush claimed we were trying to avoid war in Iraq in his March 8, 2003, radio address.

The text of the Downing Street Memo can be found on-line at *www.times online.co.uk/article/0,,2087-1593607,00.html*.

Other leaked British memos, including David Manning's report, appear at the excellent *downingstreetmemo.com*.

The *Washington Post* reported on the memo revealing the lack of thought regarding postwar plans in a June 12, 2005, article, "Memo: U.S. Lacked Full Postwar Iraq Plan."

James Fallows's article, "Blind into Baghdad," appeared in the January 1, 2004, issue of *The Atlantic Monthly*.

Bob Woodward's book *Plan of Attack* is still available in stores.

General Shinseki testified before the Senate Armed Services Committee on February 25, 2003.

Donald Rumsfeld disagreed with Shinseki's assertion at a press availability with reporters on February 27, 2003.

Paul Wolfowitz testified before the House Budget Committee on February 27, 2003. He testified before the House Appropriations Committee on March 27, 2003.

Andrew Natsios appeared on *Nightline* on April 23, 2003.

For an estimate of the cost of the Iraq War as of your reading of this sentence, visit *costofwar.com*.

Donald Rumsfeld made his "six days, six weeks" estimate in a speech to troops stationed at Aviano Air Base in Italy on February 7, 2003. He made his "five, six, eight, ten, twelve years" estimate on *Fox News Sunday* on June 26, 2005.

I highly recommend David Phillips's book *Losing Iraq: Inside the Postwar Reconstruction Fiasco*.

President Bush spoke of responsibility in his acceptance speech at the RNC in Philadelphia on August 3, 2000.

Richard Clarke commented on the President's style in *The Choice 2004*, which aired on PBS on October 12, 2004.

General Zinni's comments came as part of a May 21, 2004, broadcast on CBS's *60 Minutes*.

Chapter 13: Mission Redacted

Donald Rumsfeld discussed looting and freedom at a Pentagon briefing on April 11, 2003.

Robert Perito, James Conway, Thomas White, and Jay Garner were interviewed for a *Frontline* report, "Truth, War, and Consequences," which aired on PBS on October 9, 2003.

The 3rd Infantry Division's after-action report can be found on-line at *www.globalsecurity.org/military/library/report/2003/3id-aar-jul03.pdf*.

Thomas White was interviewed for James Fallows's "Blind into Baghdad" article in *The Atlantic Monthly*.

Many, many thanks to George Packer. He's incredibly insightful. If you liked this chapter, you'll love his new book, *The Assassins' Gate: America in Iraq*.

The *Los Angeles Times* reported on the looting of the al Qaqaa ammunition dump on November 4, 2004, in an article titled "U.S. Troops Tell of Watching Iraqis Loot Ammo Dump."

Weapons expert Gary Milhollin was quoted in an October 26, 2004, *Boston Globe* article titled "Explosives Were Looted after Iraq Invasion."

The October 25, 2004, *New York Times* article about al Qaqaa was titled "Huge Cache of Explosives Vanished from Site in Iraq."

Rudy Giuliani tried to blame the al Qaqaa Qatastrophe on the troops on *The Today Show* on October 28, 2004.

The antics of Scott Erwin and the rest of the "Brat Pack" were chronicled in a May 23, 2004, *Washington Post* article titled "In Iraq, the Job Opportunity of a Lifetime." Erwin spoke to his university's newsletter in an article posted online at *oncampus.richmond.edu/news/ricmat/volume6/607b.html*. He was also the subject of a June 3, 2004, *Richmond Times-Dispatch* article titled "A Most Unusual Semester."

The Congressional Research Service document regarding the nature of the CPA is available on-line at *www.fas.org/man/crs/RL32370.pdf*.

The results of Stuart Bowen's audit are available on-line at *www.contractwatch.org/datavault/performancedocs/cpaig_control_of_materiel_assets_iraq_7-26-04.pdf*.

For more on Custer Battles, see "Follow the Money" in the April 4, 2005, *Newsweek*. You can read transcripts of the former employees blowing the whistle at hearings convened by Senator Byron Dorgan at *democrats.senate.gov/dpc/*.

Read the results of Henry Waxman's inquiry on-line at *www.democrats.reform.house.gov/Documents/20050627140010-82879.pdf*.

The "2005 Global Corruption Report" of Transparency International is available on-line at *www.globalcorruptionreport.org*.

For more on Ahmed Chalabi, read "The Manipulator" by Jane Mayer in the June 7, 2004, issue of *The New Yorker*.

Chapter 14: Werewolves of Washington

Paul Bremer spoke to the Council of Insurance Agents and Brokers on October 4, 2004. His DePauw speech took place on September 16, 2004, as reported by the *Washington Post* in an article titled "Bremer Criticizes Troop Levels."

The *Washington Post* reported on Iraqi unemployment in a June 20, 2005, article titled "Tackling Another Major Challenge in Iraq: Unemployment."

Khalid Daoud's story was told in a July 5, 2005, *New York Times* article titled "U.S. Walls Off Its Corner of Baghdad, Annoying Some Neighbors."

For more on Condi Rice and Don Rumsfeld's bizarre "werewolves" story, read Daniel Benjamin's August 29, 2003, *Slate* article, "Condi's Phony History," available on-line at *slate.msn.com/id/2087768/*.

Bush's second inaugural address is available on-line at *www.whitehouse.gov/news/releases/2005/01/20050120-1.html*.

Here's a recipe for Uzbek rice pilaf. Franni made it for me and my staff last week. It comes from *www.geocities.com/Hollywood/2944/english.html*.

> 2 cups of rice, presoaked and drained
> 5 cups of water, or beef stock
> 1/2 lb lamb leg meat, cubed
> 1/3 cup of canola **oil**
> 2 onions, finely diced
> 3 medium carrots, julienned
> 5 garlic heads
> 2 tsp salt
> 1 tsp cumin
> 1 tsp red pepper

Sauté onions and carrots over medium heat until lightly browned. Add meat and stir until browned. Add 2 cups water, and cook over medium-high heat about 6–7 minutes, until meat is tender. Add rice and heads of garlic into stew. Add rest of the water and seasonings, do not disturb layering of rice and stew, and **boil** uncovered until rice absorbs water, for about 45 minutes. When rice is soft, reduce heat to minimum, cover pot, and let the rice steam 25 more minutes.
About 5 servings.

The *Guardian* (Britain) reported on our relationship with Uzbekistan in a May 26, 2003, article titled "US Looks Away as New Ally Tortures Islamists."

Excerpts from the cultural sensitivity pamphlet can be found on-line at *www. meforum.org/article/637*.

The Associated Press reported on the innocence of many of our prisoners in a May 11, 2004, article titled "Red Cross: Iraq Abuse 'Tantamount to Torture.' "

Colin Powell's futile attempt to question detainee abuse was detailed in the Nelson Report, an on-line intelligence briefing, on May 6, 2004.

Rumsfeld and Pace's press conference can be found on-line at *www.defense link.mil/transcripts/2005/tr20050329-secdef2381.html*.

The text of the Taguba Report is available on-line at *www.agonist.org/annex/ taguba.htm*.

The text of the Fay Report is available on-line at *slate.msn.com/features/whatis torture/pdfs/FayJonesReport.pdf*.

Senator Graham's statement can be read on his website at *lgraham.senate.gov/ index.cfm?mode=speechpage&id=221868*.

Dr. Burton J. Lee III's op-ed, "The Stain of Torture," was published on July 1, 2005.

Paul Wolfowitz testified before the Foreign Operations Subcommittee of the House Appropriations Committee on April 29, 2004. The question he couldn't answer was asked by Ohio Democrat Marcy Kaptur.

The *Washington Post* reported on Rumsfeld's use of the Autopen in a December 19, 2004, article titled "After Outcry, Rumsfeld Says He Will Sign Condolence Letters."

Newsweek reported on Ahmed Chalabi in "Intelligence: A Double Game," in its May 10, 2004, issue.

The Associated Press noted Paul Wolfowitz's puzzlement at his old friend Ahmed's behavior in a June 22, 2004, article titled "Wolfowitz Puzzled by Chalabi Actions."

The Chalabi–al-Sadr coalition was described in an article, "Iraq's Rebel Democrats," in the June 2005 issue of *Prospect* (Britain).

The website iraqbodycount.org has information regarding casualty counts in Iraq. The higher estimate comes from a Johns Hopkins study that was reported by the *Washington Post* in "100,000 Civilian Deaths Estimated in Iraq," published on October 29, 2004.

Scott McClellan refused to speculate on the number of civilian casualties on November 9, 2004.

The *New York Times* reported on the unusual compensation plan for displaced Iraqi families in "Hearts, Minds, and Flood Relief," published on January 9, 2005.

The revision of the "Patterns of Global Terrorism" report was reported by the *Los Angeles Times* on June 9, 2004, in an article titled "U.S. Will Revise Data on Terror." Colin Powell shook his head in dismay on *Meet the Press* on June 13, 2004.

The report of the Defense Science Board is available on-line at *www.acq.osd.mil/dsb/reports/2004-09-Strategic_Communication.pdf.*

Epilogue: The Resurrection of Hope

Chapter 15: A Letter to My Grandchildren

The statistics on youth voting come from pages 18–19 of the paperback edition of *How the Left Lost Teen Spirit (And how they're getting it back!)* by Danny Goldberg.

The information about Democratic victories in state legislatures appeared in *USA Today*, in a December 14, 2004, piece titled "Dems Gain in 'Hidden Election.' "

Hendrik Hertzberg calculated the total vote for Democratic versus Republican senators for a November 15 *New Yorker* piece, "Blues."

The *Christian Science Monitor* reported on the incredible growth of the Democratic donor base in "In Politics, the Rise of Small Donors," which ran on June 28, 2004.

The talk radio statistics come from a September 14, 2003, article in the *Boston Globe*, "Liberal Authors Triumphant as US Bookshelves Lean Left."

Bill O'Reilly commented on his background in an October 9, 2000, article in the *New York Observer* titled "Fox News Superstar Bill O'Reilly Wants to Oppose Hillary in 2006!"

INDEX

For a complete index of *The Truth (with jokes),* visit
www.AlFranken.com

ACKNOWLEDGMENTS

So many people to thank, so little time. With my radio show and all the other important things I'm doing, I really can't spend a lot of time or effort acknowledging the colleagues, friends, and experts who helped make this book happen. So I know they'll understand why these acknowledgments are so perfunctory and slapdash.

First, my editor, Mitch Hoffman, and his assistant editor, Erika Kahn. Thanks. Thanks. My agent, Jonathon Lazear, his assistant, Christi Cardenas, and my lawyer, Gunnar Erickson. Thank you all. Brian Tart, my publisher. Thanks. My wife, Franni. Also, thanks.

Richard Hasselberger did the cover design. Good job. Thanks. Dutton publicists Lisa Johnson and Jean Anne Rose, thanks for the great job on *Lies*. Let's not rest on our laurels, okay?

Thanks also to the phenomenal staff of *The Al Franken Show*. Much of the research for the book was accumulated during the year and a half we've been on the air. Tim Bradley, Mark Lotto, Eric Hananoki, Ayo Griffin, Rob Mackey—thanks, thanks, thanks, thanks, and thanks. And to Jim Norton, who came up with two of the lies about Sean Hannity—thanks.

Also, to the research interns—Josh Blank, Merle Eisenberg, and Joe Franken—thanks.

The rest of the staff deserves thanks, too. That would be executive producer Gaby Zuckerman, engineer Chris Rosen, associate producer Kate Sullivan, and administrative assistant Molly Patterson. You're the best. Thanks, thanks, etc., etc.

And the Sundance people, too. Thank you, guys.

To all our guests on *The Al Franken Show*. Thank you. Especially, David Sirota, Christy Harvey, and Judd Legum from the Center for American Progress. Thanks times three, one for each of you. To our other regular and semiregular guests—Jonathan Alter, David Brock, John Dickerson, Howard Fineman, Paul Glastris, Hendrik Hertzberg, Paul Krugman, Mark Luther, John Markus, Joshua Micah Marshall, Lawrence O'Donnell, Tom Oliphant, Melanie Sloan, and, of course, Joe Conason—I have one word for you all. Thanks.

A special thank-you to my terrific cohost, Katherine Lanpher. You deserve a better acknowledgment. Next book, okay?

Everybody at Air America deserves individual thanks. They won't get them. But you know who you are. Thanks.

While writing on Iraq, I sat down to talk with George Packer of *The New Yorker* and David Phillips, formerly of the State Department. Thanks. Ditto to: Naomi Klein, Richard Clarke, James Fallows, and Larry Diamond.

Sergeant Major of the Army Kenneth Preston and all the folks at the USO. Thanks for taking me over to Iraq and, more important, bringing me back.

Wait. I almost forgot Peter Orszag, Steve Clemons, Brian Greer, Joshuah Bearman, Stephen Elliott, and Uwe Rheinhardt. Thanks. But I'd never forget Brian Ross. Thanks, Brian.

To the friends who read the manuscript as it progressed—Norm Ornstein and Hazel Lichterman. Thanks. Also, Beth McCarthy and Peter

Koechley, who gave their notes through Ben Wikler. So, I'm not sure whether they even deserve thanks. But thanks anyway.

This is the second book in a row where my son, Joe, bore the biggest brunt in terms of not having as much of my time as I'd like to give him. Sorry. And thanks. And thank your sister, Thomasin, for me. And apologize for me, too.

Thanks to my departing assistant, Nate. Good luck. And to my new assistant, Casey Boyd, also good luck. Trevor Beddoe, thanks for archiving. Marie Evans, thanks for always being there for the whole family.

The acknowledgments I can't in good conscience gloss over are to Billy Kimball, Andy Barr, and Ben Wikler.

I've had the incredibly good fortune of working with Billy Kimball since 1992, when together we pioneered Comedy Central's political coverage with a series called *Indecision '92*. Billy was my producer then and is my executive producer now, guiding *The Al Franken Show* with a steady hand and constant brilliance. As he has with my previous three books, Billy has lent his comedic hand to this one. I firmly believe that America leads the world in comedy, and throughout my thirty-plus years in show business, I have worked with a good number of our nation's most gifted comedy writers. Some have planned their careers better. But none is funnier than Billy Kimball.

You may remember Andy Barr from my last book, *Lies*. He was the Harvard TeamFranken sophomore I took to Bob Jones University as part of one of that book's pranks. Andy graduated in June and immediately came on board as a researcher for the radio show and to take over the enormous task of researching and vetting this book. I cannot imagine doing this book without Andy. Although I guess it would have been possible.

It would not have been possible without Ben Wikler. Like Andy, he was a TeamFranken member on my last book. Ben's two years older than Andy, and so was able to come on the radio show at its very start as a producer. Ben reminds me of myself when I was his age, except smarter, wiser, more worldly, better read, more passionate, much much taller, and just as funny. Ben was with me every step of the way on this book. I cannot thank him enough.

And I hate to spoil the conceit, but I have to thank my wife, Franni, properly. In addition to being my life partner, best friend, etc., she took care of me, Ben, Andy, and Billy. Thanks, hon. Isn't being an empty nester easy?

And once again, anyone I forgot, blame Andy.